Extracts fro1 the reviews since the first edition

Written for the lay reader… Hugely informative…
This is just the sort of book I'd welcome as a parent of a child or an adult who is what the author calls troubled. The case studies make it hugely informative in evoking the character and atmosphere of the various services available for those with learning disabilities, autism or special educational needs. It is very different and I enthusiastically recommend it. **Dame Stephanie Shirley CH, Philanthropist and founder of research charity Autistica**

It is a hugely important subject
When I was seventeen, I worked in a small, local hospital for men and women with a variety of learning difficulties. It was incredibly rewarding. This book is about how people like those I knew are treated today. The so-called normal world should understand these lovely people better. **Dame Kelly Holmes**

…the hidden lives of people with Learning Disabilities
This book opens up interesting debates about areas of support offered to some of the most vulnerable people in our communities. The author does this so that is easily understood to the reader, in a non-jargon, non-clinical way, describing the lives of individuals with complex needs along with the services they depend upon. I would recommend this book. I enjoyed reading it. Thank you Chris. **Mark Walker, Kent County Council Director for Special Educational Needs and Disabilities**

An eye opener for the 'layman'
Written so that all can comprehend the enormity of the daily tasks which requires the expenditure of time, energy and money on a gigantic scale, but which is one that the majority of us rarely think about...

John Morgan, retired teacher

What an excellent book...
It's brilliantly, clearly written, in engaging and lively style, as well as being a major eye-opening for most of us in the 'normal' world. It's a tour de force that should be on everyone's reading list – not least because it turns out that all of us know one or several people who are in these categories. We need to know this stuff – and Chris Rowley has given us a brilliant entrée into a world we know too little about.

Anon

Important read for learning disability supporters...
The author speaks for those that have no voice. Everyone should read this book, especially if this is a subject that does not touch your life personally. **grafun**

What a great book
There can't be many practical guide books that bring a lump to your throat. I love the duality of the book. It serves as valuable resource that could be dipped into for anyone trying to navigate their way around the care provision services. At the same time, it has remarkable first hand accounts by people who have been impacted by disability and care provision. **Peter Hoare, relatives with learning disabilities**

A real eye opener
My daughter bought me this book and I have to say I was unsure about reading it at first. But the stories are full of warmth and incredible strength in the face of adversity. Glad these stories are being told. **Anon**

Full of information and a good read
I like this book. Masses of information, both anecdotal and factual, to help not just the special needs expert but also parents and mainstream teachers. It is well written and accessible and to be recommended.

Bruce Williams

Many moving interviews and informative commentary
The title of this book appealed to me immediately, indicating just how difficult it is to find a collective noun for those with a learning disability or autism. And actually, how misguided it is to try to apply a 'label' in the first place…   **Loris Clements, Communications Consultant**

A must read for teachers, nursery staff and classroom assistants
The only guide book I've read that's brought a lump to my throat! Highly recommend!   **Charlotte**

This book will shed some light on the journey many families go on…
… an incredibly thorough examination of a really complex and often emotive subject. It helps to explain the range of different diagnoses and how they can present, and sheds some light on the journey many families go on in order to access the appropriate services.
Rebecca Thomas, mother of young autistic boy

A wonderfully and thoughtfully written and researched guide
The book is insightful and full of anecdotal evidence – all written in a helpful and useful way. A book everyone should have on their shelves.
Caroline Pedley

The perfect book to allow readers to reach ther own conclusions
What I found really interesting were the detailed personal histories and interviews with the care providers etc. The descriptions of what the author observed tell us about the nature of particular disabilities and the support measures that are in place to meet their needs…
Mother of twenty-two year old autistic boy

This book does a great service
The picture the author builds up, collage-like, is so appreciative and heart-warming… I remember the term 'mongol' being used in my sister's early years – the terms are always changing. This book makes people conscious of how enriching these lives can be both for the disabled themselves and for those who support them…
Martin Gulbis, sister with Down's

"COULDN'T YOU JUST CALL ME JOHN?"

"Couldn't You Just Call Me John?"

A Layman's Guide To Learning Disability and Autism

Chris Rowley

SECOND, REVISED EDITION

"One of the highest achievements of a civilisation is the way in which it cares for its handicapped members"

John F Kennedy

"How mistaken it is to suppose that there exists some 'ordinary' world into which it is possible at will to wander. All human beings, driven by the same Furies, are at close range extraordinary."

Anthony Powell

©2022, 2023 Christopher Rowley
A catalogue entry for this title is available from the British Library
ISBN 978-0-9539340-5-8
First edition published in 2022
Second, revised edition published in 2023
by Chris Rowley
The Oak Cottage, The Green, Leigh, Tonbridge, Kent TN11 8QL

Cover design: Ashley Reuben and Caroline Woods
Text design: Amanda Hawkes
Research and Typing: Joyce Field
Published by Chris Rowley

The Author

Chris Rowley was born in Manchester. After Cambridge, he went into television, working in a wide variety of roles – studio management, programme scheduling, current affairs, news and documentaries – including World at War and a BAFTA-nominated film on the painter, Turner. Moving to the Independent Broadcasting Authority, he was responsible for the oversight of ITV's scheduling and later for the introduction of independent producers and Channel 4. He was President of The Media Society and founded the One World Broadcasting Trust – now One World Media – in 1986. He has published five well-received factual books; and founded two charities concerned with crafts. He lives in a village in Kent with his wife, Anna, a craftswoman. They have two daughters.

Other books by this author:

"We Had Everything . . . " (2000) 3 editions

The Lost Powder Mills of Leigh – A History (2009) 3 editions

The Archaeology of The Leigh Powder Mills (2009)

J J Bergin – Engravers 1894-2010 (2013)

"Just a Bit Barmy" – The Princess Christian Farm Colony and Hospital (2018)

Life & Death & Doctors 1820–1950 (to be published in 2023)

Dedication

To all those who talked with me.
Every one of them was kind to a
beginner in this complex and
exhausting world they inhabit.
I hope that I have reflected what
I was told so that the world
understands the subject and
the people better.

Foreword
by Michael Bowers

Former Managing Editor for two international publishing houses

In 2018, Chris Rowley published a history of the Princess Christian Farm Colony and Hospital, which was established at Hildenborough, near Tonbridge, in 1895. However, in this new book, he looks in great depth at the much wider subject of how people with learning disabilities are helped, educated, cared for and housed in the twenty-first century. The location for this study is, once again, Kent – but he establishes very quickly that this corner of South-East England could represent almost anywhere in Britain. The book constructs a clear and detailed picture of the sometimes fraught but often uplifting relationships between families, local authorities, schools, medical centres, care workers and, of course, those who have most need for the services provided. It is a pattern which will be repeated throughout the counties of England and Wales with differences only of detail and emphasis.

The author makes effective and empathetic use of individual stories, personally told and faithfully transcribed. They give a central structure to the narrative in almost every chapter, and they provide a telling counterpoint to the interviews and experiences provided by the specialists, the carers, and the administrators. These hard-working and hard-pressed people also have a story to tell. This book gives them a voice.

What emerges very strongly from these pages is that the problems associated with the many forms of learning difficulties are being tackled by highly qualified and sympathetic professionals, often against a background of inadequate funding and unhelpful policy changes. We are all conscious that progress is no longer inevitable. Nevertheless, as Chris Rowley skilfully highlights, going the extra mile is the norm, not the exception. There is scope for optimism.

Prologue
by Sir Richard Stilgoe OBE DL [1]

This book is the author's journey to see what the lives of people with learning difficulties and autism are like – his Canterbury Tales. He asked me how I came to found the Orpheus Centre – which teaches autistic children how to make music. My journey began almost fifty years ago.

1970. I am on a not very good television series and, as a result, get a letter from someone who runs the Tuesday Crowd, a group of disabled pensioners from Wandsworth who ask me to be their patron. Flattered, I go along to one of their meetings. I have never met anyone like them before and an embarrassed silence ensues. There is a piano in the corner, so I sit down at it. During the many periods of unemployment my chosen profession has granted me, I have played the piano in pubs, so I know all the old music hall songs that they know and we have a good, loud sing-song – including confident performances from some who had been silent up to then. When I stop, the newly-oxygenated pensioners talk with renewed energy and vigour. I have never forgotten this – the effect that music can produce, coming as it does from a different and deeper part of the brain than the bit at the front that does walking and talking. I remained patron of the Tuesday Crowd for forty years, even though the woman who originally wrote to me confessed that she had got confused and had meant to ask Leslie Crowther. It being 1970, they used words like spastic and handicapped. I asked whether it was all right to say handicapped. The pensioner said, "Of course it is. We are handicapped. The world handicaps us!"

1974. I am now part of the BBC's Nationwide – a much better and more popular programme and, as a result, get more invitations from a wide variety of groups – groups I would otherwise never have met. Often this involves opening the fete at a Special School and I usually ask whether the children do any music. "Oh no!" replies the teacher. "They wouldn't be able to do that." I have never forgotten that either. The teacher thought she was protecting the children from something they might fail at. I thought she was preventing them having a go at something they might succeed at.

1982. I am writing a musical with Andrew Lloyd Webber about trains, to be called Starlight Express. We are discussing with Trevor Nunn, the director, how best to portray trains on stage. I suggest electric wheelchairs which I had seen students drive with remarkable skill and speed. They look at me as though I am potty.

1985. Leading a horse round a paddock as vice-president of the local Riding for the Disabled (I am always flattered to be asked and am bad at refusing) it strikes me that I shouldn't be here; I am frightened of horses and wouldn't be any use if something went wrong. Nobody is doing Music for the Disabled and I wouldn't be frightened of that. Perhaps that is what I should be doing. On top of the horse is Ernie, who lives in a long-stay mental hospital in Caterham. Ernie suddenly says "Joey's dead". I ask who Joey was and Ernie explains. Ernie, Joey and Billy were all residents of the hospital and Joey had cerebral palsy, which made his speech hard to understand. Ernie could understand him and Billy could type. Between them they wrote a book about life in a long-stay mental hospital – a place where Joey definitely shouldn't have been but his hard-to-follow speech had made people assume he was dim. He wasn't. The book they wrote together changed the world and contributed hugely to the closure of such places and the beginning of Care in the Community. What stuck with me was that whatever challenges the three of them faced individually, between them they were a successful author.

1988. Dr Michael Swallow, a Belfast neurologist and brilliant musician, had started running Share Music holidays in Northern

Ireland, weeks in which 25 disabled people, 25 student volunteers and three music, drama and dance tutors worked towards a final concert on the last night – a concert of work they had created together during the week. The first one of these in England culminated in a remarkable concert in the barn theatre of what is now the Orpheus Centre in Surrey. It displayed all the elements I have mentioned: that the musical part of the brain (also the creative part) is unaffected by damage to the motor systems: that risking having a go at something and succeeding at it is more therapeutic than being prevented from doing it: and that a disabled person facilitated by a non-disabled student can produce work neither could have managed alone. Share Music continued for the next ten years and every concert produced the same litany from the audience: "I didn't know they could do that."

1997. Two things worried me. That sentence the audiences kept repeating – the assumption that, because the performers moved differently and sounded different, they were somehow less capable of invention and interpretation than other people and the fact that Share Music courses were only a week long and gave everyone involved a great high and then a worrying come-down while waiting for next year's course. So, a group of us started The Orpheus Centre, where disabled students could do this work on a proper three-year programme.

2020. The Orpheus Centre has been going for twenty-three years and is a very different proposition from what we originally began. We teach proper, independent living skills so that our students can live in their own flats when they leave (and 89% of them manage to do just that). But what keeps us special is that we focus on the performing arts. By writing songs and stories and plays and dances, the students find out more about themselves and by performing them in public and being applauded, they gain the self-confidence they need to employ the skills we have tried to teach them.

Our cohort of students has changed enormously in the twenty-three years. We began with wheelchair users who had been unfairly assumed to be not very bright and some with autism or Aspergers who were assumed to be unable to participate in 'normal' education.

In the majority of cases most of these young people would now be absorbed into mainstream colleges – not always successfully, because, however well-meaning their teachers are, not all of them have the necessary training and experience. The aim, however, is obviously right, both for the disabled young people who are no longer excluded and for their non-disabled peers who live and learn with them, support them and befriend them.

This is a marvellous change and I hope we have contributed to it in some way, but it means that those who now come to Orpheus have more complex needs – we have more autism, more students with Downs' syndrome, more with a level of learning disability who would find it hard to cope with the noise and confusion of a mainstream college. But the work we do with them still produces the same remarkable result, the same re-assessment by audiences of what these young people are capable of and the same affirmation for the young people and volunteers who work with them and feel more complete themselves as a result.

Throughout this prologue I have used 'disabled people' and 'non-disabled people', which are generally thought to be currently acceptable terms. In the splendid and scurrilous musical 'Avenue Q', John Tartaglia wrote a song called "Everyone's a little bit racist", which for my generation, however hard we try, is certainly true. The students I work with could easily write another song called "Everyone's a little bit disabled", which I believe is also true. I certainly have become convinced over the years that everyone's a little bit autistic. Experts refer to "The Autistic Spectrum". I don't believe it is a spectrum. It's an exponential curve, one of those curves that starts nearly flat and then gradually becomes steeper. Most of us are on the flat bit – a little bit self-absorbed, a little bit 'looking after number one', but trained to be part of the tribe. Some people are born further up the curve and need more support – though they may have compensating pluses like photographic memory, musical skill and, of course, the ability to write algorithms in Silicon Valley. But we are all on the same curve. (It's the same shape as the meaningless and oft-quoted 'steep learning curve' beloved of the same people who think everything is an 'emotional roller-coaster'). We all have a little bit of Attention Deficit

Hyperactivity Disorder. We all have different levels of anxiety and different intellectual capacities. As long as we have schools that select and stream, we are owning up to a diversity of ability. The wider that diversity is within those schools, the more complete society feels.

There have been great steps forward. I never met a disabled person in my youth because they were kept in special places – and there are still parts of the world where they are hidden away to prevent shame falling on their relatives. My children have been at schools with the occasional wheelchair user or visually impaired student. My grandchildren are all at schools with almost the whole range of abilities. All sorts of discrimination are alien to them because they are, in their eyes, irrelevant. We still have a long way to go before we accept that we are all different and all the same. The Covid 19 pandemic we are enduring as I write this may serve to bring us nearer together.

But one thing is certain. This book can do nothing but good in increasing understanding and lessening the gaps between 'them' and 'us' – between us all. A lifeboat that has pushed people away is an unhappy, guilty lifeboat. A lifeboat which has pulled everyone on board may feel a little full, but it's a much happier ship.

Richard Stilgoe

Contents

Why The Title of the Book?

"COULDN'T YOU JUST CALL ME JOHN?"
A Layman's Guide to Learning Disabilities and Autism

The title of this book has its origin in a conversation that I had with a lady who worked to support people with learning disabilities. I came to realise that in many ways the conversation summarised what the book is about. When I had started the book, I shared the difficulty that most people have. What does one call people who have learning disabilities? In the 1913 Mental Deficiency Act, they had been sub-divided into 'idiots', 'imbeciles', 'feeble-minded' and 'morally defective'.[2] By the 1930s, these people were called 'mentally retarded' or 'mentally defective'. And in the 1950s until the 1970s they were usually said to be mentally handicapped. I thought that the modern term was a person who had learning disabilities. However, I soon learnt that the modern terminology was a 'service user'.

I found that writing a book continually using the term 'service user' was clumsy. I also thought it unhelpful for a general reader. So, when I was talking about my problem to this senior lady – she was responsible for spending over £40 million a year looking after the housing and care of people with learning disabilities – she agreed that 'service user' was not an obvious term for the general public and that she, too, found it uncomfortable. She said that she had recently been having coffee with a dozen or so of the people she looked after and had asked them what they would like to be called. There was a pause. Eventually, one man, rather hesitantly, raised his hand. "Couldn't you just call me John?" he asked.

The phrase stuck in my mind. I realised that – probably unconsciously – John was asking to be considered as an individual. What I was hoping to do in this book was to get away from the us and them; the normal and the not quite right; the average, sensible, uncomplicated people like you and me, as opposed to the people who are and have been seen as mentally retarded, feeble-minded, idiots or imbeciles and so on. Appendix 1 gives a list of over three hundred and eighty words and phrases to indicate that a person has been considered 'not all there'.

All the people with learning disabilities and also learning difficulties with whom I talked or whom I heard about were unique. They may have 'learnt differently' or been a bit or a lot 'differently able' – terms I liked. But they needed to be understood better. They nearly all felt frustrated by their inability to fit in easily with society; frustrated that it is difficult to fit into school life; and frustrated that they usually cannot find a job – let alone a rewarding job. When I asked the Director of nearly everything at the Kent County Council[3], including supporting those with learning disabilities, what she needed most to help this wide range of people, she said that what she most wanted was not more money – although she needed that too – but more understanding from the public.

This book, therefore, aims to tell the stories of the people with whom I talked. I am very conscious that I am not an expert or someone who has had to look after a troubled child. Yet I have aimed to reflect what I was told.

I found the day-to-day support workers who dealt with the individuals who learnt differently to be amazing. They do not get paid very much but they shrug if they are asked about money; it is worth hearing their story.

The life of the parents, too, will stick with me forever. What they have to cope with is almost unbelievable but they cope – somehow. Most of the time. There was so much that I learnt.

The most memorable definition of the difference between autism and Down's came from a seven year old autistic boy. Then there was the book "The Reason I Jump" by a thirteen year old Japanese boy,[4] which allows us 'normal' people to understand what it is like to have autism.

I was fascinated, too, by the system called Portage. No one in authority had mentioned it but I was lucky to meet a husband and wife who explained how Portage teaches parents what to do to help their learning disabled child from birth – and it works.

By chance, I came across a team called CAT. They invent new technical ways to help disabled people – not to replace the carers but to augment what disabled people and their carers can do. On the schools' side, I saw many remarkable ways in which the education system helps – from two boys explaining what ADHD is like to all their school friends; to a school within a school – The Phoenix Centre – where thirty children with moderately serious learning disabilities are partly integrated, where practical, into the mainstream primary school. Further Education, including my tour of The Princess Christian Farm and the Orpheus Centre, surprised and delighted me.

The day centres I visited had a wide range of 'service users'. They are tended with such personalised care – and where I learnt what 'bicine' meant – spelt differently – taught to me by an elderly autistic lady.

Housing provision, too, varied to suit individual needs. I will never forget a profoundly autistic man who wanted to go swimming in the back garden at a residential home (it's more complex than it sounds) overseen by a remarkable, down-to-earth manager with her thirty to thirty-five staff looking after five residents.

All the so-called 'service users' I met are memorable, including the forty something, Hugh, who explained the frustration of his life – the impossibility of getting a proper job; his difficulties with bullying; the difficulties of getting his Government allowance; but, most frighteningly of all, his epileptic fits which can happen three or four times, day or night, which can result in him biting off great pieces of his mouth or tongue when he is unconscious. But, in one way at least, he has made major progress. It is a very eccentric solution – as you will hear.

Dr Peter Bench, the senior partner at the Hildenborough and Tonbridge Medical Group summarised the life of people like John who inspired the title of the book. "I think the biggest change in the care of ill people in the last thirty years has been the way we look after men and women with learning disabilities. I started my career as a doctor at the Oakwood Hospital at Barming[5] near Maidstone.

It was really an old lunatic asylum from early Victorian times. Although every effort was made to help the residents, it was pretty grim. I joined the GP practice in Hildenborough and I volunteered to be the GP at Holly Lodge, a secure home for five people with very severe learning disabilities. It had been built on part of the old Princess Christian Hospital site, the hospital where a good number of my predecessors had helped for over seventy years. I usually go up there several times a week. The care given to the residents is constructive and caring – a dramatic change from 1990, let alone earlier."

The aim of this book is to reflect the changes and the current situation, to explain about the individuals with learning disabilities wherever they are in the country. I chose to interview mainly people in the west half of Kent (nearly a million people) because I wanted to see how well the diverse parts of the system fitted together. Did the carer from social services liaise satisfactorily with the GP? Did the special needs nurse talk with the school? How well were parents involved in the complications of the system? And so on. However, when I talked with men and women with a learning disability and with the experts supporting them in other parts of the country – and I talked to people in ten to twelve parts of the country – the stories were not different. So, this is not about people in Kent. It is about individuals all over the country.

Finally: Covid. Although many of the interviews were conducted before the pandemic, the individuals in the book and the people they represent are still with us – although the pandemic will in many cases have made their support by the social services, education, the NHS and all the other groups who aim to help, more difficult.

CHAPTER 1

What do 'Learning Disabilities' and All the Other Classifications Mean?

Writing about the history of the Princess Christian Hospital between 1895 and 1995 for my book "Just A Bit Barmy", I had begun to understand a little about the wide variety of people who had what came to be called 'learning disabilities'. However, when I began to look into the situation today, I soon realised the even wider complexities. In this chapter, I aim to take readers on my journey to find out what a non-expert has discovered about the definitions of the range of people who have learning disabilities or learning difficulties or autism or the huge variety of sub-divisions.

Learning Disability – v – Mental Illness

I liked the fifty year old definition from Bill Cowell – the head of Leybourne Mental Hospital in the 1970s and 1980s. In those days, there were really only two main definitions – 'mental handicap' (today's learning disabilities) and mental illness. Mr Cowell said that mental handicap was "essentially a problem of slow learning rather than ill health." As my education on the subject progressed, I realised what Bill Cowell was saying: someone born with 'learning disabilities' is not the same as someone having one of the huge variety of mental illnesses[6]. I was told that the difference was that mental illness can be 'cured'; and that people were born with a learning disability – the main subject of this book – and will die with it. However, in reality, many people with a mental illness will often have a lifetime struggle to keep their problem at bay and most people with a learning disability can be given help to enable them to lead a more normal life. As I asked about definitions, different experts would tell me that one type of illness or problem was a mental illness, while another would say it was a learning difficulty or a type of autism. In any case, it seemed that a person with one diagnosis could vary widely from another person with the same diagnosis. Simple definitions between learning disabilities and mental illness did not always seem simple.

Learning Disability – v – Learning Difficulty

The next problem with definitions was the difference a 'learning disability' and a 'learning difficulty'. Learning difficulty seemed to be a problem with a person – usually with a child – who is slow at keeping up with their peers at school. Inevitably, parents are worried and, understandably, demand more help for their child. This help should, of course, be given; but it is not the same as having a child with learning disabilities. (One expert said that often learning difficulties went hand in hand with low IQ, although I personally did not always find this assessment at all obvious). Dyslexia is much mentioned as a learning difficulty; and as well as this problem with reading, there are other similar designations[7]. Most importantly, the learning difficulty can be overcome or at least can be circumvented by the individual who will normally adapt and end up as a part of mainstream society. On the other hand, someone with a learning disability will usually need help throughout their lives.

Learning Disability – v – Autism

The next complexity comes when explaining the difference between 'learning disabilities' and 'autism'. They often seem to be used interchangeably but, to be accurate, they should not be. One expert said, "Learning disability means what it says – the person has an inbuilt problem with learning. It can include an autistic child or adult but it can also include someone who has been brain damaged at birth; or who has caught one of the nasty childhood diseases – meningitis, and so on; or it can be someone with Down's syndrome or with hearing problems which inhibit their development and their learning." So, learning disability is the wider term; autism is more specific. Autism can, as with the other terms, cover a wide range.

The introduction of the phrase 'On the Autistic Spectrum', largely due to the remarkable English psychiatrist, Dr Lorna Wing,[8] has been immensely useful. It means that all parts of society can begin to understand that it is not a question of a person being autistic or not autistic. As someone said, "It is not like having mumps or not having mumps". An autistic person will often have certain characteristics – although to varying degrees. They find it hard to fit in with mainstream society and find it difficult to make friends. They often have difficulty in sensing other people's feelings. Some cannot read or write or speak clearly – one in four are said to speak few or no words[9] – while others, although withdrawn, are absorbed with IT and computers. They are made anxious very easily, particularly if their routine is disturbed. Yet they are usually gentle and loving. The pianist, Duncan Honeybourne, himself austistic, said it was "like having a pane of glass between me and the world". I learnt later than autism and a condition called Sensory Processing Disorder (SPD) are associated but different. However, as I never heard the term SPD mentioned as I wrote the book, I leave it to readers to check on the various websites for the differences and similarities if or when they need to. One way of looking at autism is called 'monotropism'. In essence, this means that the person is only able to concentrate on their particular interest and consequently finds it hard to be socially aware.[10]

Special Educational Needs

However, as well as the graduations between the various 'learning disabilities', 'learning difficulties' and autism, there is a further complexity – the educational classification of Special Education Needs – usually shortened to SEN. If at first it seems to be yet another way of describing the same problem, there is a reason for the educational type of assessment. The various SEN levels are used in judging the amount of help that is needed in school for that individual child, rather than relying on his or her medical or care classifications.

All these complexities of definition were made more bewildering when I asked a well-known consultant psychiatrist to check this chapter.[11] He made useful clarifications but then gave me my own copy of a WHO reference book, ICD-10, the International Classification of Mental Disorders. It is three hundred and sixty-four pages long and covers nearly eight hundred conditions – autism only has a page and a half. At that stage, I felt that, as I was writing for the general public, I would try to keep definitions simple. I have tended to use 'Learning Disability' as the generalisation, only using the term autism or learning difficulty when someone else has used it or when it is very specific.

Are Learning Difficulties and Autism Inherited? What about Older Parents?

It is not entirely clear whether or to what extent there is some genetic link between the generations of families with learning disabilities and autism.[12] In the United States, it was fashionable in the mid/later 1990s to say that high-flying computer experts (men) in Silicon Valley were the most likely to have this new and apparently rare condition – autism.[13] Research over the past twenty years has increasingly indicated that there is some genetic link. However, the details are not straightforward. I have met three families where there *was* a high achieving father who might have been diagnosed as slightly on the autistic spectrum, who each went on to have a definitely autistic son. However, I have met other families where there seemed to be no obvious inherited connection. With some conditions such as Down's, there is a clear genetic link. Yet in other cases of learning disability it is not always obvious. For example, I met one family with twenty year old twin boys. One is at university (incidentally, not reading maths or computer sciences). The other is very much on the autistic spectrum – unable to communicate socially and given to unpredictable rages. He also does not like maths or computers; and would like to be a craftsman. Nor was there any obvious autism in the rest of the family.

One danger is that, if you do have an autistic child, you may well begin to wonder if it is you, the parents' 'fault' – whether this is a family trait. In one instance, a mother of an autistic child convinced herself that she and her family must be the cause of her child's autism. She went back into her family history to find previous generations who were 'mad'. She did indeed find a distant relative who was sent to the Colonies as a black sheep; and she wondered whether he was the autistic ancestor who had provided the family inheritance. However, I suspect that most families have a 'mad' forbear in one generation on one side of the family or another. One doctor summed up the query. "We really don't know for certain whether autism is genetic. If it is, then the gene has not been identified. Maybe, in the future, it will be possible to go to a geneticist and ask him to see if any future child of yours is going to be autistic but at present…".[14]

There is another theory: elderly parents are more likely to have a child with learning disabilities. I only met one couple who were relatively elderly when they had a child who turned out to be autistic. There have been a number of reports saying that the age of the mother or the father does have a bearing on whether their child is more likely to have autism. The age of the father does seem to provide some sort of link; and a woman's likelihood of having an autistic child also seems to increase with age – but it may also increase for teenage mothers. However, the most important point is that the increased risk in all these cases is very small. For example, one 2017 study calculated "that about 1.5% of children born to parents in their 20s will have autism, compared to 1.58% of children born to parents in their 40s."[15]

One distinguished expert in the field, Prof. Francesca Happé has mentioned that there has been little research into the elderly who have autism; and suggested more research, but also more assistance is needed.[16]

I have not aimed to reproduce the definitions of all the different diagnoses and conditions which are given on the useful websites by such bodies as the National Autistic Society (NAS) or MIND; or the various more specialist groups helping with Down's, Aspergers, Tourette's, ADD, dyslexia and so on. They are all readily available. Rather I have aimed to explain the variety of learning disability or autism or learning difficulties as well as Special Educational Needs by giving examples. They start with those who are the most severely affected and move on to those with fewer life-changing symptoms.

Profound and Multiple Learning Disabilities

I have not talked face to face with the first category – the most serious – because most of these people cannot speak. Often they cannot walk or talk or hear or see or feed themselves. They form a very small proportion of those with learning disabilities. They have named illnesses – Fragile X syndrome or Prader-Willi syndrome[17] or Retts syndrome and various other syndromes. People with these conditions are classified as having 'profound and multiple learning disabilities'. To outsiders such as me, their situation is grim. In many cases, they will not get past a mental age of one or two and the majority will die young. All these people need twenty-four hour care – often with three full-time carers or more over a week. Those I sort of met briefly in a ward showed no sign of knowing or caring I was there. Yet talking to the nurse in charge in the ward at the residential home called Pepenbury, I was moved to be told "they are all different. They are all individuals."

I did, however, talk on a number of occasions with an elderly couple whose daughter has had profound learning disabilities all her life. She cannot walk or talk and is confined to a wheelchair. The parents had looked after her every hour of every day for many years; and while she is able to do almost nothing for herself, she is profoundly loved. The parents did not think it necessary to have their story told; but my admiration was total.

Nicholas's Story. Nicholas was thirteen when I first talked with his mother. He is classified as 'having multiple learning disabilities, with Lennox–Gastaut Syndrome and a severe form of epilepsy which has produced left sided hemiplegia and communication difficulties'. Basically, he has these very severe problems because he contracted meningitis when he was five weeks old, which caused substantial injury to his brain. This has meant that he and his family have had to face a huge variety of serious issues over his life. His disabilities are so severe that his mental age is more like a two to three year old. He cannot read or write and his speech is very limited. His hemiplegia, which semi-paralyses his left side, means that his use of his left arm and hand is very limited. Additionally, Nicholas has very severe epilepsy which causes him to have multiple seizures of two to three different types daily. During some seizures, he may stay partially conscious, while in others he drops to the floor without any warning, with the danger that, when he falls, he hurts himself. Twice in the last six months, he has had to be hospitalised due to serious injuries that he has sustained during a fall. Not surprisingly with all these problems, he can become frustrated and has what are called 'behavioural problems'. In his case, this means that, increasingly, he lashes out or kicks those who are looking after him – mainly his family – often without warning or obvious reason. As he is growing up a powerfully-built teenager, these outbursts can cause considerable damage to those on the receiving end.

As if these difficulties were not enough, he is often a very bad sleeper. At least once a week, he will be awake all night and likely to get out of bed and wander. Even on the other nights, he does not sleep well. As he is liable to injure himself if left alone, it means someone – almost inevitably his family – has to be awake almost all night in case he is up. Due to his age and size and his behavioural problems, it is becoming increasingly difficult for his family to care for Nicholas on their own. Because he is now a very tall young man, he is also much more likely to injure himself severely when having a seizure.

Despite all these difficulties the family, which includes an older brother, remains close. The last thirteen years have been extremely tough, but Nicholas's mother feels that they as a family have kept a positive outlook. "We have managed to come out on the other end". Nicholas has had to endure so much in his short life, with endless hospital appointments and admissions. The family feels he is wonderful to have coped. When having to describe how life is with a disabled child, Nicholas's mother uses the following analogy: "It's like an athlete jumping hurdles on a track. You have finally managed to jump over one hurdle, just to discover there is another one right in front of you. And so, it continues…". The family tries to stimulate Nicholas as much as possible by taking him on outings. However, his favourite pastimes are looking at books with pictures; spending time with his dog; and watching his favourite TV programme – the children's series 'Lazy-Town'.

Against this background, what help has been available for Nicholas and his family over the last thirteen years? According to the various caring services, Nicholas was diagnosed relatively early – when he was around one year old. From then on the NHS had provided the majority of support to Nicholas and his family. The Local Educational Authority and the Kent County Council's Disabled Children's Team came into the picture when he was four. Overall, the family feels that the NHS, Kent County Council and the organisations that the KCC have delegated to help have provided as good care as was possible in such a difficult case and with the inevitable financial constraints.

From the start, the County Council has provided a long-term care manager who is responsible for recommending what help should be given. She visits two or three times a year, either at home or at school to assess Nicholas and discuss matters with the family. The family have been provided with a number of regular care workers, the majority being helpful; and Social Service and the Local Educational Authority attend the annual reviews held at Nicholas's school. Nicholas has received support from the NHS occupational therapy team with equipment and home alterations. He also used to have respite care once a month via his special school, partly financed by the KCC Social Services and partly by the NHS. Unfortunately, this help was discontinued a year ago due to lack of capacity at the school. Nicholas's mother continues:

> "When Nicholas was five, he joined the local prep school
> where his older brother went. However, due to his severe
> epilepsy, we soon saw that Nicholas needed a more specialist
> school environment. So, when he was six, he joined Milestone
> School in Longfield, a maintained special needs school.
> However, eventually, even Milestone School could not meet
> Nicholas's educational needs, and, so, when he was nine
> years old, he was moved to what used to be called St Piers
> School in Lingfield, Surrey – it is now the National Centre
> for Young Children with Epilepsy – where he has a wide
> range of help, speech therapy, occupational therapy,
> physiotherapy and medical supervision. The teaching is
> based around the National Curriculum but adapted to
> Nicholas's cognitive and physical abilities. He benefits
> tremendously from this multidisciplinary approach to

> learning. He is picked up every morning at nine o'clock,
> with a carer as well as the driver, and they bring him back
> each afternoon at about four".

As well as financing Nicholas's place at the National Epilepsy Centre – not administratively easy as it is out of his 'home county' of Kent and providing transport to and from the school, the County Council has arranged via a charity they often use, Kent Friendz, that Nicholas goes out to a variety of clubs and activities. (Fuller details about Kent Friendz are given later). For four to five hours a week, Kent Friendz is paid to provide entertainment and stimulation for Nicholas. He loves the two carers who come every Sunday to take him out bowling or swimming or to a film. "He smiles when they arrive, which he does not normally do very often", says his mother. There is also a Saturday Club every month, again organised by Kent Friendz, as well as activities arranged by the school in the holidays where Nicholas attends their 'specialist club', which is aimed at children with behavioural problems who needs two to one support – two carers for each child.

Although the care provided by all these organisations – the Kent County Council, Kent Friendz, his school and the NHS – is very welcome and of high quality, it does seem less than ideal. The number of hours that society expects parents of children like Nicholas with severe learning disabilities to be 'on duty' seems excessive. However, the family does not complain. Indeed, they praise the people who help, although they hope that their requests for some extra home support and overnight respite care, together with the possibility of a residential school place, will be granted.

Nicholas's seventeen year old brother – of whom the family are immensely proud – says that he was probably eight when he first realised that Nicholas was 'different'.

> "When Nicholas started at my prep-school, I saw that he was
> not really like the other boys in his class. The others saw it
> too. It was not that he was bullied – they just felt he wasn't
> one of them. And over the years, when I've been going along
> holding Nicholas's hand in the street, I see people staring at
> him. All I can do is give them a dirty look. But I know he
> does walk differently and he doesn't look like everyone else.

At home, I try to do what I can. I know my parents need a bit of a break. So, I'll help Nicholas get up and get dressed and I'll change him. I'll hold his hand a lot because he really likes that – and it stops him hitting people. We're never sure why sometimes he lashes out or tries to kick people. For him, having a good time really just means someone holding his hand and going for a walk in the garden; or just watching TV programmes he knows with someone he knows. He likes things that are repetitive and really needs everything ordered in the way it has been before, but we don't really know what he likes and why – mainly because he can't really talk or tell us anything and we are not really sure how much he is understanding. The four of us – my parents, Nicholas and I – go down to the coast sometimes. And we did go away to Sardinia last summer. But I don't want people to feel sorry for us – although it would be good if they were a bit more understanding."

"Loving Olivia". Learning disabilities are often sub-divided into three – 'mild', 'moderate' and 'profound' with Nicholas being in the profound category. However, as medical diagnoses progress, there often seem to be overlaps – 'mild to moderate' or new sub-divisions, all of which seem to have three or four letter acronyms. Classification is certainly not an exact science. This is why the term 'on the autistic scale' has been so useful.

In a remarkable book, 'Loving Olivia', Lady (Liz) Astor described in detail what it was like to bring up her moderately severely autistic daughter, Olivia, until Olivia was in her teens.[18] The difficulties faced by Olivia's mother and the family, both practical and emotional, were immense, twelve or more hours a day, seven days a week and for year after year. Yet what this well-to-do and influential mother faced is only too typical of a family with a child with autism, whatever their social position. The first, early dilemma with any child always seems to be to find the right balance between excessive worrying about every facet of your child's development and, on the other hand, an unwillingness to think anything as bad as autism can possibly happen.

Liz initially veered towards the second. She admits that she found it difficult to accept what her own mother mentioned when Olivia was eight months old and not able to sit up. "It is as if Olivia hasn't arrived or woken up yet… almost as if her soul is halfway between heaven and her body." At one year old, Olivia was not crawling or reacting much to people. At two, she was still clearly well behind her peers. Professionals, while making suggestions of what might help, for some reason did not mention the word 'autism'. Liz Astor became frustrated by the many experts, often with different views, but the family was able to take on a carer to support Olivia in the period before she went to school.

The book has useful sections on getting a child what in those days was called 'statemented', meaning that Olivia, by now four and three quarters, got extra help from Social Services and the educational authorities. (This is now called asking to have an EHCP – an Education, Health and Care Plan). It was a grim fight with the authorities but one faced by many other parents that I met. The description of Olivia at two normal primary schools is again harrowing but certainly not unusual for an autistic child. There are times, too, when as well as understanding Liz Astor's great and real frustrations with the schools, one also feels sympathy for the heads and the teachers, as well as the educational establishment. Aged eight Olivia could not blow her nose, bath or wash herself or comb her hair. Although she could not write, she could talk – sometimes with embarrassing accuracy about her parents' friends. (It is clear that autistic people are not good at lying).[19] She was additionally diagnosed as having dyspraxia – where the brain cannot pass messages to the muscles. However, while she could not understand maths, she loved reading. She had her own favourite books and films which she re-read or watched incessantly. Everything had (and still has) to be done in an extremely ordered way – her way – which is completely typical of a child – or adult – with autism. There is a moving description of Olivia at eleven when her mother, while accepting all the things Olivia could *not* do, lists what she *had* mastered:

- She had learnt to walk; and to ride a tricycle around the grounds
- She had swum a length of the pool
- She had mastered a level of talking which could be understood
- She had no spite or meanness; she did not cheat, lie, bully, brag or steal
- She was not competitive and did not argue.

But she was hurt if she was laughed at and, as she had always been, she was continuously on the edge of great anxiety. The book gives a sobering list of supposed cures which were and are outside mainstream practice – none of which did much to help Olivia.[20] Above all, it gives an account of the sheer, absolute exhaustion to which so many families push themselves in order to help their child through the many long years, all the while sustained by their enormous love for the young boy or girl.

However, before I give the impression that everything to do with learning disabilities is impossible, I thought that I would give a vignette of one, not very young lady. I was impressed not only by her character but by the various services that support her. The autistic woman concerned is blind and her walking and speech are not very good. Social Services have supported her as a 'service user' since she was a child. She has a personal carer who is with her all the time. She goes regularly to the Scotts Project day centre in Tonbridge, where, when I visited, she was making small pottery houses in which a night light could be placed. She also goes regularly to an employment enterprise called 'Tuck by Truck' in Aylesford, where she packs boxes with snacks which are then taken by drivers all over the district to offices, garages and workshops. However, most surprisingly, she is a prize-winning horse dressage rider. When I asked how this could possibly work, her carer explained that there is a special riding school in Barnet to which she is driven each week. People will stand at specified positions in the ring and she is able to guide the horse towards the sound of the voice.

So far, these descriptions of people with learning difficulties have been, as it were, from the outside looking in. It seemed important to let people who have these problems have a voice of their own.

Naoki Higashida. The most obvious voice is not from Kent, not even from the UK. It comes from Naoki Higashida, a Japanese boy with moderate autism but with a remarkable ability to explain how he feels and why he and autistic people act as they do. His first book, 'The Reason I Jump', was written when he was thirteen and his second, 'Fall Down Seven Times Get Up Eight' was written when he was in his early twenties.[21] The books have been translated and promoted by the novelist, David Mitchell, who has an autistic son of his own. My thanks for being allowed to quote from both books. They are remarkable and I hope, by my giving some extracts, it will encourage even more people to read them. First, some extracts from 'The Reason I Jump'.

> *"What's the worst thing about having autism?"* "You have no idea quite how miserable we are. For us, who are always causing problems and are useless at pretty much everything we try to do, you can't imagine how miserable and sad we get."

> *"Why don't you do what you're told?"* "There are times when I can't do what I want to. It doesn't mean I don't want to. I just can't get it together; somehow my body is beyond my control. When we're being told off, we feel terrible. It's as if something that isn't us is urging us on".

> *"Do you hate it when we make you do things?"* "We kids with autism would like you to watch out for us – meaning, please never give up on us."

> *"Why do you speak in that peculiar way?"* "Non-autistic people can sort out what they want to say while they're having their conversations. But in our case, the words we want to say and the words we CAN say don't always match that well. More practice will help, however. Please never laugh at us, even when we're doing a less than great job. I can never say what I really want to. Instead, verbal junk comes pouring out of my mouth. I have no problem reading aloud or singing but, as soon as I try to speak with someone, the words just vanish. Thanks to the training I've had, I've learnt a method of communication by writing. I end up hating myself for not being able to control my actions. Whenever our obsessive behaviour is bothering other people, please stop us straight away, whatever way you can."

> *"Do you prefer to be on your own?"* "No: for people with autism, what we're anxious about is that we're causing trouble for the rest of you. THIS is why it is hard to stay around with other people. We'd love to be with other people".

"Why do you line up your things?" "Lining things up is the best fun. Other kids seem to enjoy pretending and make-believe but I never see the point of this. What I care about – in fact I'm pretty obsessive about this – is the order things come in and the different ways of lining them up. When we're playing in this way, our brains feel refreshed and clear."

"Why don't you make eye contact?" "We are trying to listen to the other person – we're fully focussed on working out what the heck you're saying – so our sense of sight sort of zones out".

"What kind of TV do you like?" "I still prefer TV programmes for kindergarten kids. We tend to prefer simpler, more straightforward stories because we can more easily guess what's going to happen next. People with autism get a kick out of repetition. What we just don't do are disputes, bargaining or criticising others. We're totally helpless in these scenarios."

"Would you like to be 'normal'?" "For us, you see, having autism is normal – so we can't know for sure what your 'normal' is even like. If a person without autism is going through a hard time, he or she can talk it over with someone or raise a ruckus about it. But in our case that's not an option – we can never make ourselves understood".

What becomes very apparent in both books is the sense of frustration. In his second book 'Fall Down Seven Times Get Up Eight', the twenty year old Naoki Higashida makes it very clear that, in the last eight years, while he still feels frustrated, he has learnt more about himself and how to control his feelings. He can now explain why, when he wants to say "thank you" to his carer, it comes out as "have a good day": or how, when he wants to say "Happy Mother's Day Mum", no words happen. The frustration at this lack of ability to say what he wants to say is enormous; and, although he has taught himself ways to release the tension, he can still have a panic attack.

"What causes your panic attacks?" "Because people with autism aren't skilful talkers, we may be more sensitive than you are. Stuck here inside these unresponsive bodies of ours, it's always a struggle just to survive. And it's this feeling of helplessness which sometimes drives us half crazy and brings on a panic attack or a meltdown. When this happens, please just let us cry, or yell, and get it all out. Stay close by and keep a gentle eye on us and, while we're swept up in our torment, please stop us hurting ourselves or others."

Changes. "In the past, I had a much harder time if the order of the day's events got switched… I didn't mind about the change of plans itself: rather, I was very nervous about how I might react to the new situation. I can't stop myself from worrying about vexing other people or getting pushed beyond my limits into a full scale meltdown."

Afterword: "Please remember: the reality of a non-verbal life is way, way harder than the verbal majority can imagine… However hard an autistic life is, however sad it can be, so long as there's hope, we can stick at it. And when the light of hope shines on all this world, then our future will be connected with your future. That's what I want above all."

Naoki Higashida is more fortunate than some people with autism. A good number of children with severe or moderately severe autism do not have their diagnosis early as he did. Additionally, from a young age his parents were knowledgeable and totally committed to his progress. But, above all, he has a remarkable ability to express himself in his writing, which, in turn, has been translated superbly.

One thirty year old woman with whom I talked had and still has a different set of problems. She had an unhappy childhood. She found learning was difficult but neither her school nor her parents thought of pursuing her troubles. "I was told so often that I was lazy, that I eventually sort of believed it", she says. Only when she was twenty-five did she get a diagnosis of dyslexia – which she had to suggest to the doctors herself. She is currently at university (and is expected to get a First). However, she now has been struggling to leave her home because she has developed an unspecified kind of anxiety crisis. Finally, she has been given a diagnosis of BPD. She learnt that this was Borderline Personality Disorder – the word 'borderline', she was told, referred to being judged to be between psychosis and mental breakdown. She was also told that the term was being changed to another – in this case with a five letter acronym – which was now thought to be less misleading and less demeaning. She is very talented in her field but lack of a diagnosis or help when she was young and a range of missed opportunities by parents, doctors and experts have meant an unfortunate life so far. It can only be hoped that rather than having a learning disability – officially the lifelong condition – she can be found to have learning difficulties or mental health problems – which, by some analyses, should mean she can be 'cured'. This case illustrates something felt by many people with learning problems – a lack of a clear diagnosis. However, even when a diagnosis is made, it can often seem obscure and masked in jargon, with not always any clarity about what can be done to help. This is not necessarily to blame the doctors or the other professionals. The subject is not a clear cut science.

While many people with learning disabilities, and particularly with autism, do not achieve very high educational levels, a number are clearly extremely good at maths and computers. A very small proportion of people with autism are even more outstanding in a particular direction – possibly eccentric but a genius. They can hear a piece of Mozart and instantly play it back; or they can see a photograph of the Houses of Parliament for five seconds and then draw an exact picture with every window and pinnacle. Elon Musk has proudly said on TV that he has Aspergers. Einstein was famously 'not very good' at maths but it is guessed that he had learning disabilities; Steve Jobs certainly had a good number of autistic traits; and one teenager I met at a well-known art school could not read, write or add up at all, but was outstandingly brilliant and inventive. For those few people with a learning disability who are unusually brilliant, there is a term for their condition: they are said to have High Functioning Autism or to be a savant. Bill Gates said, "If your society doesn't like geeks, you're in trouble." Martin Luther King Jr put it more poetically. "Human salvation lies in the hands of the creatively maladjusted." So, perhaps, one of the themes in this book gives a new perspective: a person with a learning disability does not have to be seen as a burden on society. However, only a few per cent of people with a learning disability can be classified as having this High Functioning Autism and I did not meet any, apart from the art student.

While it is repeatedly said that early diagnosis of a learning disability is important, there is one anomaly which is called 'Late Onset Autism'. A child may appear to be progressing normally, yet, quite suddenly, often at three, four, or even at five, it appears that they are different from their peers; and signs of autism become apparent. I talked to one young teenager who had a good deal to pass on to the wider world. She could be thought of as typical of a child with Aspergers – which at one point she was told she had; but, equally, she could be diagnosed as having 'late onset autism' – or as being 'on the autistic spectrum' or as having a high functioning autism or disabilities – all of which, at one stage or another, the family were told that she had.

Aspergers, Autism and ADHD

Isabella's Story. Isabella seemed to me to be a charming, pretty, serious, intelligent, polite and rather shy young lady of twelve. It was not until she was around three that her mother began to notice that Isabella was not mixing easily socially, was now avoiding other children at playgrounds, was lining up her dolls particularly carefully and seemed to suffer from real anxiety when the unexpected happened. Her parents went to their GP and it was agreed Isabella should be formally assessed. Her mother started keeping a diary of the letters, appointments, conversations and interviews. It is too long to fit into this book. Suffice it to say that, after many delays, they were told there was an eighteen month wait before the NHS could start an assessment – with the likelihood that there would then be further long delays before any specialist help recommended by the assessment would start. Isabella's parents decided to go private, even though they could ill afford it. To their surprise, they were offered an appointment with the area's top NHS paediatric consultant the following week which, after a two-and-a-half-hour discussion and assessment, resulted in a diagnosis that Isabella – now eight – was "high functional autistic". (Isabella was also told at various times that she had Aspergers. It seems that, as so often, the diagnoses are not clear but Aspergers is a sub-classification of autism.) The parents were told what this would mean for the family and, over the years, they have done everything to ensure Isabella grows up as happy and as untroubled as possible. A year ago, her parents made the decision to send her to a small fee-paying school rather than a state secondary school, as they felt that she would find it difficult to cope in a large, teenage school environment. Isabella is now in her second year at the school and it is apparent that the right decision was made. She has made strides socially and the small sized classes suit her needs. Academically, she is now starting to show her full potential as her anxiety about school has lessened. It is not always plain sailing and she knows that there will always be bumps in the road which she will have to tackle as they arise. As she is not chatty or gregarious, she often felt left out at primary school. Isabella tells me that she is good at Maths and IT and smiles because she knows that I know it is typical. "But I'm getting better with English – although I don't find it easy making up stories when I have to imagine something I don't actually know. If things go wrong at school, I don't have a meltdown – I wait until I get home! I go up to my room and put on my new ear protectors (she shows me) – I have to have them on when I go to sleep – but, overall, I think I'm learning to cope a bit better. I'm OK by the next day. I haven't got any real friends at school but there is one girl I go to dancing with – which is really my best 'happy thing'. And I've just heard I'm going to be dancing in the Tunbridge Wells Panto. I play more with the boys than the girls – the girls are soppy and just follow the boys around. I'm not very interested in clothes and things." I ask if she ever feels embarrassed by being a bit different. "Not really", she says. "And it's getting better a bit as I grow older." Isabella has given me permission to print her description of herself in her 'Communication Passport'. She wrote this a couple of years ago to help teachers and people with whom she was going to be dealing.

Important Information About Me

You will find the following information important in gaining an understanding of me!

I find social communication difficult and social experiences and situations hard.

I can get very anxious about a variety of things and I have many fears (dogs, alarms, fire, dark, thunder, fireworks, characters in stories such as wolves, vampires and zombies etc.) I can transfer fears so new ones can come up unexpectedly.

I am very sensitive to loud noise. I can find it very difficult to concentrate if it is noisy and busy in the classroom. It affects my learning and how I am feeling. And I find it hard to distinguish between loud voices and shouting. It confuses me. If you have a loud voice, I may think you are telling me or other people off. I can also be affected by light, smells and temperature.

I don't like to contribute in whole class discussions unless I choose to. Putting my hand up to contribute is rare. Please don't ever make me a focus of attention. I really can't cope with this, even if you want to make it positive!

If I don't give you eye contact or answer you if you are talking to me, please don't think I am being rude.

I can take things literally but I am becoming aware of idioms and that they don't mean as they sound – you can have a good joke about these with me to help me understand them.

I may say things honestly and to the point but this is the way I see the world.

It is not always apparent when I am feeling anxious. At times I am very good at masking it. (Signs – being clingy to a familiar adult; flushed face or very pale; I fidget – usually my hands fidget around my face and hair. I will give no eye contact and feel tearful or chew my cuffs). Signs can start off very subtly – you need to be very tuned into me to see the signs starting if you are to catch me before I shut down or opt out, etc.

If you recognise my anxiety or I opt out of a lesson etc, it is unlikely I will be able to tell you why. I commonly respond with a shrug of my shoulders if asked. There is always a trigger but this isn't always obvious.

I can completely 'shut down' if things get too much. Please don't pressure me to do anything at these times. I may need some comfort from an adult's presence but I won't respond if being spoken to and I will need time and space to work myself out of it.

I like structure and routine. I find unstructured times difficult. Play times aren't always a good place for me.

I am not very good when things change.

I am quite complex. I may appear fine for a spell of time and then suddenly I am affected by many things which affect all areas of my life. I go through this cycle again and again.

Please never underestimate how hard I work to understand the world around me. It is a known fact that a child with learning disabilities works so much harder than a neuro-typical person to make sense of their world. I have been working so hard to keep things together that it impacts on my life outside of school where I feel safe and secure enough to release these feelings.

Things I like at home

I am very good at organising. At home I like to help Mummy file and organise her work. I am very good at doing jobs. I enjoy writing lists. I like nothing more than a file of dividers to play with and organise my own papers.

I enjoy creative activities at home. I enjoy drawing but I don't always think I am very good at it. I enjoy making things with creative resources.

I enjoy role-play but with toy figures. My play is always centred on real life experiences rather than anything imaginative. I spend a lot of time role-playing schools with figures, folders of papers and books etc. School is a stressful place for me and I use my play to work my stress out.

I enjoy playing with dolls. I am quite nurturing.

I like music as long as it doesn't sound scary. My favourite is Adele. I love to sing but only if nobody appears to be watching.

I love dancing. I attend ballet, modern and tap on a Saturday and enjoy dancing and twirling around the house if nobody appears to be watching me.

I love swings, so I do really enjoy going to the park. I will swing for quite some time.

Things I find difficult at home

I need relax time – so homework can be difficult. It is not always easy allowing my younger brother and sister their own views and opinions and allowing their choice in games and play. Going to new places is often difficult.

Things I like at school

I am good at maths. I do sometimes find new concepts hard at first but I do enjoy it. I really am enjoying sensory circuits. Hanging from the wall bars is my favourite activity in this session. I am really fond of Mary, the dinner lady. She has a lot of time for me and helps me feel safe and secure at lunch times.

Slightly Milder Aspergers/Autism

The symptoms of Aspergers can vary greatly in the degree of severity. The main character, Christopher, in Mark Haddon's book (and play) 'The Curious Incident of the Dog In The Night-time' is an example of a more difficult case but I have known one boy – I will call him John – since he was ten. He is now twenty-three and I have followed his progress via his father, hoping at each stage that things would turn out well. In spite of some less than ideal periods, he is now settled with a good job.

John's Story. I had first met John when I used to listen to him reading at our local school. He was tall for his age, rather serious and a good reader. Although he could become enthusiastic when he explained about his computers at home, he did not smile much or ask questions about me, or about what we were reading, or about the wider world. His degree of Aspergers was not too serious but enough to be noticeable after one met him a few times. Luckily, as well as his supportive parents, he had an older brother, who has always looked after him. His symptoms had been picked up early which his parents felt was vital. His primary school was particularly good at providing extra, specialist help – even if it did take a bit of persuasion with the education and social service authorities. At some stages he had one-to-one tutors. By the time he reached the top of the primary school, he was caring and doing well with most subjects, particularly IT. He was a little different but he talked naturally with adults he knew. He was always polite and always looked after the smaller children and, after he left the school, he used to go back to help. The change to secondary school was likely to be a strain. It is for ordinary children and it very often is for children with such conditions as Aspergers. Although the school to which he went did have a 'special needs tutor', the man was looking after a good number of children with a range of symptoms. And the sheer size of the school, with a wide variety of children, meant it was not always easy or pleasant for John. He did get singled out as different, although actual physical bullying was kept at bay by his elder brother – a respected athlete. John obtained his GCSEs, continuing to be keen on maths, science subjects and IT. He went from the secondary school to West Kent College and from there got a trial job at a well-known shop dealing with top of the range hi-fi goods. However, at the end of the apprenticeship, the firm did not wish to pay him full wages and he left. I suspect that the job was not ideal for someone who did not easily chat with customers. However, matters turned out well. After more studying at West Kent College,[22] which both he and his parents felt did a good job in helping people with a range of learning difficulties), he ended up at twenty-one in charge of IT systems at a leading school locally. So, in many ways John's life has been a success. He is a bit different and it does mean that he does not make cheerful, jolly friends easily. He has not yet had a girlfriend but he is close to his family who value him.

The next person, David, *does* have a computer wizard as a father but David himself has never had a passion for IT or maths. I have known David for well over fifteen years since, as an exhausted sixty year old cross-country runner, I used to race against him as a seventeen year old. David has said that I can quote him, because he wants to explain how being on the mild end of the autistic spectrum can still be a hurdle, although, as he says, "obstacles can be opportunities to be overcome and do not mean being excluded by society."

When I first met him, I did feel that he was different. I could not imagine him drinking with the lads. He seemed friendly but had a slight hesitation in his speech, which he explains as trying to find himself at that time. I heard about his aspiration to go to university. He had a creative flair, though he was also interested in science and history.

David's Story. "Looking back, no one talked about Aspergers or anything like that in my early youth. I was treated like any other kid. Whilst I liked this equality, it meant I had extra things to learn, as well as the regular teenage issues. I would often use video games to escape from reality, and I recall being shy and doing tasks differently. As I grew up, I found I was interested in writing and in art – I'm no Picasso, but I can draw. And athletics gave me a new form of escapism that was good for me physically and mentally. When I was fifteen – just before my GCSEs – an educational psychologist told me I had 'mild Aspergers', but it didn't make much of an impression on me and I've been completing the jigsaw of information ever since. I had little in the way of learning support, apart from extra time when I sat my university entrance. In some ways, I feel the school curriculum needs to include classes on life and social skills. That would benefit nearly every young student. I say this, because I have a memory of saying 'hi' to a girl – and having to go into the bathroom afterwards. I remember thinking to myself – I cannot be shy forever: this is not how I want to live my life, and I should just stop being shy. From then on, I felt a new sense of energy and confidence, though I still had a way to go. My first secondary school had been big and I felt left out, but I changed schools and that helped a lot.

I don't recall being bullied – except once – and it seems strange even to look back on the incident. There was a group of boys who took against me. First, they called me names and threatened me. Finally, one day the leader tripped me up from behind. But then – after a pause – he leant down and helped me up. And, peculiarly, after that the whole group seemed to look up to me. It was almost like it was a test or initiation.

Anyway, I went to university and read journalism. I made a point of going to the university bar and talking to my peers about their courses while drinking a beer. Taking an interest in what they had to say helped. I did go clubbing with friends and have the drunken photos to haunt me. It was a fun experience that helped shape my character, although I prefer the intimacy and relaxation of a small pub. I've had my share of dates and girlfriends, which I attribute to my earlier pep talk to myself. It means I had a life like anyone else, and experienced the same relationship ups and downs necessary to function in society. After graduating, it was tough to get a worthwhile job. However, I gradually built up a portfolio, particularly with magazine features and marketing. I'm writing a health book with a fresh approach, and have a flat with my girlfriend. I now realise I'm unique and this is a plus – imagine being a carbon copy on a production line. We all have our own abilities, and the more I learn about the world, the more I see that everyone has at least mild signs of a learning condition. They either haven't been diagnosed; or they try to hide and not admit it. There are things I can't do well, such as cook, since I worry about the gas – but baking is fun. We tend to split the household chores, as this is most fair. I feel that I picked up a lot more knowledge *after* education. A big part of this is learning what I wanted and not clouding myself with details. The main point is to start. I now run less than I once did, partly because I found a way to try other activities, although running did give me added confidence. Over the years I have found good people who lift others up, and I've got better at facing those who challenge you. Life is actually pretty good. Looking back, I see a boy who was yet to mature. I might have matured quicker with more informed, formal support and it might have given a boost to my confidence, but it made me who I am. And I sometimes wonder if I could help kids with mild Aspergers. You need social teaching to explain life, and a kind of mentor to challenge you. It is never too late. The key is learning to live with who you are. I don't look down on autism because I experienced Aspergers in a mild way. It can have huge pluses. If it's difficult, then that makes it more rewarding to accomplish. And being different is a testament to your character".

ADHD

Having described the lives of people with some of the different degrees of autism, the next type of difficulty worth describing is Attention Deficit and Hyperactivity Disorder – again increasingly being diagnosed and more regularly appearing in the media. The condition – which was often just called Attention Deficit Disorder (ADD) – is now mainly known as ADHD. Although sometimes classified as somewhere on the autistic spectrum, other experts are inclined to say it is a type of personality disorder. However, whatever the diagnosis, ADHD can be very difficult not just for both the child and the parents, but also for the school. It means that children – much more often boys than girls – cannot concentrate and feel they have to move around. Until fairly recently, it was often seen by their teachers and the other school children that the child was disrupting a class: and it is true – they were. In the past, their behaviour often meant that they were criticised for being inattentive or stupid or both. This in turn means that the child loses confidence and can become upset or aggressive.

There is a moving description by a nine year old and a ten year old boy in the Schools chapter of how they feel and what can be done to help. The school's Special Educational Needs Officer had discussed the condition with them and their parents. She persuaded them to do a presentation to their school friends. It taught the two boys to understand themselves better; and, with the support of the teachers and the parents, they are learning to cope more easily. Additionally, the presentation helped explain matters to the other children. One of the several ways to help such children is to do what are called 'circuits' which are done before classes begin. This routine goes some way to let out their energy and their tensions. These exercises are again discussed in more detail in the Schools chapter. While ADHD normally affects children and becomes manageable as they grow older, there can also be adults who suffer from the problem.

Having a Meltdown

I had heard a good deal about a boy or much less often a girl or an adult, "having a meltdown". It often affects those with learning problems. I wanted to understand what happened; what it felt like for the person experiencing it; and what could be done both to prevent it or to make it less awful when it was happening. A very experienced Special Educational Needs officer (usually called a SENCO) explained what was called the 'Rage Cycle' and she produced a description which she had been given which she in turn had adapted. The Meltdown or 'Rage Cycle' typically runs through three stages – the rumbling stage, the rage stage and the recovery stage. During the whole cycle, the child is not really able to think or talk rationally; and allowance has to be made.

The Rumbling Stage: In this first stage, the pupil exhibits specific behavioural changes which often signal the impending crisis. At this point, it is imperative that the teacher intervenes but without becoming part of a struggle. The teacher can often help the pupil regain control without stopping the class routine. It can help to redirect the pupil to focus on something other than the allocated task at hand. Creating a 'cool zone' outside the classroom where the pupil can go to work in a less stressful environment is also often successful. Even at this early stage, the pupil is not thinking logically and will most likely react emotively to any adult statement. Teachers should be calm, show as little reaction as possible and never be confrontational. Under no circumstance should the teacher engage in lengthy conversation about "who is right" or "who is in control". During this stage the teacher or teaching assistant must think of things for the child to do with which he/she is familiar and likes doing – often reading or such things as playing with Lego – things which will make him/her relax down. The teacher must be flexible so that the child can meet the 'new' goal – to get back to a state when he or she can once again become teachable.

The Rage Stage: If a pupil's behaviour is not diffused at the rumbling stage, a tantrum, rage or meltdown is likely to occur. At this stage, the child is disinhibited and acts impulsively, emotionally and sometimes explosively. Initially, if the rage stage has not yet become too serious, the best plan is to get the child to the cool zone but only if he or, less often she, can be moved without physical assistance greater than a gentle touch. Sometimes, it may be easier to remove the other children. Again, adults should be non-confrontational and use few words. It is essential that the teacher remains calm. The adult should not take the pupil's words personally – the child's mouth is on "automatic pilot", saying words that are unplanned and not meant. Adults should disengage emotionally. The meltdown will most probably run its course. However, the rage or meltdown can progress into shouting or crying, plus physical violence to staff or other pupils: and throwing or breaking things – a complete loss of control, frightening to themselves and others. However, this worst case scenario can usually be avoided by watchful work from staff. Priority should be placed on helping the pupil regain control and preserving his or her dignity.

The Recovery Stage: Following the meltdown, the child may have contrite feelings and apologise; or he or she may become sullen and withdrawn; or deny that inappropriate behaviour occurred. Children at this stage should still be considered fragile. If they are not given enough time to calm down they may enter the cycle again. Most often at this stage the child is not ready to learn – he or she is not in a 'teachable moment'. However, the child can be directed towards tasks, with which they are familiar and which they like – something within their comfort zone. This is not rewarding bad behaviour; rather it is helping the child to return to a 'teachable state'. This is not the time to discuss the rage behaviour with the child or attempt to discuss relaxation strategy. The ONLY time a pupil can learn is when they are back into a 'teachable state'.

Most teachers and teaching assistants, let alone the SENCOs, will have had experience of meltdowns. They will know how best to deal with the individual who is likely to suffer from them. However, some children – particularly girls – bottle up their frustration and rage until they get home. It is then difficult for the parents. They do not know what has caused the problem. Is it a one-off incident or just a general frustration that the child has felt? They may wonder whether they are just having to put up with a normal young person's angst. Nor have most parents had the training about meltdowns that the school staff will have had. One girl used to arrive home and explode. Sent upstairs to calm down, she would go round and continuously slam the doors. So the father took all the doors off! (History does not relate what she did instead.)

Dyslexia – and SpLDs

The term Dyslexia is now widely used and the general condition understood. The 'word-blindness' or difficulty with reading can nowadays be identified fairly easily by schools and help given to the child. However, this support is surprisingly recent. It was not until the 1970s that the subject became more of a mainstream issue – the actress, Susan Hampshire, did an excellent job in publicising the condition – but until then, children with what would now be clearly dyslexia were often thought to be stupid or just 'slow readers'. Even by the 1980s and 1990s, children with this type of problem were often missed.

I remember meeting one eight year old boy. He was being badly bullied and called 'dummy'. However, he managed to hide his serious worries from his parents and his teachers, until the mother began to realise what was happening. The story eventually had a happy ending primarily because of two things – a computer typing course designed specially to cope with dyslexia; and one particular teacher who built up the boy's confidence and provided help which eventually enabled the boy to get his GCSEs. The Government eventually laid down guidelines (including such things as extra time for exams) but this was only around 2010. (Incidentally, having dyslexia or the other similar types of difficulties, does not indicate a low IQ). Primary schools I visited, too, now all routinely checked for such problems. So, there has been progress in the last ten or twenty years. While treatment and support will certainly help, it will not mean reading or the other problems magically vanish – they will linger but will not ruin a life.

One headmaster I talked with recently reeled off a long list of conditions, all of which he said the school absorbed and helped. I knew about dyslexia but there was dyscalculia – problems with numbers; dysgraphia – problems with writing; dyspraxia – problems with co-ordination; dysmorphia – problems with body image, and I suspect, others. I learnt that they had a group name – Specific Learning Difficulties (SpLD).

Down's syndrome

Down's syndrome is usually thought of as a learning disability, rather than on the autistic spectrum. I particularly liked one story which I felt showed the difference between Down's and autism. I was talking with a mother who had an autistic son. He was aged seven. The son needs order; he is not good a relating to others in his class; and has no obvious friends. Although somewhat dyslexic, he is both lucid and candid. He has explained his current predicament to his mother. In his class, there is a Down's girl. She is talkative, demonstrative and wants to hug him – all the time. The son has told his mother that he has had to tell the Down's girl that there are hugging relationships and friendship relationships. He only wants to be friends.

Down's is something that is apparent at birth and, nowadays, can be increasingly easily detected when the mother is pregnant. There are about forty seven thousand people with Down's in the UK, with roughly seven hundred and fifty children born each year, and slightly more (about 55%) being boys. Their life expectancy which, between 1900 to 1960, was thirty or forty, is now much higher. The child (and the parents) will experience considerable problems, although the severity of these problems can vary. Now that Down's can be diagnosed during pregnancy, the dilemma faced by parents will be complex. Doctors will tell the parents the facts – including the strain that they will potentially have to cope with over the next twenty or thirty years – as well as the joy of having a totally loving child. The result is that 90% of women in the UK faced with this situation today have a termination.[23] However, the parents that I have met who have a child with Down's may have had to struggle but would not change what has happened. For an outsider, a person with Down's syndrome is obvious. They walk differently; are inclined to be tubby; have a funny voice; and a very noticeable round face. Yet the child or the adult will be gentle; can usually be taught to cope with life as long as they have support. I liked another statement by a man with Down's who, when thinking about the rush of everyday life around him, said two inter-related things. "Maybe we could all slow life down – inclusion is everything." Having just read an article about a family's struggles to bring up their twelve year old Down's son, I foolishly said to the father of a charming twenty-three year old Down's young lady, how much I admired and sympathised with what he and his wife had gone through. He looked at me with puzzlement. "There are no problems. She is totally wonderful. She is probably the best thing in our life."

Obsessive Compulsive Disorder (OCD)

There are various conditions – including Obsessive Compulsive Disorder – which, while they are not classified as on the autistic spectrum, are often considered a type of learning disability.

Obsessive Compulsive Disorder is usually called OCD. It can be very debilitating, yet it is often seen by the public as someone who feels he (or she) has to place his pens and pencils in a straight line. While the need for symmetry is certainly one of the characteristics, OCD is more clearly described as the uncontrollable and repetitive nature of doing a particular thing. It usually starts in early adulthood. There can be many symptoms but they are often classified into four groups.

- Compulsive washing and anxiety about contamination
- Concern about potential accidents, leading to compulsive checking
- Arranging objects in a symmetrical way
- Unacceptable taboos and mental rituals

The people concerned will often realise that what they both do and feel is irrational but are unable to control themselves. A good proportion of people with OCD will either grow out of it or learn to control their worst symptoms. However, in the worst cases, OCD can radically affect his or her daily lives for the whole of their life. In these severe cases, therapy can help but, as yet, there is no total cure. It does seem that the cause is often to a degree genetic and this applied to some of those I met – but not to others.[24]

I heard of two particular cases. In both, the people concerned know or sort of admit that they have OCD. The first example is described by a younger sister, whose older sibling has had OCD for much of her life. The whole family has been blighted by the problem.

"My older sister has OCD – you are never completely 'cured'. It is always there in the background. It was noticeable from when she was about eight years old – we don't know why it started. There was something 'not quite right'. The family tended to assume it was her way of getting attention: and she certainly got their attention. In fact, an oft-repeated phrase of my childhood was that we had 'to keep the peace' because of her or we couldn't do something because 'she did not like it'. Problems would generally happen in the evening – I guess because during the day she had to go to school. Before bedtime, she used to have to run up and down the stairs a certain number of times, and, if this was interrupted, she would have to start again from the beginning. As part of this (we had an old-fashioned toilet cistern), she used to have to pull the toilet chain each time. As you can imagine, in those days the cistern did not fill up quickly, and if it wouldn't pull, this would cause her to rage and to have to start her routine all over again – right from the beginning. The anger and the rage happened if the 'habits' or 'routines' were interrupted in any way. Of course, she was always very tidy. She meticulously cleaned her bedroom every Saturday morning. It would take several hours and everything would always be in its place. And there were things that annoyed her; my dad, mum and I could not play piano in our downstairs lounge if she could hear it upstairs, no one could sing or whistle because it annoyed her, I couldn't practise my violin (I had to do it at school). And she did not seem to worry about her behaviour if friends came around. If she was in a mood, everyone would all know about it.

"It could be very embarrassing for the family. My parents did get our GP involved, but he said that he had never seen anything like it. I don't think there was an awareness of OCD in those days. For me, it is only in the last twenty – maybe thirty – years that you hear the term Obsessive Compulsive Disorder mentioned, read about it, see programmes about it. After the GP visit, I recall my sister did spend some time in hospital where she underwent what I think was electro therapy. Whether it helped I don't know, but the extreme tidiness, or the jealousies or more general obsessive behaviour patterns and the arguments did not stop. There are many other examples that I could give that happened over the years, but generally, she still has problems – problems with coping, with her self-esteem, which has always been low, with anxiety, and she is quite self-obsessed. OCD never goes away. It is something she will always have and those around her have to live with. Because with any suggestion of seeking further medical help, particularly nowadays with mental health and anxiety high on the agenda, she will always find an excuse. 'There is nothing wrong with me.'"

The second case also concerned someone who is now middle-aged, in this case a man. Again, his problems had not made life easy for his family, his acquaintances or the people with whom he works – or for himself. On occasions he cannot control himself and flies into rages. He is exceptionally worried about order and the condition of his house and belongings. There is autism in the family which did not seem to apply to the first example above. It is tempting to 'blame' people with OCD for their bad or eccentric behaviour. However, in the more serious cases, that is to miss the point. They cannot control themselves.

However, not all cases are debilitating. One mother told me about her adult son. He is a distinguished scientist but, nevertheless, he has to keep everything in his life clean – to an extreme degree. He constantly has to wash his hands and to disinfect all the things he has touched. Yet he is not only very conscious of his OCD but he cheerfully tells everyone about it. His life is not ruined. As always, everyone is different.

Tourette's syndrome

Tourette's syndrome is sometimes said to be a learning disability but some experts class it as a neurological disorder. (I am not sure it matters?) People with Tourette's syndrome have slightly similar symptoms to OCD in that the person cannot control themselves. However, the symptoms primarily concern what are called their 'tics'. These tics can take the form of repeated and uncontrollable physical movements – such as blinking, eye rolling, grimacing, jerking or touching particular objects. Occasionally, the person cannot stop twirling and I did meet one such elderly, severely autistic man – it was very strange but moving. The vocal tics are most often grunting, tongue clicking, whistling, coughing or repeating a word or a phrase time after time. The public commonly thinks that repeated, uncontrollable, extreme swearing is a common characteristic. In fact, only one in ten people with a vocal tic will swear.

The syndrome often starts when a child is between five and nine and it is more common in boys. While there is no cure yet, the symptoms often improve or disappear as the child grows older. In the more severe cases and when there is no improvement after a year, there are therapies and drugs which can be prescribed.[25] I did not meet anyone with a diagnosis of Tourette's but one GP said: "I did have a family with Tourette's in my practice. Not violently swearing, but the father came in to see me in his early forties wondering if he had it? He had identified it in his son, and in himself. I can't remember whether any treatment worked, or was even offered. I think just being reassured that it was unlikely to get worse – and in that he was indeed correct – stopped him worrying to much about it." I was pleased to see that a short discussion by young people with Tourette's on the web had been viewed over 4.7 million times. This must have increased understanding. "You just can't hold it in – it's such a strain," said one young man. There was also a documentary on TV which is described in the chapter about the difficulties in finding a job if you have a learning disability.

(Peter the Great[26] seems to have had Tourette's – he had facial tics, and an uncontrollable temper as well as epileptic fits).

Most of the sub-divisions of learning disabilities have their own groupings or societies. So, there is information not only from the well-known groupings such as MIND or SCOPE or the NAS, but also from lesser-known societies such as PDA (Pathological Demand Avoidance). As well as national headquarters, many have local sections. I have often been told how helpful these places to meet people with similar experiences can be.

Hearing Impairment

At the beginning of this chapter, hearing difficulties was mentioned as a potential learning disability and clearly a child with severe or even moderate hearing loss is indeed going to need extra help. Although I met only one family with the problem – and they were obtaining very useful support from the school – it seems helpful to mention the National Deaf Children's Society (NDCS) which, as with so many of these specialist organisations, provide impartial advice not only for younger children but also for young adults and their parents.

Borderline Cases and Non-Intervention

As will have already become apparent from the examples in this chapter, there are often overlaps between the various sub-sections of learning disability and learning difficulty. Throughout this book, there are further examples of children and adults who have had complex evaluations resulting in borderline diagnoses or several diagnoses. It is not easy for experts. As each person is different, there become more and more sub-divisions. I liked the honesty of the diagnosis of PDDNOS which the patient found later meant Personality Development Disorder Not Otherwise Specific. But I doubt it helped. When the diagnosis is finally made, it is not easy for the parents either. This can be particularly the case for less well-off families. Professor Anna Vignoles has pointed out that middle/upper class parents obtain more help for their children than the less educated.[27]

There can be a different approach for the parents, especially if the child's difficulties do not seem too serious. It could be called non-intervention or doing nothing – apart from watching. Some years ago, a boy's parents were perfectly happy with their eight year old son's progress at school and not particularly concerned with the fact that he was finding some spellings difficult. A teacher suggested they get him tested for dyslexia. However, when the parents talked with a relative who had been an English teacher, the relative very strongly advised against it, saying the boy could be distressed and become labelled. Nor was there any major problem with the boy's actual reading. So the parents did not follow up on the idea. The son went on to get a good number of top 'A' levels including English A*; continued to university; and is now a journalist on a national newspaper. It can sometimes pay to be brave and not to fuss too much.

I talked with another family who are also trying what is, in effect, this calculated denial. They, too, did not wish to make their child feel 'different' or 'ill'. They are intelligent and prepared to put in a great deal of thought to help their son who in this case is now fourteen. The boy is doing well at school – particularly in maths and IT. Let's call him Vic. He clearly does have Aspergers or autism – even if it is not very severe. The mother explains their approach.

"We have two sons – now aged twelve and fourteen. We began to notice signs that Vic – the older one – was a bit withdrawn and seemed not to mix with other children much. Of course, we looked into things in considerable detail and it was clear that he had some form of autism: but, after a good deal of thought, we decided that we did not want him 'labelled'. We did not want other children or teachers to pick him out as being different or as having an illness. Probably above all, we did not want *him* to feel he was an outsider – someone who was not part of mainstream society. So we have brought him up normally and, just as we would tick off either of the boys for coming in with muddy boots all over the house, I tell Vic off if he does not behave 'normally'. So, if someone comes to the house and Vic is sitting in the corner with his computer and doesn't look up, I say 'come on Vic, say hello to Mr Whoever' and encourage him to look the visitor in the eye. Things like that. We know his 'little ways' and try to steer him into being as normal – whatever that is – as possible. Mainly it seems to be working. But I don't know if it would be right for all children with similar problems or even if we are doing the best for him. It just seems right to us."

The Old Way

For hundreds of years there was another way forward for those we today say have learning disabilities or learning difficulties. Society just let them get on with life – helped in practical ways where they could and – unless they were a danger to their neighbours or themselves – thought of them as part of the ordinary world. One very senior NHS dignitary was pondering the seeming huge increase of children with learning disabilities over the past ten or twenty years. "I wonder if it really is getting more common. I suspect that in my days at school – the 1960s – we just thought of some boys as lazy or stupid, just as you'd reckon another was fat or spotty. They may or may not have had learning disabilities – or learning difficulties – but all of them grew up OK."

I know a man in his eighties who has plainly had some form of what would today be classified as autism all his life. In many ways he has lived his life within the wider community. He has been married twice and has children. He has held modest jobs and he continues to look after himself, although nowadays not very well. He has not been very go-ahead but then many of the population are in the same position. Yet, underneath the seemingly regular life, he has had considerable troubles which do not need repeating here.

He did not have much help sixty or seventy years ago, nor did he want or expect it. Many of the diagnoses of today did not exist then. Schools and doctors and social workers did not recognise or have the means to help. Would the man have lived a fuller or happier life if he had the support available today? I do not know for certain: but I suspect that he would.

CHAPTER 2

Numbers:
"Are We All Really A Bit on The Autistic Spectrum?"

The Difficulty with the Figures

What is 'normal'? What isn't normal? There is the often-mentioned phrase "we are all a bit on the autistic spectrum", said by people who see themselves as normal but wish to be sympathetic to those who are not quite as normal as they think they are. (Incidentally, the phrase infuriates many of those who really do have recognised learning disabilities or autism).

So, trying to estimate how many people there are with any of the varying classifications of learning disability is complex. Even if detailed definitions are given, the large numbers who are on some borderline or other means the figures are unreliable – often extremely unreliable. There are some figures which are clear. For example, people with Down's syndrome, or the people admitted to hospital in a particular year with an eating disorder. However, the majority of figures have often seemed to be estimates and the estimates often seem to include overlapping diagnoses. One suspects that one person gets included in figures several times. Often, too, a charity or support group is likely – for the best of reasons – to include a higher rather than a lower estimate.

The difficulty for the officials – whether they are from government or Social Services or the NHS bodies or the education world – is that they have to say 'yes' or 'no' to individual cases about whether they allocate – or do not allocate – money and/or resources. The demand for help from all the service providers is dramatically increasing. All the GPs with whom I talked; all the NHS and Social Services officials; and all the schools all say the 'demand' – and 'demand' is the word used by them – for support for a perceived learning disability or difficulty keeps increasing.

Increase in Demand

What are the causes of the increase? One school of thought has been that there is a real explosion in the number of people who really can be considered autistic. Some US experts argued that not only was there a genetic background, but that particularly bright and numerate parents were inclined to have autistic children. Another US theory said the 'fault' was that of bad upbringing by the parents; and yet another blamed a wrong diet (which needed special supplements only provided by the particular expert). These ideas – together with the often extremely expensive 'cures' which were prescribed – are described by the award-winning American reporter, Steve Silberman, in his huge book 'Neurotribes'.[28] Silberman's conclusion, in simplistic terms, is that numbers of autistic children are not increasing but that identification of children with potential learning problems is becoming better. While this conclusion had largely been accepted in the UK earlier, there are still some UK experts who are dubious. They wonder whether there are one (or more) external causes. Increased stress on children was mentioned by one top NHS expert with whom I talked. Others have cited pollution; an increasing number of premature babies; food allergies or bad or unfortunate parenting – including divorced parents; or the general problems of disadvantaged families. None of these seem to have any totally convincing factual basis.

The majority of UK experts believe that the increase is due to better diagnosis and increased parental concern. Children, who would previously have been thought of as lazy or stupid; disruptive or inattentive; unable to answer clearly; or even being seen as a bully, are now classified as having learning difficulties or to have ADHT or Aspergers. They are now noted as having Special Educational Needs. However, one doctor said to me, "I am worried that nowadays far too many children are classified as having a personality disorder and that every GP and consultant is swamped with parents insisting their child is classified with something. They just have to say 'yes' to anyone who feels their child is a bit different. But everyone does

NOT have autism." The Government is inclined to favour the wider diagnosis theory and schools are encouraged to concentrate on helping each child achieve his or her best possible educational standard, with less emphasis on the medical diagnosis.

Overall UK Figures

However, to look at the question of numbers. In the 1950s, it was thought that four people in ten thousand might well have autism. Even in 1979, one of the world's greatest and best loved experts in the field, Dr Lorna Wing,[29] thought the figure was one or two in a thousand. In the 1970s, some estimates suggested that maybe 250,000 people in the UK had learning disabilities. It is now said to be around 1% of the population.[30] This would mean a large increase to perhaps 600,000 for the UK. The National Autistic Society (NAS) say that there are "around 700,000 people in the UK who are on the autistic spectrum. Together with their families, this means that autism is part of the daily life for 2.8 million people."[31] The KCC say that each year they have a hundred new cases which they classify as having learning disabilities, although they also have a good number that they turn down. Another study[32] said the number of people in the UK with some form of autism was more than one in every hundred – again probably suggests the figure of 700,000: and the British Institute of Learning Disabilities gives a figure of 210,000 people with severe and profound learning disabilities and a further 1.2 million with mild to moderate learning disabilities. Yet, another estimate of the number of people in the UK who have some form of learning problem – a slightly different definition – is one and a half million, or over 2%.[33]

The figures mount up. It was calculated that 10% of the total population has some sort of "Personality Disorder". I have forgotten the source – perhaps because I was beginning to find the figures bewildering or, sometimes, even meaningless. The figure presumably includes all the children with Special Educational Needs (said to be between 5% and 10% of all children in England) and all the children who are a bit below average in one subject, as well as all the adults with some sort of learning problem. It maybe also includes all those with Obsessive Compulsive Disorder, Tourette's and so on. (And maybe bad-tempered men – and 'difficult' teenagers. I do not know: but it does not sound a useful statistic.) And none of these figures includes people who have never been diagnosed – either because they do not want to be diagnosed or because they have just got on with life in spite of their problem.

Life Expectancy

I asked several people about life expectancy for people with the various learning difficulties. I was usually told that it was not something to be discussed. However, the leading autism research charity, Autistica,[34] analysed some Swedish research which said that, on average, people with autism die sixteen years earlier than normal people – fifty-four years old. The main cause is epilepsy followed by heart attacks and suicide. The Government agreed (April 2018) that more should be done to reduce the gap – often, in the words of Autistica's Jon Spiers, "from entirely preventable causes". Another survey[35] said that people with a learning disability were four times as likely to die of preventable causes as the average person; and fifty-eight times more likely to die before they were fifty.

Children and Special Educational Needs

Yet more statistics – this time just about children. In 1959, it was thought that autism affected around 5 in 10,000 children. By 2010, it was considered to be double the figure from fifty years earlier – a hundred in 10,000, or 1%. It is nowadays suggested as a rough indicator that 5% or between three and three and a half million children have Special Educational Needs, with 1% of school children in England at special schools[36]. However, this figure includes not only children with autism but children with all types of learning difficulties and physical difficulties.

The problem with all these figures is reflected in what I was told by the KCC officials. They emphasised that even their actual figures were fraught with statistical complexity. Does the number include the proposed, new classification of up to twenty-four years old (or sometimes up to twenty-five)? Are further education students included? Have the parents agreed their child should be formally classified? And so on. However, most school experts agreed the average is about 5%. The same statistical problem occurs with adults but I was given the figure of six hundred and nineteen people with formally classified difficulties in the Sevenoaks, Tunbridge Wells and Tonbridge and Malling Councils' area of around 360,000.

Figures Relating to Sub-Divisions

There are numerous other figures relating to the many sub-divisions of learning disabilities. The figures for people with Down's have been mentioned. There are also figures – much less accurate because of the difficulty with definition and diagnosis – for the variety of really serious but less usual forms of autism. Epilepsy is often associated with autism. Yet even in Victorian times, it was understood that the two, while often associated, were different. For a hundred years, from around 1830, many people with epilepsy were put in lunatic asylums, presumably because the family did not know what to do with their epileptic relative or the person was an embarrassment. Over the last sixty years, there have been two stages of drug treatment but, even so, for people with autism, there is still a distressing risk of seizures. It is reckoned that about 600,000 people in the UK have some form of epilepsy (about 4% of the population) and that over 30,000 are newly diagnosed each year. Around 30% of autistic people have epilepsy which tends to develop in the teenage years. The link between the two is not yet clearly understood. However, as examples in this book show, it can be a devastating complexity in the already difficult life of a person with learning disabilities. The South East of England is lucky to have a national centre of excellence in Surrey in the specialist school, Young Epilepsy, which is discussed later in the Schools chapter.

Looking on various specialist websites, it becomes clear that the number can become not only large but variable. For example, one website said that there are 200,000 people in the USA with Tourette's syndrome; but in the UK the figure is said to be 1% (so 600,000-700,000). I have never knowingly met someone with Tourette's but the symptoms can vary so widely, perhaps I did not realise. Nor did any teacher with whom I talked mention a child with Tourette's. Yet one estimate said that one in ten children have Tourette's in some form. There are said to be 700,000 or 750,000 individuals – children *and* adults – in the UK with OCD – Obsessive Compulsive Disorder – which could mean that in just South West Kent there will be several thousand people with OCD; and a village of two thousand might statistically have around twenty – which does sound high. 5% of British children are said in one radio report to have ADHD. However, while again the figure seems large, the symptoms of a child – usually a boy – with ADHD can be so wide that figures are not always useful. (2% of adults are said to have ADHD). When one looks at figures for the group known as Specific Learning Difficulties (shortened inevitably to SpLD) – such as dyslexia, dyscalculia, dyspraxia and dysgraphia – the number gets larger and larger. One website said that 3%–6% of the UK just had dyscalculia. Presumably, this means up to four million of us are not very good at maths – which may be true. We are just part of the mainstream population, rather than being on the autistic scale – unless the condition is serious. Nor do any of these figures include babies who, for a number of reasons, have been born with brain damage – often called TBI. (Grimly, there is a website to tell you how to sue your hospital if it happens). In fact, the Tunbridge Wells Hospital, where I talked with the experts, has very few babies born with brain damage each year and they get very specialist treatment.[37] People who have been brain damaged at birth and are included as having a learning disability have an extra difficulty which was explained by Sarah Richards, the head of Superior Care, a firm which supplies care workers. "My team look after quite a number of clients who have brain damage. They are all different, of course, but they often say that they wish they had Down's or were really obviously autistic or had had a leg blown off. 'Then ordinary people would feel sorry for us. As it is, when we do slightly strange things, people don't understand.'"

Male/Female

To look at one other statistic for sub-divisions of learning disabilities: boys versus girls, and men versus women. It used to be said that males were more likely to have autism. In the 1960s until 2000, it was usually said that the ratio was around 7:1. This reduced to 5:1 and is nowadays said to be more like 2½:1.[38] However, there are increasing doubts about whether even 2½:1 is correct. There is a sense that girls could have as many or nearly as many autistic problems as boys, but that the problems show themselves in different ways. One Special Educational Needs Officer (SENCO) said, "It appears that boys are more likely to have these types of problems because their symptoms are more obvious – more extreme. They disrupt the school lessons; they are seemingly never concentrating; they shout and end up with public meltdowns. Girls are better at masking their distress. They can copy what other girls are doing. So, on the outside, they put up with all the issues at school. They wait until they get home. Then the meltdown happens. Tantrums and often very severe trauma and distress as it all comes out. I sometimes call it the 'silent disability' – sometimes the school does not realise it or, at least, the seriousness of it." Another SENCO agreed, adding that girls are more likely to mature with a group of supportive girls and consequently be better at disguising problems.

The Nearness to Everyone

If the rough national figure for people with a more formal classification of learning disabilities is 1%, then in a small market town such as Sevenoaks or Tonbridge of around 100,000 people, there will be over one thousand. Sub-dividing the number still further, a theoretical village with two to three thousand people might expect on average to have twenty to thirty people – children and adults – with some sort of learning disability.

To see if some of the figures seemed reasonable in practice, I contacted a senior social worker in another county who had lived in a village of around two thousand people for many years. She said that she knew of at least fourteen people in her village who fairly clearly were or should be formally classified as having some type of learning disability. Two had Down's and four or five children were classified as definitely needing SEN help at the local primary school. Several older pupils needed extra help at secondary school. Two people were autistic and wheelchair bound and she suspected that three or four adults had Aspergers or forms of autism which had never been diagnosed, let alone helped, when they were young. Probably over half of the fourteen had had assistance from the

Health Service or various parts of Social Services. She said that she was sure there were others in her village with lesser problems, or those whom she did not know or who fitted into their community without much fuss. She rang back later to say she had thought of more people. Her final comment was that, with constant government cut backs, help to these people was becoming more and more difficult to provide – in her particular county anyway.

In one four hour period I mentioned this book to three people, a taxi driver, an old friend and a radiographer taking X-Rays of my knees. It turned out that all three had close personal connections with what I was writing about. The taxi driver had a thirty-four year old step-son with cerebral palsy with other associated learning problems. "Everyone's very sorry for him but he gets a really good service from our council – we're Tower Hamlets. But when you have to live with him, he's pretty difficult actually – not really very nice." The old friend had a granddaughter who was mildly autistic. "She's lovely but she's having a rough time – no one's fault really." And the radiographer said that as a student he had worked at the Princess Christian Hospital as a carer. "It was a good place for people with autism. I liked it. All very cheerful." The point of mentioning these three quick conversations is to illustrate what I have often found while writing this book – that a great many people know someone who has a learning disability or difficulty. Yet few of us realise how common learning disabilities are in the population as a whole or how near a family affected by it is likely to be in our own city, town or village. One GP reminded me of the old Yorkshire saying: "All the world is odd save me and thee – and thee's a bit queer."

Talking with a very experienced care manager, she said "I don't know how many people have real, formal learning disabilities; but over the years I've met and looked after many hundreds. If even 2% of those classified as having a learning disability were difficult – a danger to themselves or others – I'd be surprised: the others don't deserve to be hemmed in." I have used all the varying statistics in this chapter just to show how near we are to people who need our help but, even more, our understanding.

CHAPTER 3

Housing: Where Do You Live If You Leave Home?

The majority of adults who have a learning disability will have left home and need special housing and support. So, I thought that I would look at the different types of accommodation and the different types of support that are provided for them. The seriousness of the person's disability will be the main determining factors for the kind of housing that is best for them. Where the learning disability is what is classified as 'profound', there will need to be considerable extra facilities and extra staff. When the learning disability is mild, there will normally be a group of flats or bungalows with only a manager who keeps an eye open for his/her 'tenants' to make sure they are not having problems.

The KCC is responsible for housing for people with a learning disability and it employs various sub-contractors to provide the housing and the care. The current aim is to reallocate people from larger residential units into small flats or houses. In 2016, a hundred and one service users were moved from the former to the latter and this trend has continued. Each person is asked what type of housing they would like and every effort is made to ensure that they are given the accommodation they want. If they have family, the person will want to be near them. It will also often be important that they are with their friends – people with whom they have been living before. Their level of satisfaction is monitored. One of the first groups of housing for people with learning difficulties that I visited is called Pepenbury. It is useful to describe it early in this chapter, partly because I thought it excellent and partly because it illustrates the wide range of people who need – and receive – extra help with housing and appropriate support.

Pepenbury

Pepenbury was founded in 1927 when a group of parents, all of whom had children with what was then called mental handicaps, felt that more had to be done to help them. Eighty-five years later, the organisation moved to farm land between Pembury and Tunbridge Wells. I was shown round by Roger Gibson, their then Chief Executive.

> "We explain our services by saying that, we have about fifty people living here but, including our day-care people, we have over two hundred and twenty families whose lives are touched by our work. But you have to remember that the UK has around one and a half million people with some form of learning disability: so, the number of people – the parents and others – who are directly affected is huge".

Pepenbury has residents from all over the country, not just Kent; and, of the £6 million annual turnover, roughly 50% comes from KCC's Social Services and 50% from the thirteen other Councils who have people at Pepenbury. Local charities and individuals not only help raise money but also help to increase understanding by the public which Roger Gibson considers vital. The care can cover residents who need help for a few hours a week to those who need one-to-one, round-the-clock support. Some will be able to progress with help and training towards successful independent living; others will need life-long residential care. For example, there are some who have severe behavioural problems, who need full-time supervision on at least a one-to-one basis. Residents use not only the thriving Day Care Centre at Pepenbury itself but also go out to many other facilities in the area for supported activities such as sailing or riding. There are also a fair number who live in sheltered accommodation away from the main site but who come to the Day Care facility, which provides many on site learning facilities as well as a place to socialise. Great emphasis is given to providing education for anyone who will benefit from it or who just wants to learn and there can be a wider range and level of subjects.

The statement which follows was written by one of the residents who gave it to me and asked me to print it.

ONE OF MY DREAMS IN LIFE IS FOR PEOPLE TO HAVE EQUAL JOB CHOICES AND NOT BE TURNED DOWN BECAUSE OF AUTISM.

IT IS VERY UNFAIR AND UPSETTING THAT WE ARE BEING DISCRIMINATED.

WE ARE INTELLIGENT BUT PEOPLE IN GENERAL DO NOT SEE THIS AND THINK ALL PEOPLE WITH AUTISM ARE UNABLE TO WORK.

EXAMPLE: I GOT 'B' IN MY MOCK GCSE AND AN 'A' IN MY ORAL. AND NOW PREPARING FOR THE REAL THING IN JUNE.

AND I KNOW A FEW PEOPLE WITH ASPERGERS / AUTISM WHO WENT TO UNI. AND THEY HAD NO PROBLEM.

THIS PROVES THAT PEOPLE WITH AUTISM ARE NOT BELOW AVERAGE ABILITY.

WE JUST WANT TO HAVE A FAIR CHANCE IN LIFE TO BE ABLE TO MAKE THE MOST OUT OF OUR LIVES.

There is training for the staff at all levels, from new arrivals to experienced nursing or supervisory staff. Many of the staff have been at Pepenbury for a great number of years. In January 2015 four staff celebrated a hundred and fifteen years' service at Pepenbury between them.

I spent three hours there. I walked from the car park below the old farm buildings, past the children's play area where outside families are particularly welcome. I am passed by a man singing – not very well but certainly cheerfully. He goes into Pepenbury's cafe and says to the pretty girl behind the counter "You were charging me four million pounds for two cans of Coke yesterday. What's it today?"

Roger Gibson's office is part of a converted – nicely converted – pig sty, Roger, having moved the admin staff out of its original block to turn it into tenanted flats. We go to see the flats next. There are eight, beautifully fitted-out, which are for people with less severe learning difficulties. They pay their own rent and water rates and do their own cooking, cleaning and shopping, all paid for out of their housing and social security benefits. The tenants do have – and from talking with one they do need and receive – a bit of help and advice. This part of the system is called 'Supported Living'.

The other forty-two residents at Pepenbury who have more severe problems are classified as 'Registered Care' users. Their support is paid for and overseen by the KCC Social Services Learning Disability team or, as we have seen, by other out-of-the-area Councils. The first of this type of residents we visit are the very severely physically and mentally handicapped. The nurse in charge describes some of the problems faced by the eight residents – each with different and, to me, horrifying symptoms and diagnoses, none of which I have heard of at this early stage – Fragile X Syndrome, Prader-Willi Syndrome, Pelmans Syndrome, Rett Syndrome, and other diagnoses. Most are not just almost permanently in bed but cannot talk properly or feed themselves. I feel appalled sympathy for them but I cannot think of them as individuals because I am frightened of their condition and do not know them. The nurse – who quite clearly does know each of them – explains that knowledge about these conditions is progressing and that the medical help that can now be given to these individuals is getting and will get better. But throughout the conversation runs her concern for these people as individuals – separate people with their own likes and dislikes and their own special, one-off circumstances. I feel bad that I have not asked more about each of them.

The next building is a huge contrast. We go to the Art Workshop. Some of the people in the room live on site and others come in as part of the day centre service. The Workshop is run by a hugely energetic lady. (I have met many art teachers. This one is good.) Currently, the major project is on bees; and ten inch papier-mâché bees sit in what will become a hive, surrounded by everything to do with bees. The class is intensely occupied – too busy to look up. On to the next building. It is the main day centre. Staff, residents and visitors are chatting. I am introduced to a thirty or forty year old lady – to my inexpert eye, probably with Down's. Yes, she has a funny voice and looks a bit different: but she is completely clear that while she used to like living at Pepenbury – which she did for some years – she much prefers living in her present sheltered accommodation flat in the nearby village of Pembury. "I can go to the shops when I want, buy what I want, and come down here when I want". A really special lady – but perhaps I have not yet talked to enough people who are like her – it is the early stage of my research.

We continue into the educational part of the site. There is an IT Room – a long line of computers which Roger Gibson tells me are used for a wide range of education as well as entertainment. Next door there is a small 'Quiet Room'. It has a sofa, a mattress on the floor; low lighting; and bubbling water in a changing coloured tube. "Sometimes when an individual is feeling very stressed out, it really does calm them down to just come in here and relax," says Roger. We pass through a separate pottery building and, while we have a word with the teacher, one of the seven or eight men working with the clay starts shouting. I am not sure if he is just shouting or shouting at us. Nor is it clear to me why he is cross. What is clear, however, is that the other potters think that he is out-of-order and he is told in a kindly way to behave. He stops shouting and goes back to work.

I ask about violence – not because the man seemed dangerous: just because I know the public do worry about it. Roger has a double answer. First, if there are very occasional dangerous incidents, it is nearly always one resident hitting or losing their temper with another patient – not against staff, visiting families and certainly not outsiders. The second part of the answer is that staff get to know what triggers the frights or annoyances of individuals and are able to head them off. This answer about violence is undoubtedly truthful when it applies to Pepenbury. However, talking to staff in other facilities outside Kent, it is clear that many staff are at times frightened by their charges. A good number say that they have been threatened or attacked. Roger Gibson does accept that life can be unpredictable. He mentioned one man with moderately severe learning difficulties who was normally allowed to go off by himself. He developed a liking for the Pembury Barclays Bank when he realised people went in to get money. However, the niceties of the banking system were not totally clear to him, so to start with he went into the bank and demanded money. The Police were called and matters sorted out. The man now goes into Barclays and the staff know him. They even occasionally give him five pounds which encourages him to leave. "He has also gone into the big local Tesco's. You should *see* what he has done on a couple of occasions. I *have* seen it. It was chaos. But now Tesco's know what to expect and they seem to put up with it all". We walk out of the pottery room into the gardening section. There is the biggest bed of rhubarb I have ever seen; and at the end is an old man (with four remaining teeth) who is sitting in the sun on a stool leaning up against a garden shed looking entirely happy. "He spent all his life in Leybourne Grange mental hospital until he came here ten years ago", says Roger. Of course, I do not really know but I am fairly sure that he is much more content in his sheltered accommodation at Pepenbury than he was at Leybourne. Roger confirms this. We go into the greenhouse and polytunnels. There are half a dozen people there, all working away potting up plants and chatting. One is a teacher but I am not sure who. All the plants are being made ready to go into the Farm Shop by the cafe. We do not go into the next building. It houses the residents with the most profound behavioural problems – as opposed to those with physical difficulties who I had seen earlier. They have live-in carers twenty-four hours a day with one-to-one attention. It sounds like Holly Lodge which I later visited and which is described next.

By the end of my tour, what have I learned? I had had my views about the great care given by the staff in this type of life confirmed – together with their professionalism. My understanding that every resident is different and each needs to be dealt with as a person and not as a group has been reinforced. I also feel that generalisations about people with learning disabilities need to be better explained to society so that people in the street see those at Pepenbury and others like them just as other people in the street – not oddments that should be kept out of sight.

Pepenbury represents similar residential homes throughout the country for people with learning disabilities. It has been recently absorbed into a large grouping, Aspens.

Holly Lodge

Holly Lodge, which I visited next, was started in 2012 by two large Kent County Council's housing sub-contractors, *mcch* and Avenues. It was to be a special unit for those with particularly severe learning difficulties – 'profound' is the official designation. The manager is Mel Bentley, a cheerful, supremely practical lady with wide-ranging experience. She has worked in hospitals, overseen dementia patients and trained carers of the mentally ill. She has a staff of over thirty to look after her five 'tenants' – as they are called – three men and two women – each of whom has their own flat with a sixth flat for staff. The award winning unit looks after predominantly younger people, normally under thirty-five. It was specially designed with safety in mind, including having no sharp corners to help prevent accidents. There is specialist medical help available when needed, but their regular GP for ordinary aches and pains, cuts and bruises, coughs and colds, is Dr Peter Bench – who is highly appreciated by Holly Lodge's staff. "I wish they'd clone more like him", says Mel Bentley.

Dr Bench is carrying on the tradition of four generations of doctors from the Hildenborough Medical Group, who had looked after the 'boys' and 'girls' at the Princess Christian Hospital – which was on this site – for sixty years. When Holly Lodge opened, the needs of the three tenants who had already been cared for by *mcch* or Avenues were already clear. With the two new tenants, the normal procedure of assessment applied, with the *mcch*/Avenues team, headed by Dan Gower-Smith, the Manager of Avenues South East, very much involved in working out the detailed individual needs. (Dan's job is described later in this chapter).

Learning about the day-to-day running of the unit gives an insight into the complexity of caring for those with a profound learning difficulty. All the tenants are physically strong and almost continuously active. Four are autistic, and one lady has severe Down's symptoms. They are not really aware of how the world operates, being bound within themselves without understanding others in a normal way. Mostly, their speech is severely limited. Nouns are often used as a demand to have something or to do something, if they can speak at all. Repetitive but not always meaningful phrases occur when the person wants something but when the request is answered, it may well get no particular reaction. Communicating by signs is often the way that the tenants make themselves understood and it was no coincidence that, on my second visit, the staff are in the middle of a deaf and dumb signing course. All five tenants need a routine but it has to be *their* routine. Any interruption or change to their own routine makes them fearful or unpredictable or violent – or all three. So, the work of the staff is demanding, not least because of the minute by minute need for supervision but, allied with this, the constant repetitive nature of just watching another human being – who could at any second do something difficult or inappropriate or dangerous. Each tenant has to have at least two carers with them all the waking hours of the day. On their daily trips into the outside world there are often three carers for each tenant.

Joseph's Story. Taking a week in the life of one tenant will give an indication of life at of Holly Lodge. When I arrive, Joseph (not his real name) is shouting something that turns out to mean "watering can". He is waving one in the air. He has suddenly decided to water his small garden – which all the tenants have. He appears to be a bit over thirty. He is tall, good looking and well-built but with a slightly unusual walk. His voice is loud and imperious but not easily intelligible. On a normal day he will always line up everything into precise patterns. He does not really look at anyone. He gets up with the oversight of two regular carers. He washes and shaves and duly puts everything back in its exact place. While Joseph does not insist on dressing in a particular piece of clothing for the day, he does have a 'style' of what he wants. It is fairly straightforward – a tee-shirt and tracksuit trousers plus trainers. Interestingly, however, when he is going out, he realises that he has to put on more formal clothes and he does so almost automatically without fuss. He tidies his room and hangs up any washing that he has done. He is then helped to get his own breakfast which he eats with his carers.

On Monday mornings, Joseph always goes to Barclays Bank in Tonbridge in the Holly Lodge van. He is accompanied by three carers, sometimes four. The bank and Joseph have come to know one another and what to expect – although at first it did take an effort by both sides. He writes his own cheque – countersigned by a named carer on which the bank insists. Then he likes to go to Greggs in the High Street for a coffee and his own special cake, preferably going to a regular seat with his carers. Greggs is his particular favourite, although he also quite likes Subway. The journey to and from Tonbridge can be stressful – both to him and his carers. As Joseph does not like any change to his routine, even a red traffic light worries him. A road diversion is a major concern to him; but the very worst thing is a blue flashing light from a police car or an ambulance, which totally terrifies him. At this point, he is likely to get violent out of panic. As an indication of just how upset he can be, Mel Bentley explains that they badly need a new van with toughened glass windows to cope with him.

After the bank and the café, he goes to his regular greengrocer on the way back to Holly Lodge to buy his vegetables. "Although he is not a vegetarian, he has a thing about vegetables and we have to encourage him to have other food – meat and so on – so he gets his iron and vitamins", says Mel. At lunch time, he helps prepare his own food, washing and cutting up the vegetables or peeling his own potatoes under supervision; but he is frightened of the hobs and the oven because he sort of understands that they are hot and, therefore, dangerous. So, carers do the actual cooking for him. However, all the cutlery is normal. Once again, the carers eat the meal with him. Joseph does not want to eat with the other tenants: it would be out of his routine and he would not interact with them anyway. The afternoons could involve an outing but, bearing in mind the stress and activity of the Monday morning, Joseph is more likely to be encouraged to do what Mel describes as "low arousal activities – things we know from experience that he likes and which will keep him occupied and calm. He likes doing things with pen and paper. What this actually involves is him scribbling – but they can be very colourful! He also has two sets of bricks which he is very keen on. One set consists of small bricks – Lego – and the other set consists of larger plastic ones. He usually likes making towers – which he can do for ages". The carers will again help him with his evening meal and then perhaps they will watch a DVD together. Joseph particularly likes 'Friends' and 'Batman' and, because they come in a box set, he will sit and watch them for an hour or an hour and a half at a time – which he can do day after day. Like most autistic people he really likes repetition.

Then finally to bed – once again with a detailed ritual. He has a bath with, as ever, a carer in attendance. Everything has to be correct and exactly as it always is. The shampoo has a pot of one colour, the body wash another and there is a further one to hold the water to rinse himself down. After the bath, he might well make two towers and would normally be in bed by ten o'clock. That was one day. On the other days, Joseph's routines are generally the same but with the daily outing varying. All the tenants go into the outside world every day. On some days, Joseph goes to Knole Park to get some exercise. It is always the same walk, with him heading to the café where one of the ladies behind the counters has become a special friend. Once a week he has a meal in the local pub with his parents. On another day, the tenants sometimes all go together to a special park in East Peckham where there is a play area with swings and plenty of room to run around. The tenants love this. As an extra treat, they have also all been to the cycle park at Gravesend. However, although the five tenants may go out on trips together, they do not mix in a normal way. There is an annual barbecue.

At the end of my visit, Joseph's main carer arrived in the office and explained that Joseph had "asked for a swim". This, in fact, means that he sits in a small plastic pool which the carer fills by hand with about ten or fifteen buckets of water. However, although Joseph did sit in his pool for a moment or two, he then kicked the water out and indicated that he did not want to have anything to do with water. The carer was relaxed – he had seen it all before – but to an outsider to the Holly Lodge world, the staff seem to have the patience and kindliness that most people could hardly comprehend. When asked what politicians could do to help people with severe learning difficulties, Mel Bentley said: "It would be good that the carers were given more money. And we need to have more special units like Holly Lodge". Both seem eminently reasonable.

The Scotts Project Trust

The Scotts Project Trust, just outside Tonbridge, is another of the residential resources used by the KCC. It is only when you meet a group of people with learning disabilities that it becomes clear what huge differences there are between them, each needing their own particular attention. In the abstract, this thought is obvious but until the room is full with the variety, it does not strike home.

The café at the Scotts Project may prove the point. Outside the café, there are three Down's residents potting plants for the Nursery Centre. In the café itself, taking orders for tea, coffee and cakes is a young man, also with Down's who is helped by the café's guiding supervisor lady. The supervisor also advises two other residents who are doing the bills and working out the change – with some difficulty. In the kitchen are two Scotts day centre regulars who have been helping make the cup cakes and an apple and sultana cake but who are more specifically learning about clearing up. "I don't actually make the cakes; the staff do that", says one. At one table there is a father and his very lively daughter who has Down's. She lives at Scotts and I have met her on a previous visit – the father has given help to the organisation. At another table there is a group from the outside who have four people with a range of fairly severe learning difficulties. One man sits for the whole hour rocking on his chair saying absolutely nothing. Another starts shouting unintelligibly until he is asked gently by one of the carers not to. He stops but otherwise shows no expression at all. Another man, probably about fifty, sits silently until he gets to his feet and stands in the middle of the room, his feet pointing in. He then starts to move round delicately in a small circle, knees going high but, most noticeably, with his elbows out and his hands pointing to his face, fingers splayed like a ballet dancer pretending to be a crazed magician. Round and round and round he goes. No one comments. He seems to be content. When the group leaves, he and the others are helped through the door, none of them showing any expression, not sad or cross, not worried or cheerful, just nothing: yet they understand they are being asked to stand up and to leave. Do their carers know what they are thinking or feeling? In any case, the carers clearly do a more than worthwhile job in looking after their charges on an outing.

The Scotts Project is a remarkable example of how two parents have done something positive. They had an adopted daughter, Henny, who had cerebral palsy. They decided to start a new centre for people like her. In 1990 Jill and Denis Scott were told that Henny, by now aged twenty four, had outgrown her special school. Their amazing fight to create The Scotts Project began. Starting with jumble sales and coffee mornings, their faith was justified when one of their supporters, who happened to work for a famous businessman and philanthropist, talked to his boss about the project. A large cheque arrived out of the blue the next day. But it took a further seven years of lobbying local councillors and writing to the local press before the charity was able to raise the £1 million needed to open the new building which has now become the home for fifteen people with learning difficulties.

To be shown round the houses by Jill Scott, aged eighty-two, is quite an experience. The first part of the Scotts Project consists of three inter-connected homes called Peters Row. Each part of the building has five residents and each part has its own large, perfectly equipped kitchen, sitting room and laundry room. Each resident has their own bedroom which is their private place. The five work together to prepare meals (with some help from their carer) and to look after each other. It was moving to see one girl with Down's helping her friend who cannot speak but has a machine into which she can type her words – which then come out with an American accent. The third of the inter-connected buildings has recently been expanded to cater for those with more severe physical difficulties. The staffing at Peters Row consists of an overall Resident Manager and a Deputy; and each of the three buildings has its own Team Leader and staff. There are also staff on duty at night. More recently, the Scotts Project acquired two separate buildings towards the middle of Tonbridge which are for nine people who are more able to look after themselves. These have a Manager and a Team Leader plus six other staff, one of whom is always rostered on the night shift. This means a staff/resident ratio of 1:1 which seems very good for people who are part way to being 'in the community.' Kent County Council Social Services call these outside homes 'half-way houses' and are pleased with the care provided. Just as importantly, sometime later when talking with two of the men who live there, they are very happy and mention a former resident who has moved into his own flat in Tonbridge – whom I also later met.

A separate development was the opening in 2000 of a day centre based in two beautifully converted barns which Jill Scott persuaded the developers of the new adjoining estate to rebuild. (One guesses that the developers, keen to obtain their planning permissions, were 'enthusiastic' to help Scotts: but that's another story). The Scotts Project only caters for those with relatively mild learning difficulties and who have lived within one hour's drive of Tonbridge. In the past, it has tried to help people with 'moderate' autistic problems but found they could become very disruptive to the other residents; and, with regret, the criteria for residents had to be changed. KCC, of course, has to be sure that all the houses provided for those with learning difficulties are of a good standard. Not only is it their legal and moral duty but, in large part, they are paying for the care of the residents. The Trustees of the charity continue to raise money to finance their plans for the future, including a new block for ten to twelve people to live communally with some background help; and extra facilities for the day centre. (The Kent County Council does not pay for capital expenditure). One parent of a child at Scotts mentioned that she had been asked by the Chairman, banker Tom Hoppe, to come to give her views. She said that she had commented on some aspects of training which she felt could be improved. He agreed with her suggestion and action was being taken. But 'hats off' for asking for comments. Training is needed for both the residents and those who come to the day centre but also for the staff, who receive lessons and advice – particularly from a District Nurse. There is also a masseuse who also comes in to teach the staff.

I also visited Scotts day centre, which is officially called 'The Development Centre', in the lead up to Christmas. It currently helps seventy to eighty people a week, some of them residents but mostly people from the outside who have a range of learning disabilities. Being shown round for several hours by the supervisor of the Centre, Claire Davies, is enough to get an impression but, clearly, a full book could be written about the people there – both the 'supporters' and the 'supported'. The Centre aims to help individuals develop as well as provide something for them. *[The problem in describing what I saw and who I met is that some of the people, quite sensibly, did not want to be identified, particularly as my description would be very simplistic. So please accept circumlocutions to try to get round the problem].* First, the staff. As is often the case, those working at the Centre have been doing their job for a long time. Claire Davies says "I'm a new boy: I've only been here for seven years," although she has been in this type of work for nearly twenty-five years. "But Scotts is the best". And to work at the Centre, either as a part-time teacher or as a full-time staff member requires a cheerful sense of dedication. My guess is that wages are certainly not a driving force but I did not actually ask. The pottery class has five learners with four people helping. The teacher goes round her pottery makers adjusting and advising each. They are making small pottery houses which hold a night light – being made for Christmas. A hugely energetic young man talks constantly – he lives in supported housing and wants to get back to watch a particular Christmas film. Another has a carer but does not talk unless prompted, although, as I leave, she bursts into a wonderful description of her pet rabbit. On to the cookery class. Here the majority of the nine 'supportees' live in their own homes with their parents; two are in Scotts own supported housing down the road; and one lives at Scotts in Peters Row. One of the girls, Katy, is active on the local Partnership Group representing the views of the disabled to the Authorities. The men who live at the Scotts houses half a mile down the road come up by themselves on the bus. They would walk "but the Highway Authority will not let a pavement be built", says one. Several of the men work on the other days at a local charity, Spadework, training for horticultural work. Another man is employed regularly in a mainstream garden centre. "It's got pretty busy this week – the Christmas trees have all arrived". What are they actually cooking? "Thai curry" and I watch as the splendid lady teacher, Sue, "been doing it for years", tries to get her charges to actually work. "They have to learn not just the cooking but laying the table and serving. AND the washing up!" One man, who is eating at the table with the others, keeps laughing loudly for no apparent reason. The others touch him to quieten him down. "What you don't realise", says Sue "is that for ages he would only eat by himself. Now he stays for lunch and eats with the others. It's a momentous change". Then on to the Journalism Group, led by Paul, an ex-media man with help from a lady who also teaches "gardening and faith" – quite a combination. There are fifteen pupils there seemingly with a very wide range of abilities. They are working on the Scotts newsletter – which has video links on the website. They also work on various leaflets and gain experience about envelopes/labels/franking/postage, etc. At this session, seven live at St Peters Row, four live at Scotts supported housing down the road; the one who used to live at Scotts supported housing but who is now living with a friend in Tonbridge (a great progression); and three who live with their parents. Finally, I go to an IT session where five people are being taught (at a higher level than mine). What I have not seen are the art sessions, the gardening, the drama and the chess – which involves Tonbridge School boys. Tonbridge Girls' Grammar School also help with other sessions, including dancing and even quick cricket. However, I suspect that I may have missed listing all the potential activities. Another aspect of Scotts that I have not directly seen but which I have heard about is the increasing help given for what is called 'life skills'. This ability to look after oneself rather than to rely on carers or parents clearly has to be done on an individual basis and Kent County Council care managers are keen to encourage it. As I was told: to enjoy going to a dance class may not be as useful as learning to put one's clothes on by oneself.

Jill Scott says "I keep saying that I'm going to slow down". In reality she does not seem to do so. She comes in three or four days a week; knows every resident intimately and cares for them in a sergeant-majorly type way. She oversees the massive and perfectly kept garden "although I have recently stopped doing the heavy digging – it is almost solid clay". She is pleased with the ways the Scotts Project has progressed but is always looking to their future plans. Her biggest concern is that Government will concentrate its funding on the most severely handicapped and that funding for those with less severe problems – but nevertheless those who still badly need help – will have their funding cut. This worry is shared by many others in the field.

Watercress Court

It was suggested that I visited Watercress Court by Tunbridge Wells Borough Council's Head of Housing. She said that looking after people with learning disabilities was not something that fell within a local council's remit like hers. It was KCC's job to look after housing those with learning disabilities; but she had heard Watercress Court was good. However, I became aware as I researched the book that virtually all parts of the UK have similar homes. On my visit, I met two of the people who oversee this pleasant building in the village of East Malling, with playing fields on one side and a meadow used by the scouts on the other. The first was Clare Maher who looks after housing for a wide variety of people all over Kent, including Watercress Court for her company, Housing and Care 21. Watercress Court had been specially built in a joint PFI between the KCC and Housing and Care 21 ten years ago to house seven people with moderate to severe learning difficulties. (Once again to reiterate that 'moderate to severe' is a formal designation which in actual fact to an outsider like me means there are extremely serious problems). The housing – called 'independent living' – provides each person with their own flat for which they pay rent to Housing and Care 21, mainly from their Government housing allowance. Its success can be judged by the fact that none of its seven tenants – they are *not* called 'service users' – has left since it first opened. I asked Clare how a new tenant would be chosen if a flat were to become available. She said a representative from the local District Council and a specialist from KCC's Learning Disability Department would talk to the applicants, with her present as the future landlord. There could well be half a dozen shortlisted people. Such flats were much sought after. I looked at one of the self-contained flats and briefly met three of the tenants, one of whom was clearly less able to cope than the other two. I asked how much support the four men and three women received. I learnt that it varies depending on the person but it averages ten hours of one–to-one care each day and there is a flat for the overnight carer who is available to cope with any night-time issues. I had a brief talk with one man, probably in his thirties, who said that he would get Clare and myself a cup of tea. He forgot but he was very keen to be kept in the picture about everything. He particularly liked helping Clare with her weekly fire inspections. He lives in a first floor flat and the team have been trying to persuade him to walk up the stairs for the good of his health. But, laughing, he steps into the lift. I was not sure whether he knew he was being naughty. Another tenant has been allowed to keep two rabbits on her balcony which overlooks the pleasant garden. In the cold weather, the rabbits live in a store room.

I also met Katie Ashworth who works for the housing charity, *mcch*, as the Service Co-ordinator for Watercress Court and another similar home. It is her job to ensure that the required number and suitability of carers are in place to support the individuals for which her organisation is responsible. I asked about finding staff, particularly as I had heard that it was not always easy. Katie said that she was lucky at Watercress Court. There were easy transport links and it was a good place to work. She had a full team and seldom had to employ agency staff – who were much more expensive and did not know her people. However, she knew that in other parts of Kent, it was difficult.[39] When she had worked in Chatham, she had advertised for two years and still did not find the right person for one particular role. She had also heard that in Ashford and Canterbury, there were difficulties in recruitment. I asked what caused the difficulties. She said that in her view it was primarily the money. "You have to be very dedicated to work at a carer's job on what is usually the minimum wage." Katie has worked her way up over the past nine years. Now that she is in a senior managerial role, she deals with her thirteen clients on a personal basis and with the twenty-four support staff, as well as two, more junior managers. "We should not have to rely on staff goodwill and their sense of dedication but this often happens." Katie clearly knows the people she supports well. While I was there, one of them arrived back with her carer from a visit to the hospital. The lady had been told that she needed an operation. She was in tears with fright. Katie made her a cup of tea and comforted her – the kind of caring I have seen time and again.

Having described some of the main complexes where people with learning disabilities live, it is worth looking at the two main not-for-profit groups that KCC principally uses to oversee its housing and to provide and support staff – *mcch* and Avenues. Both have contracts for millions of pounds each year and provide support staff for many hundreds of people on a day-to-day, week by week basis throughout the year.

mcch

'*mcch*', was formed twenty-five years ago. The initials originally stood for Maidstone Community Care Housing Society and it was a consortium formed to help provide care for what were then called 'mentally disabled people', particularly when they left the many mental hospitals all over the UK. By the end of its first year, *mcch* was managing seventeen residential properties with fifty 'patients' – as they were then called – living in 'ordinary houses in ordinary streets', all achieved with a staff of six. Today, *mcch* has expanded across the South East, including some London boroughs. It now helps with a wider range of people with learning difficulties, including individuals on the autism spectrum but also people with mental health needs. *mcch* employs around one thousand four hundred staff and supports one thousand five hundred individuals with a learning disability. *mcch*'s Director of Operations until recently has been Karen Reed. She started her career as a trainee nurse at Leybourne Grange Mental Hospital near Maidstone, went to two other hospitals, before returning to Leybourne as a senior nurse. As 'Care in the Community' began to be put into effect, she was seconded to help the group which eventually became *mcch*. She explained the process of helping a new individual referred to them – almost always by a Kent County Council care manager. The care manager and the specialist team under the then KCC boss, Penny Southern, will provide a detailed assessment of the person and what help is needed. *mcch* will then meet the individual and, where possible, the family and usually with the care manager, too. They will discuss details of the housing need – often a location near the family is vitally important – and what day-to-day assistance is needed. If there are physical difficulties as well as mental ones, these will obviously have a bearing on what kind of housing is needed. Sometimes, agreeing what is ideally needed is the easy part. The ideal has to be balanced by what appropriate housing is available which is relatively near where the person wants to be and lies within the funding allocation. Over the last few years, the situation has become more difficult by the Government funding cuts and the increasing number of individuals requiring appropriate housing and support. Their youngest supported person was five and the oldest was ninety-two. *mcch* gave me some examples of the people they support. Pat is an eighty year old lady. After many years living in a house where she shared a kitchen and lounge, she now has her own flat. Her previous housemate has also been moved into her own flat in the same building. Another *mcch* service user, Nathan, moved into a new self-contained flat. "I really like it. There is a nice courtyard where I keep my rabbit. The staff give me some support to help me be more independent. I like going into town and meeting my friends, and I also like going cycling." Another example is about two people who, a long time ago, used to live together. They got separated and had not seen each other for years. *mcch* reunited them and filmed the event so they could relive the moment and talk about it with their friends and staff. So *mcch* concerns itself with more than just housing and providing support staff. It actively seeks to look after the mental and physical health of its service users, to integrate them within the community – as far as the community wants – and to link the service users in with the sometimes bewildering array of services which can be available from the KCC, the voluntary groups, the NHS, the various governmental bodies and the educational system. Karen Reed is particularly interesting when talking about the changes she has seen over the last thirty years for people with a learning disability.

"There was, quite understandably, great anxiety about the winding down of the mental hospitals, such as Leybourne. The staff were worried about their futures but, at least as much, they worried about the residents, many of whom they had known very well for years. And the residents – many of whom had been there all their adult lives – were apprehensive: Leybourne was their home. All their friends, all the people they had known all their lives, were there. Staff could see that the change to 'Care in the Community' was a good idea in principle but they thought the process of actually getting there was going to be difficult – even if the money needed was going to be available. I remember one man whom I knew well who said he would <u>never</u> leave Leybourne: that, even if we moved him, he'd come back. And he did, too! I still keep in touch with some of those we had to re-house and their families. As *mcch* has taken on more services, commissioned by the KCC and other local authorities, I continue to meet people that I knew at Leybourne. One person I met who now lives in the Bexley area remembers his time at Leybourne very fondly and we have had many chats about his time there and laugh about some of the situations and the staff that he remembers. He now has his own flat in a supported living scheme and when I asked if he would like to go back to Leybourne, he said 'No: happy where I am'. Many people have fond memories, as well as some stories that make you shudder now but, at the time, they seemed to be the norm and accepted practice. The fond memories are usually about the people they knew and friendships they had. In some cases, the freedom, as they saw it then, was to wander around the grounds in a safe environment within their closed community, albeit they could not leave the grounds without support. Nowadays, they can usually go out when and where they like into their own town or village, even if, quite often, they require support."

When I asked what the best term to use about the people this book covers, Karen Reed laughed and said it had always been changing. "It was a challenge for *mcch* – and other providers in the sector. They used to say – and still sometimes still said – phrases like 'those with learning difficulties' or 'those with mental health problems', although they are now meant to refer to them as 'service users' – which is probably a bit better than 'clients' or 'patients'." At one stage, she said she had asked a group of the people that *mcch* supported what they would like to be called. After a bit of a pause, one said, "Couldn't you just call me John?" She felt this was very logical, even if it was not perhaps the perfect group word which everyone had sought for as long as she could remember.

The Avenues Trust

The Avenues Trust is another large, not-for-profit company with a South East Division covering the whole of Kent and Medway, plus Surrey and a small piece of Essex. It has an annual income of around £14 million and around four hundred staff. Like *mcch*, they are commissioned by the county councils to organise support for people with learning disabilities and autism, but also with some mental health issues and dementia, either in residential homes or in their own homes. Dan Gower-Smith has seventeen years' experience of working in the social care sector and now is the Regional Director for Avenues South East. He has a staff of two hundred and fifty generally full-time people who help around two hundred service users, although he never mentioned the term service user which was a relief. In the local area they have five small homes which have between two and six people in each. Avenues do not own these houses. Their role is to provide the support staff who look after the very varied needs of the people in the houses – their food; transport to access the local and wider community; and their medical needs under the direction of the NHS professionals. As with other care providers, support needs are sometimes one-to-one full-time care over the twelve to sixteen hours of daylight, plus night care. Other clients or service users will only need an occasional visit through the Avenues' 'outreach' services. Dan Gower-Smith emphasises – what I have heard so often before – the wide range of people they look after. "We will initially receive a call or an email from the council's Social Services or a family member about someone who needs support. An assessment will have already been completed by the KCC care manager and so we will have a summary of the wishes and needs of the person that we are potentially going to help. If it is for new housing, we will see whether we have anything suitable in the right area. Sometimes we have nothing available – it's not always easy to find the perfect solution – but if we do have a possibility, there will be lots of meetings with our Service Manager and the person concerned, often with the parents, the care manager and other people in the person's life. Then, if everything looks promising, they will all troop along and meet the manager of the prospective house and will look at the house or the flat. So, it is all a careful process involving all the different experts and services to make sure everything is going to work. Avenues can offer advice to people from the age of nine but we generally start supporting people as young adults. We are aiming – just as you heard from Penny Southern at the KCC – to end up with as many people as possible in their own homes – 'Supported Living' – which could be in a block of flats or a house for three or four people in an ordinary road. Currently 40% of our people are in this type of Supported Living Housing, with the other 60% in Residential Homes – the latter where the more severe cases who need more specialised care are likely to be. Avenues also provides support workers for a good number of people living at home with their parents which is part of our 'Outreach service.'"

Other Housing Providers

There are a large number of other housing providers in Kent which support people with different levels of housing needs. For example, 'hft' – formerly the Home Farm Trust but now, fashionably, in lower case – is a national group. It has a pleasant grouping of bungalows in Edenbridge which, in conjunction with Avenues, looks after around thirty-five people with learning disabilities. For those with less severe learning difficulties, there are many individual flats with minimal management help. I talked to those living in several other housing units and to the manager of others. The buildings varied from modern, purpose-built, en suite flats to the not so modern. One manager of one not-for-profit housing trust for nine men explained that their location in the high street was much preferred by its residents to being in the countryside or on the edge of a town. They had a small garden in which the residents could relax but they could walk down to the shops or catch a bus whenever they wanted. Another charity group, MacIntyre Care, had a modern group of flats in Sevenoaks for those with the need of only general support. It was much praised by those who live there. I gather it is typical of the best of this type of accommodation. However, as ever, you cannot please everyone all the time. I was told about one new development – the erection of a state-of-the-art, new block of flats called 'The Pines'. It is run by Avenues for the KCC and both are proud of it. It replaces four bungalows which used to house six people in each. But not everyone thinks the new arrangements are an improvement. The debate is an old one. Are larger, often older, units with close-knit friendships between their residents but with perhaps not so many modern fixtures and fittings, better than individual, modern flats where perhaps the service user is more in control but perhaps more isolated? I heard strong, well-informed but unattributable views from those who felt the Pines new development was a backward step. Yet the authorities really are pleased. I did not talk to any of the current residents or staff, so I cannot take sides.

CHAPTER 4

Living at Home and Leaving Home

There are many difficulties for the parents who have a child with a learning disability. They have to think how to cope in the early years; choose a primary school, then a secondary school, followed by the complexities of finding useful further education courses; and probably look into obtaining possible jobs. The next choice is when or if to leave home. In many cases, the choice to finally leave for good can be the most difficult – certainly the most emotional – choice of all. It can sometimes occur when the child is a teenager. If the boy or girl has severe learning disabilities, a parent may realise that, however much they would like the child to be based in his or her own home, it is becoming untenable. The KCC care manager will be able to give advice. I have heard from a good number of families about the varying reactions to the advice. Several realised the inevitability. Two were filled with guilt that they could not cope. And a few were clear that they intended to cope until they or their child died. However, usually it was a mix of every emotion – which can change with the changing circumstances. If a specialist weekly boarding school such as Young Epilepsy is chosen in the first instance, it is only a partial leaving home.

Some parents, particularly those with a child with milder symptoms, cope until their child is in their late teens or is leaving formal education. The decision is then radical. Does the young adult continue to stay at home or do the parents have to encourage their much loved child to leave them? One mother – who had considerable experience of people with a wide range of learning disabilities – explained how she and her husband, together with their son, whom I will call James – reached a decision when he was twenty-one.

James's Story. At a young age, James was found to have a rare form of learning disability – tuberous sclerosis – which meant that he also had a range of physical problems. After going to a special primary school, he went to 'Young Epilepsy' in Lingfield, Surrey, which all concerned thought excellent. However, James had to leave the school when he was twenty and his mother and father realised that they now had to make the decision. They had looked after him all his life but had always realised that, long term, he should not live at home. It would be restrictive for him and mean he was not with people of his own age. Additionally, if he continued to live at home, there would come a time when he would be acting as the carer for his elderly parents and after their deaths, he would not easily be able to adapt to life on his own. So, they began to discuss the matter with him..

When they had all agreed the principle, they looked all over Kent and then all over Surrey and Sussex for a suitable home for him. It had to be in a town so that there were a variety of things for James to do; and it had to be a life with mainly young people. And ideally, there needed to be a young and dedicated staff. Eventually, they found a group of shared flats in Folkestone which seemed to all three of them to be suitable. It worked. James, now aged thirty-four, leads a full life, going to college two days a week, plus weekly swimming and visits to the gym. He loves listening to music which he can play whenever he wants. He can walk along the beach and easily go to his favourite MacDonalds. And he gets home to his parents for occasional weekends. So, considering James is still relatively seriously disabled in a number of ways, there has been a relatively happy outcome.

However, life is not full of happy endings – certainly not in the area of learning disability. Care managers are very well aware that when someone with learning disabilities reaches adulthood, it is nearly always best for the family to look ahead. Yet it is clearly very difficult for the parents. They will certainly know their child and his or her abilities better than anyone. They know what he or she likes and what he or she is able to do (and not able to do). They know that making friends is difficult. They know what is frightening. They know what makes their child – however old he or she is – laugh. Many parents do start thinking about the problem even when their child is young. However, to think about it, is not the same as being able to make the decision that their son or daughter should actually leave home. Completely naturally, they want to help their child whom they love as long as they can. One father told me that, as his autistic son grew up, he had said forcibly that he and his wife would *always* look after the son – "Over my dead body will he go into a home." However, some years later reality arrived and they could not cope. The son did end up in a home, although they visited him frequently.

So, the decision for a complete move away from home is quite often not made until the son or daughter is twenty or twenty-five. It can be wonderful to have your disabled child at home with you, watching him or her grow up, hopefully getting a little more able to cope with everyday life – although in their own way. I know one couple and their twenty-five year old daughter who lives with them. The family is very happy – if always at full stretch. Yet I know that the parents are conscious that they will probably not outlive their daughter and are making every effort to ensure their daughter will, in due course, be able to live an increasingly independent life, supported by the various agencies as necessary. Another man now in his forties, who came from a relatively well-to-do family, agreed in his early thirties to move away into his own house. It is fairly near his parents and they are there to give friendship and practical advice. He does lead his own life. However, the parents do have a constant longer-term worry about his future when they will not be around.

Alan's Story. However, as the KCC experts had explained to me, as well as being difficult for the parents, it is not easy for the care managers either. One couple with whom I talked at length had started thinking about what was best over fifty years ago. In the mid-1960s, the wife had given birth to a son whom I will call Alan. It was not until Alan was ten weeks old that the news that he had Down's syndrome was broken to the mother. (The father was not even asked to be present). Such advice as there was in those days seemed only to be available in London. The local GP appeared to know nothing; and Social Services seemed to be non-existent or to provide very little support. Against this background, the couple had little alternative but to cope on their own. It is not necessary to give details of the battles that they have fought over the half a century in order to provide a calm and supportive home for Alan and to find things for him to do which he enjoys – for three hundred and sixty-five days of the year (minus the respite care which Alan loves). Both parents agree that there have been major improvements over the period. Their new GP is knowledgeable and sympathetic (even if they have never yet met the learning disability nurse who is apparently attached to the practice). Their individual care managers have normally been constructive and charming. "A few were not so good: but most were." The range of activities is dramatically better (even though one that Alan particularly liked and was good at was stopped due to lack of KCC funds). I listened with sympathy to the stories of meetings that they had with their local MP – "he was wonderful"; frequent meetings with KCC councillors and the KCC experts, the voluntary organisations and even some lawyers. However, most of these meeting did not result in what the parents sought.

Yet I also had some sympathy for KCC Social Services and all the experts who could not and cannot accede to every individual request or wave a magic wand to 'make everything all right'. It is clear that this couple have spent a lifetime getting Alan as full a life as was possible in the era in which he grew up. It is also very clear that the system – if occasionally not ideal – is dramatically better than it was. However, the story has not ended. Alan is now over fifty and his health is getting worse. His hearing has deteriorated which makes it even more difficult nowadays for him to mix with others at the day centres and at other activities he attends. His walking is reasonable but he is developing more and more autistic traits. Increasingly, everything has to be in its exact place, and his detailed routine is very important. He is inclined to ask the same questions over and over and he is very time conscious. He can wash and dress himself but needs supervision when he has a shower to make sure the water is not too hot. He can make toast and a cup of tea but not prepare a meal – "although he does do the washing up", says his father. He loves doing things like jigsaws – very complex ones – but it is a very solitary occupation. He used to have a friend who shared his love of computers but, when the friend moved away, it left Alan without anyone close except his parents. Forty years ago, he was classified as 'uneducable', which infuriated his parents. They accept and have always accepted that he will not progress on to GCSEs but they have proved that he has become able to do more things than were forecast by the experts all those years ago.

Alan's parents are now approaching eighty. More pertinently, they know that neither is in the best of health. Indeed, the father was thoroughly ill when I last talked with him. In general terms, they have known that, at some point, Alan will have to start living away from them. So far, they have not actually started looking for somewhere but know they will have to begin soon, although they do realise that it will be a dramatic change for all their lives – particularly for Alan. They ask themselves how Alan, with his increasing need for routine and decreasing ability to cope with life, can possibly cope without them. They know from talking with others that 'supported living' – they do not like all these politically correct wordings – can be good but they have also heard that it can be appalling. They knew a girl who was keen to go into supported living but it went badly wrong when the authorities moved her from her home without preparation or notice. The result was that she became very distressed and is now back at home again. All this makes Alan's parents wary. It is not an easy predicament. His father continues. "All his life, we have had to look after him. After he was eighteen, his parents – us – weren't allowed to interfere officially. The authorities seemed to be able to do what they liked. They have all these politically correct phrases. I'm sure that they are well-meaning but sometimes they think you've got to get people like Alan to do just what they – the officials – want. I know that you have to have guidance. Someone like Alan has to be guided and it was us, not them, who should do it – and have done it. Eventually, we had to get a Power of Attorney so we could do what was right for Alan. But one size – one system – doesn't fit all. So now, when I and my wife are not very well, we have to think more seriously about what will happen longer term when we are not around. We will have to do some looking. But it isn't going to be easy – for us or for Alan". I guess that the various care managers who have aimed to help Alan and his family over the years would have tried to persuade the family to look ahead. It was probably one of the reasons why the father felt that he and his wife were being bullied. But I ended up feeling worried about everyone – including the 'officials'.

At no point has any parent actually said that they would feel guilty in putting their adult child into sheltered accommodation. However, I am sure it is something most parents do feel. One parent briefly but movingly mentioned the position they were in with their middle-aged, very severely autistic daughter who is in a wheelchair. Although the daughter had been in a specialised care home for a while and had seemingly adapted to it, things had somehow gone wrong – I do not know why. So, the two parents had taken over again. They have some outside KCC help and the daughter is taken to a day centre in a specially adapted bus: but this support does not cover many of the one hundred and sixty hours each week. The mother concluded: "we will continue to love her and look after her until we die."

Another case, where the whole family was desperate, concerned a twenty year old son. All the symptoms seem to indicate that he was on the autistic scale – somewhere. Perhaps in an overloaded system, he was not autistic enough. The father is self-employed and in his late forties. His wife is ill and the son is often proving almost impossible to live with. The father has been having to spend so much time dealing with the family problems that he was finding it difficult to earn enough money to support the three of them. The difficulties with the son had started six or seven years ago and had become worse. While the parents began to think that the son was on the autistic scale, the various experts, including the GP – who did not seem to them to be very knowledgeable – said that the son was not autistic. The son was not very academic – finding school difficult – and he did not have many/any friends. He lives at home in a village which he hates and can have fits of rage, which, while the parents sort of sympathise, can be very frightening. The son was eventually referred to a specialist clinic in Tunbridge Wells – after a huge amount of effort by the father. By this time though, the son was on marijuana and the clinic said that they could not or would not treat him until he was off it. In the meantime, the son is desperate to obtain a job – which he has so far found impossible –

and to leave home. He has decided that he would like to try to become a cook/chef but, so far, that does not seem to be progressing. He has even just failed his driving test. The situation has become so bad that the father is desperate. His summary was that he was faced with a choice between looking after his ill wife or coping with his son. Yet the son has nowhere to go and is getting more violent. The three of them could not continue in the same house, the father said..

The KCC Social Services are well aware of these types of issues. They have developed one way of bridging the gap between being at school or college when the child is usually living at home and going out into the wider world. It is called the 'Transition Service'. One is housed in a well-converted, former school near Maidstone and is run for KCC by *mcch*. It has seven flats – each with its own kitchen – and it caters primarily for eighteen to twenty-five year olds. Help is available as needed by each individual and, although it can be for twenty-four hours a day in some cases, it is more often much less. A stay can be up to three years before the service user is found their own accommodation, where, with the experience that they have gained, they should be able to live a fairly independent life, albeit still with the relevant support. It was suggested that I talked with some of the service users but, after discussion, it was thought to be intrusive. The KCC mentioned that, nowadays, there were probably fewer families where parents of a child with learning difficulties kept a young adult – or adult – at home for what they, the KCC experts, considered too long. Perhaps this is because the facilities, the accommodation and the care provided are much better than years ago? There is also a new KCC scheme called 'Shared Lives'. It is a kind of fostering scheme for people with learning difficulties who may be willing to try living away from home for a long or a short trial period in a home of a sympathetic outsider. I did not meet anyone who had participated but there is a leaflet and a website.[40]

CHAPTER 5

Social Services Support

Twenty-five years ago, when the small Princess Christian mental hospital near Tonbridge was wound down, the prime responsibility for looking after children and adults with learning disabilities had passed from the NHS to the Kent County Council – the KCC Social Services. Has the new system of Care in the Community been successful? The system currently is certainly not straightforward and this book describes how it works, or occasionally does not work. The KCC itself does look after some of the Social Services aspects of this care; but it contracts out much of the day-to-day work. The schools system in Kent, which is in part overseen by the KCC, has a wide range of other schools for which the KCC is not responsible. The NHS, again using contracted out services to organise Community Health, has to integrate its work into the KCC Social Services and the educational system. And astride all this support, is the question of money – government funding and County Council funding.

It is, therefore, perhaps not surprising that many parents with whom I talked had spent months or even years finding their way round all the services that could be valuable to their son or daughter. Sometimes even an expert did not know about help available in another department. The reasons for the complexity are not just because there are the three over-arching services – Social Services; the NHS; and the fee-paying and maintained school systems. Another level of complexity for parents is the three-letter-acronym syndrome, which is, in reality, the experts talking amongst themselves – as every profession does – to the detriment of public understanding. This trend goes hand-in-hand with new services and new procedures – all with catchy and ever-changing titles, although each service in itself is nearly always very useful. The difficulty in describing all the services in a straightforward way is compounded by one of the greatest strengths of the system – individualised care. It is the fact that each person being supported is different and treated differently that makes simple descriptions of their care complex. (There are various websites.[41]) However, over three years of talking with all levels of the Social Services, the NHS and school/college experts, I have been impressed by their practical and forward looking commitment. Each care manager, responsible for each individual, aims to guide parents and those needing help through the tricky waters to a relatively calm harbour.

Paul Carter CBE,
Former Leader, Kent County Council

I thought that I should start by going to the top of the KCC to obtain a statement about their overall policy towards learning disabilities. I, therefore, asked whether I could have ten minutes with the then Leader of the Council, Paul Carter.[42] I was told 'no'; he would set aside an hour. It turned out to be an hour and a half's discussion. He started by saying that the Kent County Council has a wider range of responsibilities than most people realise. They oversee social care services for older people and children taken into state care (including unaccompanied asylum-seeking children). They are responsible for around 70% of Kent's primary schools and about a quarter of its secondary schools. They manage the council tax benefits and also Kent's roads, the subsidised bus services and the footpaths. They organize disposal of household waste; and – particularly relevant for this book – support for people in the county with learning difficulties. As ever, where policy has grown up over many years, with an adjustment here and an addition there, the whole field of what the Government pays for and how much the KCC council tax and other sources of KCC income contribute is immensely complex and changes frequently. It ends up by needing specialists to understand the system.[43] However, there is a clear trend. Central Government is giving the County Councils less and less each year. At the same time, it often demands that the

County Councils must do and pay for more. Additionally, throughout most of the last ten years, the government offered a financial incentive to county councils not to increase council tax and forbade any increases above a level deemed acceptable to government (usually a very small amount) although, more recently the Government has allowed councils to increase council tax by up to 5%. These permitted increases, while welcome, do relatively little to offset the cuts in Government finance to the KCC and the increasing duties imposed on them. There are rises in the cost of services due to inflation and the extra need for services because of the growing population. And, where learning disabilities and difficulties are concerned, there is a large increase in demand, especially from parents. These interviews took place before Covid 19 and the increases in refugees from across the Channel and from Afghanistan, all of which has placed ever more strain on the Kent County budget – as it has on all social service budgets across the country. The KCC provided me with a mass of financial details. I have put some in the notes but the important point for this book is what the KCC has been and will be doing for Kent people with learning disabilities at a time of severe financial cut backs. For this reason, I first asked Paul Carter how he saw the problem of doing more, or at least the same, for less[44].

"I was elected as a KCC councillor over twenty years ago. Sandy Bruce-Lockhart, who was then Leader, asked me to look after education for the county which I did willingly for the next eight years – I was interested in it. The education job involved helping to oversee the education of over a quarter of a million children but it also included 'Special Schools' which moves into what you are writing about. There was a fashion at this time that all children with a learning problem, whatever their disability, should be placed into mainstream schools. Extra help would be given to the ordinary schools so that they could integrate the children with the very wide range of difficulties in mainstream schools. I did not agree with this policy and Kent has preserved its Special Schools – and improved them. We now have twenty-six, most of them classified as 'outstanding' by Ofsted or at the very least 'good';

and every one of them is a new, purpose-built building. The one in Tonbridge, Ridge View, will be the last to be finished. The Headteachers are all fabulous – you've met some.

"I was rather pleased when Baroness Warnock – who had been a big critic of what the KCC was doing twenty years ago – got up in the House of Lords the other day and said she accepted that she had been wrong. We are finding, too, that there seems to be more not less call for schools for children with a range of special needs. I think that it is partly that more babies who have severe physical and other problems are surviving nowadays but it may also be that more children are being better diagnosed – or both. But, just for example, Valence School in Westerham, which primarily looks after severely physically disabled children – it is a wonderful place – is dealing with many more difficult cases these days. And, in addition to more children with more complex needs, we nowadays have to look after these young people until they are twenty-four. I agree that it probably is a more rational cut-off point but it is yet another expense we have to factor in.

"On the adult side, we feel we have looked after people with learning disabilities pretty well.[45] We are proud of the way we have been able to find good housing which is suitable for individuals – to allow them to be with their friends; and to have as much independence as they are able to manage. It was not that easy when the old mental institutions like Leybourne Grange or Barming or The Princess Christian Hospital, all of which you know about, were being wound down twenty years ago; but generally, the KCC was able to put people who were friends in the mental hospitals into sheltered accommodation together. We have run a special scheme 'Your Life, Your Home' which looks at each individual to ensure they are happy with their housing and that, where possible, there can be a choice between different types of accommodation. We have also got some innovative support packages which enable people to maintain their independence.

"We had closed a few day centres which created uproar initially. But we closed them because they weren't very good. They were sometimes too centralised and had no links to the local community. We were sure we could do better. I remember one case. We promised that, after a year, we would ask the people who used the new service to let us know what they thought of the revised arrangements. We did the survey and 75%-80% thought that things were better.

"I understand that some of the smaller, more specialist organisations for people with learning disabilities are nervous that decreasing amounts of money overall may mean that in future the KCC will have to concentrate our resources on the larger organisations; and at the same time they fear that we may be tempted to use contractors rather than our own staff. But I can assure you that where units or organisations – however small – are seen to be doing a good job, we will continue to support them.

"The KCC was one of the first councils to take on outside specialist firms to help with learning disabilities. They were charities but they were given a remit from us to look after certain aspects of our care for our people with learning disabilities. They do much of our care in specialist housing and look after a wide range of individuals. We know that there is sometimes a feeling that these firms – some are after all businesses as well as charities – sometimes do not provide the same continuity of care that parents in particular think should be given to their child. They wonder whether more regular staffing might be given if KCC staff were used; but we feel our 'contractors' do a good job and we have moved to giving a greater proportion of our learning disabilities' budget to this sector – and that includes helping the voluntary organisations.[46]

"The National Audit Office reckons that County Councils like ours have lost 30% of central government money over the last five years. But, so far, I am convinced that we have kept up the overall standards pretty well and, as far as helping those with learning disabilities is concerned, I really do feel we have <u>improved</u> what we do to help – even though I do not think the general public know how much really wonderful work is done. I rather wish they did. And thinking generally and looking back over the last twenty or thirty years, I really do feel that the world for people with learning disabilities or learning difficulties is a better place – maybe life is better for nearly everyone."

The Director for Learning Disabilities and Mental Health in the West Kent area for some years has been Mark Walker (although he has moved to an even grander role which covers the whole of Kent). His West Kent team (which covers the Maidstone and the Faversham areas as well as the South West Kent area) has forty-five experts, who include speech therapists, occupational therapists (OTs) and physio therapists, as well as nursing and medical/psychological specialists. Additionally, they can call upon NHS assistance where it is needed.

Pivotal to the department and those it looks after are the care managers who are allocated to individuals. Each service user is then assessed and, where it is necessary, formally classified as having learning disabilities which in turn can warrant special help. The West Kent team as a whole look after 1,722 people who are registered with them, although they are aware that there are always others on the borderline of learning disabilities, who ideally should receive some assistance if there were not the inevitable financial constraints. To demonstrate the growing requests or demands for help, Kent as a whole adds an extra hundred 'service users' each year, in spite of what is clearly a rigorous examination of each case. (Parents, who have had to deal with the examination, have repeatedly said how difficult it is for their child to be accepted for help.)

The type of problems that Mark Walker's team have to overcome is wide-ranging – from very young babies (nationally three or four children in every thousand are born with some form of handicap) to disturbed old people, an increasing problem. The degree of the problem faced by each can vary from those whose problem is clear but not very severe – to those who are dangerous to themselves or to society, who need constant supervision within a relatively controlled community. Mark Walker's team look after all children, mentally and physically disabled/disadvantaged; but they only cover adults with learning difficulties (i.e. not those with only physical disabilities).

The special assessment is drawn up for each individual so that particular needs can be addressed. Then, Kent County Council's Social Services provide some of the assistance directly – in about

10% of the cases. For the majority of the 'service users', however, the care is contracted out to professional groups – nearly always charitable trusts which have a variety of residential care units. As we have seen, in South West Kent the main groups are Avenues, *mcch*, the Scotts Project and Pepenbury.

As so often, there are also instances where the system seems less than ideal. While saying that the following story occurred in a London borough rather than in Kent, it is important to mention it as a warning of what can happen when money becomes tight or the oversight by the authorities is lax. This case was told to me by a former partner in one of the world's top accounting firms. When he retired, he had volunteered to help a south London charity which was contracted by the local council to house those with learning difficulties. The charity was buying up large suburban houses, putting in cheap partitioning to make very small rooms and 'selling' these services to the Local Authority. Virtually no oversight or help was provided. It became clear to the retired accountant that the charity was in the business solely to make money for the trustees and he resigned – detailing his concerns to the authorities.

However, to return to the care in Kent. Whilst clearly every part of Social Services and the National Health Service ideally needs more money, Mark Walker is firm when he says that Kent has a good record for planning and implementing its responsibilities for learning difficulties and mental health. He mentions the Care Act which became effective in April 2015.

"A good number of Councils around the country had problems in coping with the new Act; but we were prepared and there were sensible consultations beforehand. I haven't seen any problems arising from it – although in the longer term all Social Services departments face difficulties, particularly with increasing numbers of elderly patients with various mental or learning problems. What many people forget is that around one in three of us are going to face some kind of mental problem in their life. This has not been recognised by everyone – not only is it not always fully understood by the government and the various Councils, but it is not really recognised by the general public either".

Day Care Centres

The Kent County Council has sophisticated Day Care Centre facilities which Mark Walker's department organises internally. Currently, there are fifty-six adults who are helped in the Tonbridge, Edenbridge and Sevenoaks area. The range of care is huge and Nikki Jones from the department explains.

"We have four main Day Care Centres and you're welcome to come and see us." (Descriptions of my actual visits come later). "We aim to help our people in a wide variety of ways – to suit their own needs. It can be to look after their physical or their state of mind needs. We have got what are called 'Sensory Rooms' which are specially designed to have a calming atmosphere. They can be used for 'challenging' patients but also for the severely disabled who can be given smells or things to feel and touch. There is one man who is virtually blind and the Sensory Room helps him; but some Down's syndrome people use it too. But we also give help to quite a number of service users who just need a bit of general help to equip them to lead ordinary lives. We call it 'independent living' and typically it would be to show a man or a woman how to plan a shopping list, get the money ready, go to the supermarket to buy the shopping and then to come home to cook the meal. Some of our service users can be encouraged to take courses at West Kent College; and the Sevenoaks Library runs special courses – including a poetry one. There is a drama group at Trinity Arts in Tunbridge Wells and there is music therapy available for individuals if and when the care managers think it could be useful. One of our most unusual facilities involves a trampoline. For some time, we have had one very severely mentally and physically disabled person. He gets taken to the trampoline, hoisted on to it and very gently rocked. We also involve our service users or patients or clients or whatever one calls them as much as possible in linking in with the community around them – although that's not always easy".

As I met all levels of expert in the field of helping the people with learning difficulties, I asked all of them about money and the future. Mark Walker's boss is Penny Southern about whom Paul Carter had talked with awe! (She was Director of Disabled Children, Adult Learning Disabilities and Mental Health when I first talked with her but then assumed even wider responsibilities before retiring). She is clear that, despite the significant financial pressures that local authorities are under, funding has been available to transform services for people with learning disabilities to meet demand, as well as run everything more efficiently.

> "In the 30 years I have worked for the KCC, we have always had to respond to the challenges of growing demand and less money. But we have done this by improving our services, making them more efficient and managing the demands in a proactive way so that our frontline services are protected. Many of our changes have been in prevention, supporting people with a learning disability safely to increase their independence, as well as increasing support to the carers. We also try to make sure young people have as much opportunity as possible to live as full a life as they can. There will be difficult times – for instance when they move away from their family home – but we hope, with our help, they can happily live in the new accommodation, accessing local services and becoming part of a community."

Another senior manager, Richard Brabbins, heads a KCC team of thirty who look after adults with learning disabilities in North West Kent. Half his staff are care managers. Richard himself has had nearly thirty years experience in helping people with learning disabilities. In that time, he has seen a number of gradual but positive changes in how support is given.

> "I think the biggest change is in attitude. The experts – people like me and my care managers – no longer feel that they are the ones imposing decisions on our people. The Care Act in 2015 reinforced this trend: people with learning disabilities have a right to make up their own minds. So, for example, if a person with Down's or Aspergers or is

somewhere on the autistic spectrum gets Government financial assistance – say for housing – nowadays we hope that we will help them have a home that they really want (and for which they will pay out of their grants). This has led to smaller units with more help for them as individuals. We try to encourage them to tell us what they want. There are what are called District Partnership Groups which aim to give them a voice if they feel the hospitals or the police or any part of the system could be improved. There was one instance when one of the DPGs – another of the many acronyms – persuaded the authorities at Bluewater to provide better facilities for the disabled. It happened – which was great. We try to iron out inequality, too. So when we found that the annual GP health screenings were missing out some of our people – our service users – we were able to ensure the system covered them more consistently. Over the years, we have been making all the services that we provide more local, so that service users have day centres in the town where they live and where they know people and can get to the centre more easily. This local basis also helps us help them to get an appropriate job. Finding a job is never easy for the general public but for many people with learning disabilities it is even more difficult, but is something they really want.

"On our side, we have been aiming increasingly to integrate our teams that look after each individual, so the social service experts and NHS experts will all meet together to discuss the needs of a particular person, with them or their parents usually there. You could have a speech therapist there or a specialist physio or someone who is an expert on the housing side. So I am pleased with the progress we have been making. But, of course, we know there is more to be done. Some of it will be dependent on money but that is certainly not the only thing. We would definitely like to have the availability of more varied housing – more options for our service users. We have too many of the larger residential homes with slightly too many people in them. They are good of their type – well run and

with pretty good facilities. But many of our service users would ideally like their own homes or to be sharing with one or two friends. We have even been piloting a scheme where someone with a learning disability lives with a host family. In spite of the difficulties of finding suitable jobs, we are continuing to think of new ways to help. We've got a KCC scheme called Kent Supportive Employment which talks with employers as well as our disabled people, so both sides can understand the other better. Incidentally, we'd like more firms to work with us on this. Finding a job is not something that we start on when the person reaches eighteen. We will have known about them before – probably from when they are sixteen – with our care managers liaising with the child's care manager and with the family. So, we'll know the young person and will have a good idea of the kind of job they could do. You asked about how many years a particular care manager would be with a particular service user and his or her family. It will vary but it could be up to ten to fifteen years. The problem is often staffing and recruitment. Good care managers will get promoted and some may get poached by private companies in the care sector. And a few will leave for other jobs. In areas where there is a labour shortage – places like the Bluewater area – there will be lots of other jobs available which pay more; and in rural parts, it can also be difficult to find the right people. But the wages we pay are not that bad. A care manager who has finished training earns around £27,000 which goes up as they get more experienced."
[Author's note: these were figures from 2018]

The support staff directly employed by the KCC to look after learning disability matters may seem small – under three dozen full-time and part-time people to cover children and under two dozen for the adults. The answer is simple. These staff are largely the care managers who are assessing the needs of those who are receiving help or who are likely to need help, together with staff who look after the excellent Day Care Centres. All the people who arrange the care – the housing, the daily oversight and support, the medical needs or the education needs and so on – are contracted out by the KCC or provided by the NHS or the various schools and further education bodies. (These are all discussed in more detail later in the book).

West Kent's Adult Learning Disabilities Team

Richard Brabbin's opposite number for adults in South West Kent area is Julie Read. Currently, she has the six hundred and nineteen adults mentioned above who are formally registered as having learning disabilities in the area. The team of thirty-five mixes social services experts with NHS professionals. There are two 'senior practitioners' who oversee, advise and train younger team members; seven care managers with another seven care manager assistants. The specialists include seven community nurses, two occupation therapists and three speech and language therapists. The average case load for each of Julie's care managers is forty-five people with a learning disability – quite a task. I attended one of their once a month meetings at which the whole team assemble to review the ongoing cases and to agree what should be done. Julie says:

"We know that there are and will be people with learning disabilities and their parents who are upset when we start trying to help them. They can often be full, not just of grief, but of blame and anger at what has happened. We understand these feelings and all of us try to help as much as we can. But we cannot always achieve a perfect solution. We can usually improve things but not provide a cure".

As well as helping children, there are close ties, too, between the different specialist staff who look after an adult. His or her care manager keeps an individual 'client file' which is continuously updated. It includes all the likes and dislikes, risk assessment points and medical details. It will have input from day centre staff, GPs and specialist nurses, carers and support workers; and comments from the clients. If there are any problems at the sheltered accommodation or other homes, these, too, will be reported back and dealt with. I was given an example of how the liaison between the various parts of the care service worked. One of the Day Care Centre staff guessed that a particular service user had a urinary infection. They contacted the person in charge of the particular sheltered accommodation unit who sent a written report to their regular GP who in turn dealt with the matter. There is also an annual review. The KCC is in the process of introducing a computerised version of the service user's records, which will not only be able to contain more information but will be instantly available to anyone involved with the client. Not everyone I asked about these digital changes was hopeful about an easy introduction of the system.

KCC Support for Children

There are some children where it will be clear from birth that they and their families are going to need support all their lives, but particularly in their childhood years – for example, children with Down's or cerebral palsy. In these cases, the family will immediately be referred by the hospital – in South West Kent, it is the new Tunbridge Wells Hospital and its acute maternity service – to the KCC Support Team. For many more cases, however, the health visitor may see early signs of a problem when the child is one or two years old. Again, the relevant authorities will move into action and a range of support can be offered including Portage, where the parents are trained to give the child carefully calibrated work. There is an Early Support Team and one of their key workers will co-ordinate the variety of experts needed for the individual child. However, sometimes autism and other similar problems only become apparent once the child starts school – often with the symptoms appearing relatively suddenly. In these cases the school's' Special Educational Needs Officer – the SENCO – will liaise with the parents, the school and the GP. A KCC team manager will be notified and an individual care manager allocated. The care manager will then do the assessment. At the present time, there are only relatively small delays in this part of the process. This KCC assessment will, amongst other things, either allocate appropriate KCC support workers or give the parents an allowance for them to buy in their own help. Currently, in Kent, seven hundred and fifty parents out of one thousand (so over half) take the latter course of an allowance. However, the next stage is where the delays seem to start – when the NHS becomes involved. The problems are discussed in more detail in the NHS and schools chapters.

Staff

There are two types of job, both of which are necessary to look after people with learning difficulties. There are the 'professionals' who have degrees and specialist qualifications – the doctors, community nurses, speech and physio and occupational therapists and so on. And then there are the various levels of care management and the support workers. This section looks at the people who provide the day in/day out care.

The definition of the people who actually support people with learning disabilities, either in their homes or when they go to and from the day centres or go to a film or shopping, seems to vary. I had heard them called 'carers' or 'care assistants'. However, I was told that technically a carer was someone who looked after the service users in their own home. So, a parent was a 'carer'. People who were paid to help the service user in their supported living flat, for example, or to take them to interesting places were called 'support staff'. However, often the terms seemed interchangeable. I met probably thirty support workers and many carers; and I heard about many more. In the vast majority of cases, their patience and understanding seemed difficult to comprehend to an outsider. I talked with one carer of about fifty. He said that until he was thirty-five he had done probably ten jobs – builder, driver, barman, and so on. Then sixteen years ago he had fallen into care work – which he now loved. "Anyone can do it but not everyone will stick it", he said with a laugh. "I probably do forty to fifty hours a week. Sometimes seven days a week if someone needs helping out."

His colleague, Clare, agreed. She too had had a variety of jobs before trying caring for people with learning disabilities which she had done for six years now. She worked part-time, nearly always looking after one particular lady whom she takes out to the shops or the cinema or on trips, as well as helping out at home. "I don't think of it as a job. Just me going out to meet my friends." When I visited day centres, I met many other support workers. I thought them all – at various levels – to be knowledgeable and dedicated. And in talking to parents and the service users themselves, I never heard complaints.

Recruitment

The heads of several organisations with whom I talked said that their biggest challenge currently was recruiting support workers. So, I asked about support workers' wages,[47] how best to select the right people and to train them, and how, if they eventually wanted to, they could progress. I gathered – this was in 2019 – that the starting wages for a new, full-time support worker with some basic training and employed by the KCC, or more often, groups responsible to the KCC was around £16,200 p.a. plus reasonable allowances, overtime and increments. This increases to around £19,000-£20,000 p.a. for a Senior Support Worker. The next grade up – which would involve management duties – is an Assistant Service Manager who would earn around £22,500, which could in turn lead to being a Service Manager. A Service Manager will be responsible for the direct oversight of between fifteen and thirty support staff at various locations. They might earn around £30,000. (Various care providers have different titles/structures for roles). While these kinds of wages might seem reasonable for some parts of the country and even in some parts of Kent, the cost of living in South West Kent is particularly high and the salary level, therefore, comparatively less favourable. I heard of residential homes where it was impossible to obtain local support workers and, in consequence, the necessary staff were coming down from London by train, with taxis to take them from the station to the home – all at very considerable cost and with little continuity for the service users.

Karen Reed, the then Director of Operations at *mcch*, summarised the difficulties of finding good staff. "It is the worst I have ever known it in forty years of working in the care sector. Social Care has in recent years gained media attention and what the public hear about is usually negative. Of course, it is right to highlight where care and support falls short or abuse occurs but I feel the media coverage has impacted on recruitment. Fewer people are now wanting to enter social care as a career. It really is true, too, that social care is in crisis due to the financial constraints that have hit the local authorities. This in turn impacts on the funds available to provide support. Another problem is that people thinking about going into the various caring professions sometimes assume that it is just about providing the actual care and support to someone who needs it. They are surprised by the amount of paperwork that needs to be kept – the support plans, risk assessments, outcomes and goal setting, compliance monitoring and much more. So, the money is very low; there is the negative media coverage; and there is the not very realistic expectations of new support staff. All impact on the sector's ability to recruit good staff."

In all my discussions, I only heard one instance of a carer/support worker in the area letting down her profession. It made headlines in the newspapers. A woman carer had stolen three lots of money from her elderly charges. The sum was several thousand pounds and the world was encouraged to feel outraged. I suspect that the story will have been seen by many of the public as typical, whereas, in reality, it was a complete exception; but it probably did not help recruitment.

Care Managers and Support Workers

A National Audit Office report[48] in 2018 underlined the difficulties of finding care workers that we have heard about if we read papers, or watch TV programmes, or listen to Radio 4. It put all the facts together and recommended that society should pay these people more and plan better for the future. It said that there seemed to be no national strategy; that not only were care workers given insufficient money per hour, but that the pay only covers time spent in a house looking after their client, not travel to and from the client; that the hours are incredibly long – up to sixteen hours a day; and that there are shortages of staff; and that the retention rate is very poor. There is little prestige or career prospects; and that there is less overall money being spent than there was six years ago. All this at a time when the need for such services is increasing and will increase still further as the population ages. I met quite a few support workers and heard their upbeat and positive stories. Not one of the twenty or thirty support workers with whom I talked brought up the question of pay until I specifically asked about it. Even then, while they usually admitted they got very little and really needed more, particularly in this expensive part of the country, they would return to talking about the other aspects of the job – a job they loved. Pay was more often raised by their bosses or their bosses' bosses, who, in most cases, were finding it difficult not only to recruit new staff but to retain them. Brexit and the pandemic are not necessarily going to make matters easier.

I asked one young support worker informally about a typical day. He laughed and said that currently his life was not very normal. He works at an 'independent living' house. Currently, it has two tenants, both men, both of whom he really likes, although they are very different. The first is a moderately autistic young man with whom he can easily relate because the man is very similar to his – the carer's – own twin brother. "We do all the usual things together – day-to-day life things – shopping, going to the cinema or bowling and I'll take him to medical appointments and things like that. And he goes off to see his parents for a bit of each week." The other man is middle-aged and has always been seriously autistic. He had lived at home but he experienced a series of incidents – including being severely beaten up. So, at this moment, he was not in a good place and he needed special help. The young support worker had become close to the man and was fond of him, even with his current problems. However, in reality, he was too inexperienced to cope. Cheeringly, the authorities were clear that the young support worker was getting out of his depth with the second man and changes were being made. The man would be receiving extra help and, with luck, the situation would improve. However, the young support worker was clearly right to say that his 'typical day' about which I had asked didn't really exist.

There can be cases where the service user is so disturbed that they are a danger to others as well as to themselves. I heard about and saw several such people and came to understand that their sometimes violent behaviour is normally because they become frightened – not because they want to hurt anyone. One case, which illustrated the complexities, reached the High Court[49]. The authorities were being criticised for keeping a disturbed sixteen year old boy in solitary confinement in a Young Offenders 'prison'. The judges decided that the authorities had been wrong. However, the newspapers did not have the time, space or perhaps the inclination to fully explain the case. In reality, the boy was extremely violent. Others in the Young Offenders Institution wished to do him harm. The 'confinement' was the only way the authorities could find to save him from injury. There will be occasional instances such as this one, but newspaper reports may well make the public feel that they are frequent. In reality, I was assured that, within Kent at least, the KCC has its own 'secure units' and these have been praised for the sensitive way they deal with people with these rare but severe problems.

Training

I asked the senior managers and most of the support workers I met about the details of staff training. The answers varied. Sometimes there was a very detailed syllabus, with progress through levels of exams. In other cases, there was a much more informal type of training. For example, when I asked some support staff about their training and qualifications, they described an initial week of intensive induction at the base from where they would mainly be working. This week seemed to cover everything – the types of disability, the range of work they would be doing, and how to do it – including the various safety issues. The second week would be spent working alongside an experienced mentor who would not only be teaching but would also assess the potential of the new person – did they have the right attitude; and could they learn the skills needed to be taken on? The mentor would also assess whether the new person would be able or want to progress to more senior types of work, although many do not want to: they want to stay looking after 'their friends'. Most of the support workers with whom I talked agreed that the vast majority of 'training' came from doing the job and getting to know each of the people they looked after as individuals. As I listened to these experiences from support care staff, it sounded quite like the training done by the Princess Christian Hospital staff and the way they looked after their 'boys' and 'girls' twenty or thirty years ago.

However, while the somewhat informal training – 'the learning on the job' – certainly occurs, it seemed that much more structured training was often now happening. In the KCC's own departments and in the larger contracted out services, there were increasingly detailed syllabuses with subsequent exams. (The web certainly helps with these developments). I asked Dan Gower-Smith from Avenues South East, with its two hundred and fifty staff, how they went about choosing prospective new applicants. "Values," he said. For him, it was not whether the person had done a similar job before but whether they had the right attitude to really care and support people who have a learning disability.

"If they are the right type of person, they can be taught how to become good at the job. For us, like most organisations, training starts with a six month induction course. There is some classroom work and e-learning, as well as practical work with a mentor This leads to a certificate. After that, the training is on-going, with courses on various more specialist subjects and refresher courses, including, where appropriate, management training."

There are various levels of qualification for the levels and types of job. The basic Care Certificate uses a mixture of e-learning, workbooks and supervised learning on the job. Then there are QCF qualifications[50] from Level 2 and 3 for support staff up to Level 5 for managers, together with other qualifications[51] particularly for managers. I talked with one manager at the Tonbridge Day Care Centre who was studying to enable her to progress up to the next, fairly high managerial level. I was impressed by the amount of work and the breadth of learning that it involved. Karen Reed of *mcch* also sent me two pages just with the headings of the subjects their staff training involved. There was an induction course which included thirteen aspects of care. This was followed by eleven headings of courses which were mandatory for all support staff to attend. Workbooks are completed and managers supervise the staff during their probationary period, regularly reviewing their progress. This was only the first page. The second page covered more specialist subjects – epilepsy, dysphasia, PEG feeding, positive behaviour support, moving and handling, makaton, catheters and Prader-Willi syndrome were just a few examples.

However, as I have mentioned, the amount of training seemed to vary and one senior manager did wonder aloud whether there should be a national system for training support workers and the grades up the ladder.

However, there was a stark contrast between the systems described above and some firms within the private sector, particularly, when looking after clients who were disturbed or elderly or both. I talked with one firm, Superior Care, which provide occasional support workers for the KCC's sub-contractors They seemed efficient and caring and were adamant that their training was rigorous and ensured that each support worker was competent for each type of client they were employed to look after. However, I heard of another well-known firm which employed an eighteen year old girl waiting to go to university to look after an elderly lady who, quite clearly, had serious dementia – the old lady kept seeing swarms of bees in the room and could become very distressed. With no training whatsoever and no response from the firm for the requested help, the girl eventually contacted the old lady's children who were doctors. They again did little to help. The girl left. This was not a case of providing help to a person who was registered as having learning disabilities but does illustrate that some private care providers are much less good than others.

I had expected to meet support workers from abroad. (I had met many in both hospitals and in old people's homes). Perhaps, by chance, I met hardly any. Where there are currently foreign workers, it may well become more difficult to recruit new ones after Brexit.

However, the fact remains: social services staff are increasingly difficult to attract. A report in October 2021 ('Skills For Care') said that there was a record number of vacancies, 8%-9% and the situation was getting worse.

Transport

There are numerous and varied things for people with learning disabilities to do. However, very often, there is the question of transport. How do children get to and from school or to and from the special clubs or places to visit? If they are adults, how do they get to and from work; how do they get to the shops or to a day centre once or twice a week; or to a hospital appointment on an occasional basis. All the authorities make an effort to teach their people how to catch a local bus or a train; and sometimes it is possible to walk where one needs to go. Sometimes parents are able to fit a journey in, perhaps with the school run when they drop off their other children. However, where none of these is possible, the KCC has a sophisticated system of taxis and drivers, supplemented by various voluntary groups. Many parents and adults are very grateful for this service, so, I thought it worth a brief heading on its own. Shane Bushell was the KCC's Client Transport Manager for Special Educational Needs when I needed to know what happens. Each day he was organising six thousand journeys. The majority were for children going to and from special schools but there were a good number of adults to be ferried to a place, too. He employs around six hundred carefully vetted drivers – and parents told me that the service was of huge value and that the drivers are very kind.

This massive, daily, logistical operation is supplemented, although only to a small extent, by a number of charities, often with volunteer drivers. The largest of these is Compaid (which also runs computer courses.) Their transport service covers most of West Kent. "We are what is called a pan-disability charity," says their CEO, Stephen Elsden. "So, we do help people with learning disabilities but we also help the elderly and the disabled. We have over twenty buses and take over a thousand people a year to where that individual wants to be." I also talked with one of Compaid's volunteer drivers, who said how rewarding he found the job. "I earn about a hundredth of what I used to earn in the City but it's great. Many of the people I carry around would never leave their sitting rooms if it wasn't for me. We are their window to the outside world." There are a number of other transport services – some given help by the KCC and others run by volunteers. People told me about Dial-A-Ride, Kent Karrier and Dial-2-Drive. I did not ask them for details; but, no doubt unsung heroes all.

CHAPTER 6

The NHS – and the Police

The NHS plays an important part in the lives of adults and children who have learning disabilities – and their parents and carers. There is help available from a wide range of services 'from the cradle to the grave'. The two major NHS hospitals in West Kent provide help, particularly if the child is born with a learning disability; and the GPs are there to give advice and pass the patient on to specialists as necessary. However, the major NHS contribution to the well-being of those with learning disabilities (and, to a certain extent, those with learning difficulties) is a much less well-known group called 'Community Health'.

I learned two general things about children who may have some kind of learning disability or learning difficulty. The first is that it is important to obtain a diagnosis early. The second may seem to be at odds with the first: it can be complex for even experts to make the diagnosis and, in any case, it can be difficult to get to the experts. My views about the complexities of assessing children who may have autism were reinforced when I watched a specialist video featuring one of the country's leading experts from the country's most famous children's hospital. He gave details of the assessment of a primary school-aged boy. The tests had taken a year – about a dozen had been undertaken, all by well-known experts in their particular field. He came to his conclusion. The boy was normal. Then he added that the father was Chief Executive of a major UK company and that the mother was a well-known lawyer. My conclusions were that it helps to have influence; and that the assessment phase of treatments for potential autism can indeed be complex and lengthy. It was obviously unlikely that the NHS could afford anything like the service provided in this instance. This example also reminded me of a concern that I heard from a good number of professionals. Well-educated and forceful parents could be extremely demanding and difficult. One NHS expert said that she realised every parent would fight to get the best for their child but she found some of the better educated ones were dismissive of NHS professionals who they felt might not be first-rate, yet fought to get to the front of the NHS or school queue for help. Another social worker told me of a child whose parents were convinced, against advice, that their autistic son only needed to 'be stretched' to bring him into line with his peers. They bought a piano and the boy had lessons. They hired a maths tutor to help the boy. The result was that the child had a complete breakdown.

For the very young, a diagnosis may have already started to be made when the child is first born or is very young – for example, children with Down's, whose prognosis is known at or before birth. However, sometimes it is not until the child is two or three, or even four, that symptoms of the various types of learning disability can start to appear. The parent may notice something first or a health visitor or a teacher may begin to have concerns. The child may not mix or becomes absorbed in his or her own world; or there are signs of frustration leading sometimes to rage; or their speech or other learning skills start lagging behind their peers; or he or she becomes over anxious in a new environment and away from mother and home – more than in a way common to any child. The problem always is that any or all of these types of behaviour can be part of growing up for most children. So, at this stage it is sensible – if worrying – for a parent to talk with their GP, as well as the teachers of the child.

It is a truism to say that every child – and every parent – is different. Most parents with whom I have talked, watch their child's progress almost every day. They compare how soon their child crawls, walks, says its first word and so on, with other children. They discuss it all with friends and health visitors, read books and consult numerous internet sites. As every child is different, about half the children will be below the average at any one week by definition. How much and when should the parents worry? Friends, grandparents, sisters and, at a later stage, teachers, will probably start by being reassuring. "Every child develops at his or her own pace" will be agreed. But parents will still want more information. If there are even slight doubts, they will want to know whether something bad is happening and whether, in the old phrase, "something should be done". Help is available. Some will be via Social Services. Much will be available when the child starts school. But much expertise is within the NHS services. This chapter looks at the various parts of the NHS and what each does to provide support, first for children with learning disabilities; and then, as they grow up, for adults.

The Main Acute Hospitals: The Tunbridge Wells and Maidstone Hospitals

West Kent's main NHS Hospital Trust has two major sites – at Maidstone and Tunbridge Wells plus a subsidiary one at Crowborough, East Sussex. When I first enquired, the Care Quality Commission (CQC) classified both main hospitals as "requires improvement"[52] and the Trust which administers both hospitals has been in Financial Special Measures – one of the first five NHS Hospital Trusts in the whole of England to be so classified. However, the general public seemed to find both hospitals first rate – apart, of course, from the waiting lists, with a survey for 2017/2018 finding that over 93% of the 35,826 people who had used the hospitals saying they would recommend the service. In my discussions, the Tunbridge Wells Hospital was criticised by two families who felt not all the general staff were sufficiently aware of the problems and anxieties of people with learning disabilities. However, from the point of view of this book, it is not the main, acute services that normally deal with learning disabilities; it is the Women and Children's Department and, in particular the Maternity and Neo-Natal unit which are classified by the CQC as being 'excellent'. I talked with Jenny Cleary who is in charge of these services.

> "Pregnant ladies have the option of tests at the end of their first three months. They are non-invasive and will give a good indication about whether the baby has Down's and one other horrid but rare condition – Edward's syndrome.

If it does look as though either of these conditions are likely, we explain things to the mothers – the parents. We are lucky that we have a really good Down's Society locally and they help the mother – and the father – make a choice if Down's is definitely found. The vast majority opt for an abortion. I sometimes wonder about it because I know wonderful Down's people and do we want everyone perfect – everyone the same? But it will never be an easy choice and we well understand that. At eighteen or nineteen weeks there are another set of tests. These look at limbs, heart, spine, liver and so on. Again, if it looks as if there could be problems – and they are very rare – there are carefully planned consultations and counselling for the parents. We have got much better at these discussions – we have now got a special room – but it is always difficult. In those cases, if the mother opts for an abortion, it can only be up to twenty-four weeks. A midwife is allocated to each pregnant mother – whether there are potential difficulties or not – and will follow the baby through until after the birth, when she will make probably two visits at home in the first couple of weeks, or more if there are problems. At this point the health visitor takes over. Of course, not every mother wants to have the birth in hospital. Currently, it is 87%, with the other 13% preferring to give birth at home. We leave it up to the mother and only try to insist on a hospital birth if there could be problems. It is funny how the fashions change. It used to be mainly at home. Then in the 1960s and 1970s, the experts wanted to get everyone into hospital. Now it is flexible. Last year, we looked after nearly six thousand births, with just over five thousand two hundred here at Tunbridge Wells – the acute maternity unit – or at the two other birth centres, one at Maidstone and one at Crowborough. That meant there were seven hundred and seventy-five births at home. Out of the six thousand births, only a handful had problems. Of course, these do not include a number of children with learning difficulties and autism where they often don't become apparent until later.

"But wherever the child is born, there is an automatic set of tests at birth – 'The Examination of the New Born'. These check all the main physical aspects including hearing but also for various rare diseases – cystic fibrosis, sickle cell anaemia and other unpleasant things. If there are doubts, there are more tests and, where necessary, discussions by our experts with the parents. Then extra, specialist help can be laid on by the KCC's learning disability team. We also have learning disability specialist nurses who will be involved. One relatively new development is the Children's Centres. There are around eight in South West Kent, so always somewhere nearby for the mother and baby to go to. The idea is partly to save the Health Visitors having to spend time in travelling to see every new baby at home: but it is also good to get new mums out of the house, meeting other mums as well as getting the necessary checks at the centres. So we aim to provide a seamless service from when the pregnancy starts until the child goes to school – it helps being a 'Women and Children's Department'. I feel very lucky here at Tunbridge Wells in not having any staffing problems. We have a full complement of midwives, special nurses, consultants and so on. And, if we ever have vacancies for trainees or interns, we are swamped with applicants. It's a really good place to work – a lovely hospital."

One grandfather told me of his six year old granddaughter who had been born with multiple autistic problems. The family were repeatedly told that she could not survive but with huge help from the Tunbridge Wells Hospital, she has progressed into a cheerful – if still disabled – child. The Hospital has an open-door invitation for the child to come to them anytime, day or night. The family could not be more grateful.

Still thinking of the help given by the Tunbridge Wells Hospital, I remembered that when I was talking with one of the KCC Day Care Centres, they had mentioned how the Matron at the hospital and some of her staff there talk with groups of people with learning disabilities. The day centre staff said how useful it had been in helping dispel the fears that their people had of hospitals and operations. At the same time, they said they had been told by the Hospital staff that it was useful for them to talk with organisations such as the Day Care Centres or the Down's Society so that the staff better understood the feelings and problems of people with learning disabilities.

Children's Therapy Service and the Dolphin Centre

Once the new born child has been identified as having learning disabilities, either at the time of the birth or slightly later by the Health Visitor, a number of NHS specialist services are available. The Children's Therapy Service is one. In South West Kent it is based at the Dolphin Centre at Tunbridge Wells. The Centre is part of a Kent-wide scheme to provide an integrated therapy service for children who have learning disabilities/autism but also those with physical difficulties and needs. The team is headed by Karen Corrigan, with around sixty therapists – physiotherapists, occupational therapists and speech and language experts. The Centre has a number of roles. First, it supports young children from birth until seven in a scheme called Care Co-ordination. If a child has a recognised problem at birth, the Dolphin Centre would be contacted, usually by the hospital. The Centre then provides expert help. For example, a child might have swallowing difficulties and one of the Dolphin's speech therapists would immediately be allocated. The second role is to give physiotherapy or occupational therapy or speech and language assistance to children between seven and nineteen – either in their home or at a school. They also provide regular help to special schools. For example, Karen has around ten therapists of different types at Valence School in Westerham – which is described in the Schools chapter. The Dolphin Centre also provides training courses for teachers, teaching assistants and Special Educational Needs Officers, covering a wide range of subjects including such things as 'sensory circuits' – exercises which can be done at the start of a school day to prepare a child who has, say, ADHD for the classroom; or set up a course to help children who are non-verbal. These courses can be either in groups or occasionally for individuals. They can be held at a school or, more often, at the Dolphin Centre. The courses seem much appreciated by people who have attended with whom I talked.

Portage

One specific method of helping the very young about which I was told initially by some parents and later by some experts is called Portage. The aim is to teach the parents how to help their young child on a day-to-day basis from birth until pre-school. The system in Kent had originally been based in the local maternity unit at the old Pembury Hospital near Tunbridge Wells. I was told it was started about thirty-five years ago by a Dr Robards who, as well as being the consultant paediatrician there, also had a special interest in learning disabilities. He formed a team to which any new born baby was referred if it was clear – or even likely – that they would have learning difficulties. This would include a Down's syndrome; or a cerebral palsy child; children who might have been injured while being born; or infrequent but devastating illnesses such as cystic fibrosis and other problems – including epilepsy if it had become apparent this early. Having had a diagnosis from the senior paediatrician in the hospital, the team would work with the parents – even when they were still in the hospital – but, much more importantly, at home, often with weekly visits so that help could be provided regularly. This could continue up until school age if it was needed. I thought that it was useful to include a description from a mother and father of how Portage had helped them. The parents, Lorna and Bill Belither, who used the system some years ago, were clear that their child would not be where she is today if it had not been for Portage.

"It started while we were at the hospital. We were told that our daughter had Down's. It was not a good time. So to have immediate help was wonderful. Directly we got home, our Portage worker arrived. She was called Linda and she became a close friend. She still is. She was a specially trained volunteer and she came one morning a week for most of our daughter's first four years. One of the problems with Down's babies is that the muscles are very floppy. It is vital to get them stronger. So, Linda taught us a whole range of exercises that we had to do – to teach our small daughter how to roll over, to sit up and to crawl and so on. At first, some of the exercises seemed a bit rough to us as new parents – pulling her up by her arms, pumping her legs when we changed her nappies and so on. But Linda would explain it all. And, if she didn't have an answer to something that worried us, she'd find out. She also helped with speech and language and about how our daughter could acquire 'social skills' – getting on with people. But above all she taught us how we could do things ourselves to help. Without her teaching, our daughter would never have ended up as the lovely and lively young lady that she is today."

However, treatments and the organisation of them evolve and about ten years ago, the system, originally run by the NHS and based in hospitals, was changed, so that it became part of KCC Education, and was not based at hospitals and no longer used volunteers. Not everyone with whom I talked thought that this was an advance, so I asked Tracy Harvey, the current head of Portage locally, how things worked now.

Tracy has been part of Kent's Portage service for twenty-four years and is an enthusiast. She has a team of thirty staff to cover the whole of Kent with around nine in West Kent "which is not our busiest area by any means," she says. Each year, her team will support well over nine hundred Kent children – around three hundred and forty at any one time – whose ages will range from birth until their care is taken over by the pre-school specialists.

"Ideally, we would like to follow up our children to make sure things are progressing well at school but we have a waiting list of around a hundred and twenty children most of the time, so we just can't." Sometimes a child will be referred to them at birth, either from the neo-natal paediatrician at the Tunbridge Wells hospital or the midwife "but we will look at applications from anyone. When the child is a little older, it could be a GP or the district nurse or the parents. Our criterion for accepting them on to the waiting list is that the child is at least six months behind a 'normal' child. The treatment we give is either weekly or fortnightly and our aim is always to involve the parents.

Between us, we must make things not only better but fun for the child. Other departments will tell parents what to do – which is fine and often the best way; but we work <u>with</u> the parents; and every child will be helped in an individual way. We recruit our staff from a variety of backgrounds but most will have had some teaching or SENCO experience. Of course, we give the newcomers formal training and mentor them to begin with but the vital thing is that they are able to get on with the parents and their child. It's a long term relationship and it has to work. We are very lucky in Kent. The KCC Social Services, which pays for two thirds of our service, with the other third and overall management coming from Kent Education, is hugely supportive of what we do. We have had no cuts – although I have to say that we have had a relatively big increase in demand. Some other County Councils have dramatically cut back Portage budgets or even abandoned the service. But we like to think that what we do is really valuable. The parents certainly think so. I still get letters, sometimes years later, with donations or photographs of how the child is doing or a note of how they are still using what we taught them to do. Oh, and when we can't cope with an extra child because of the waiting lists, we arrange group sessions for parents with similar aged children to try to help."

West Kent's NHS Community Health Services

Kent, like most counties, is divided into a number of regions for the provision of NHS services. I began to get the impression that these areas were being consolidated. The Sevenoaks, Tonbridge and Tunbridge Wells area which is generally called SW Kent seems to be in the process of being merged with Maidstone into a West Kent area. This could have both advantages and disadvantages. It could mean that specialist expertise within the wider area was more readily available. Alternatively, it could mean 'patients' having to travel further and that, more importantly, the local relationship both within the teams of experts, and between the experts and their own patients was lessened.

However, to return to the service which is currently being provided. The government provides each NHS region with money. In spite of many genuine stories in the media about NHS waiting lists and mistakes, the budgets are increasing and many more patients are being treated. More doctors and nurses are, seemingly very belatedly, being trained in England. There are regional bodies called Clinical Commissioning Groups – known as CCGs. West Kent has its own CCG. I asked David Holman, its Head, how the system works. Because the overall task of looking after people with learning disabilities falls within the three areas of responsibility – his NHS services; the various types of help provided by Social Services; and the increasing support given within schools – I asked whether the three worked together satisfactorily?

He said that he thought cooperation was good – in part because many of the top people had worked together for a good number of years but also because the system of looking after people with learning disabilities had not had reorganisation after reorganisation. He added that there is almost a constant interchange of information between the three services so that potential problems are picked up early on an informal basis. People like him have been concerned with the quality of care for people with learning disabilities since the days of the Princess Christian Hospital which had survived into the late 1980s/early 1990s and which he had known about as a young care manager[53]. He went on to explain the present NHS structure in West Kent. The NHS gives his CCG money with overall guidance about what it wants to see for such areas as mental health and for learning disabilities (which I learnt was nowadays often called 'LD'). As a commissioning organisation, with approximately ninety staff, his CCG has to allocate contracts to groups that will provide the best services. With learning disabilities, for a good number of years they have given the contract to the Kent Community Health Care NHS Trust – guess what? – always known as KCHCT. The CCG also allocate monies to Kent and Medway Partnership Trust (KMPT) and to some KCC services. In theory, they could commission a Health Care Trust from another area or a private group – for example Virgin Health Care – but in practice they have found KCHCT does normally provide the support very satisfactorily. It is the KCHCT which then provides a range of services for people with learning disabilities. Although GPs are separately funded and overseen, they work closely with CCG and KCHCT, with each doctor's practice having a specialist community nurse to give advice. Recently, the CCG had funded an experienced doctor as the Clinical Lead for local GPs who will work with them on the care given to people with learning disabilities. Occupational therapists, physio-therapists and speech therapists which the KCHCT allocates where they are needed, particularly in partnership with schools. And, in some cases, specialist help is provided for adults – usually via GPs.

Part of the contract given to KCHCT is devoted to assessing whether the quality of the service given is satisfactory. Both Dave Holman's CCG and the KCC's learning disability team are currently devoting a good deal of effort into checking what their 'service users' think of the service or services they are given. Nearly all the feedback seems to be positive. There is said to be '94% patient satisfaction' for its various remits, including preventive medicine and the community hospitals as well as the services for people with learning disabilities and the CQC rates KCHCT as 'good'. But always, for Dave Holman and his unit, as well as for the Social Services teams, the mantra is "Patients at the Centre".

I asked Dave Holman about the future. He was confident that West Kent – his area – would continue to provide a good service for those with learning disabilities – as far as was ever going to be possible when the individuals had such very diverse needs and when their care was an inexact science. However, he did wonder about two things. Firstly, why did there seem to be an increase in the number of children being diagnosed as on the autistic spectrum? He suspected that there _were_ more troubled children and that it was not _just_ that more parents demanding more help for their own child. He wondered whether the stress put on children today could be having an effect. And, secondly, he wondered whether society could be more inclusive to those with learning disabilities. In that aspiration, he echoed what the KCC's Penny Southern, his long-term colleague, had said. Although he recognised that people had got less abusive and were more prepared to accept people who were different, he still felt that there was a good way to go.

Kent Community Health Care Trust – Children

As we have seen, the Kent Community Health Care Trust receives money from the CCG. The KCHCT person who oversees the NHS services for children with learning disabilities for the whole of Kent is Clive Tracey, who has a background in nursing in both the NHS and the private sector. He has a total of around hundred and sixty staff made up of OTs, physios, speech therapists, audiologists, specialist nurses and specialist doctors. In West Kent, they deal with about one thousand two hundred appointments a month. (There were over 77,000 contacts in the whole of Kent over a recent six month period). I only give these statistics to indicate the large number of children with learning difficulties that seem to need and usually receive NHS support. Clive Tracey emphasised the importance of early diagnosis and treatment. He felt that one reason why they had been able to cope with the increasing demand was the fact that this earlier treatment meant quicker improvement and that the overall case load could – in theory at least – go down. The earlier treatment could also often mean that there was a need for more therapists and fewer high level staff such as paediatric consultants. The system was internally training up more junior (Level 4) staff, such as therapy assistants who could continue with treatment once it had been established.

I asked about his overall funding. Clearly, he would not criticise the CCG – whose people he knows well and respects. He also knows the current NHS financial constraints. He said that, of course, money was a challenge. It was publicly known that the NHS in Kent was likely to be £400m in deficit for the coming year unless more funding was provided. However, he and his team were constantly looking for new ways of doing things which would benefit patients but cost less. He agreed that on the staffing side, there were occasionally types of jobs which were difficult to fill. However, he felt that within his part of the NHS, it was not necessarily a matter of low pay. It was sometimes difficult to assess where a gap in particular skills might come, although, in some cases, it was clear that not enough people of certain professions or skill were being trained. And you had to expect younger, more junior staff to move on. I asked about the future. He felt his team was providing a really good service now but he did wonder about the longer term. Groups like his have made all the efficiencies they could. In the future, they would also probably have to involve parents and carers even more. But at some stage, if more money did not arrive, you had to do less well or think about rationing the support given. He hoped neither would happen.

However, for younger children with learning problems, the waiting list for assessment and then for treatment does appear to be a major concern. Some assessments come within the KCC social care's remit and some are the concern of the NHS. When I had talked with the KCC's Penny Southern, I had been assured that there were no <u>social care</u> assessment delays in Kent. By law, these have to be carried out within twenty-eight days; and, in Kent, they are. However, talking with a range of experts and with a good number of parents, it seems that the demand for <u>NHS</u> assessments and then the provision of follow-up help, greatly exceeds what is possible to provide. The theory is that, when a child really seems to have a problem with which the GP and the school cannot cope, they go to the NHS experts. In practice, this then becomes a protracted struggle. And these interviews were all done before the Covid pandemic. I hear that the delays are now even worse – not just in Kent but over most, if not all, the country.

One mother who, in fact, was knowledgeable about learning disabilities and, therefore, was able to be more pro-active than most parents, told me what had happened to her and her daughter.

"Our first concerns for our daughter began at the age of four, just before she started at the playgroup in a primary school near Tunbridge Wells. When she got to the school itself the symptoms got worse. She displayed very high anxiety levels; made frequent toilet visits (these were extreme: they could be every few minutes); had major meltdowns and sleep disturbances (many wakings in the night, with, again, a meltdown); she was extremely clingy and would need a lot of reassurance from me all the time.

"At school, I would leave her every morning in tears – the teacher would have to pull her from me. And she didn't mix socially. Every school holiday was hard because she would be worrying about returning to school. Any change was hard for her. At first, I didn't do anything; but the summer before she started in Year 1, things got even worse. She displayed the same anxiety behaviours only in a more extreme way. She also began to get red raw hands from going to the toilet so frequently and then over-washing her hands.

"After Year 1, I went to our GP by myself to discuss my concerns. The doctor mentioned Aspergers and suggested I involve the school before taking any further action. So, I made an appointment to see the school's Special Educational Needs Officer – the SENCO – and the form teacher. The SENCO didn't even know who my daughter was and asked me to hold off trying to get a formal referral so that she could find out more about her and observe her. (I felt it was ridiculous that she hadn't already identified my daughter's problems and was very frustrated and cross). We agreed to meet again in a month. However, on reflection, I wasn't very happy about the school, so I went back to the doctor and we got the formal referral process going. We were referred to see an NHS paediatrician and saw him a month later. He didn't feel that it was Aspergers but wanted to review things in six months. He agreed she was a very anxious child but we left with no strategies about how to help her.

"I met the teacher and SENCO again. The SENCO had not done a single observation of my daughter but the teacher had been looking out for her. I was told that they would continue to keep an eye on her but, at that stage, nothing further would be necessary. I began to question once again whether the school was right. My daughter had not improved socially; she still tried everything to avoid going to school; she still cried every morning; her anxiety was sky high. We felt that we weren't getting adequate support from the SENCO. We decided to try to move schools and we were lucky enough to get a space in a different primary school. Within weeks, we felt there was a little improvement but after the summer holidays everything became worse again. I went back to our GP and he referred us on to the NHS specialists again. So, we went to see a different NHS paediatric specialist, who asked for more information from the school. I had good support from her teacher for Year 2 in the new school, who kept observations for me. The school filled out a special questionnaire, did some formal observations, together with the formal assessment.

"All this was then sent to our doctor. But the answer came back that they had discussed everything with the area's leading paediatrician and, at that stage, they felt there was still not sufficient evidence to warrant a full assessment, which would lead to specialist help. However, we were told to come back again in a further six months. We were lucky that the new school put in place a Care Around the Family (CAF) plan and the school and I continued to gather observations and evidence. I felt there was more than enough to suggest Autism Spectrum Disorder – ASD. (I had previously done a good deal of research on girls with ASD). Through the CAF plan, we were able to get agencies involved and, eventually, our daughter was put on an ASD waiting list. After a month or two, I checked how long the waiting list for the NHS ASD assessment was and was told a year and a half."

The above narration of the difficulties faced by one couple is certainly not unique, even in my experience. In many ways it was probably 'better' for several reasons. The mother had experience of autism; and the second primary school was pro-active. Five years later, the daughter is now at secondary school. She can still have problems of much the same nature as she had when she was younger but they are nothing like as severe and she is learning how to cope.

So there seems to be problems for the NHS with children's assessments, particularly for those who are not the most serious cases. Professor Anna Vignoles[54] has explained that it is almost inevitable there will be increased parental pressure for more help; and that there does seem to be a distinct lack of resources in this area. A Government report on the subject – not the first – was issued in October 2020, accompanied by assurances that there would be improvements.[55] As all types of treatments become more complex and as more and more parents all wish for the latest and best, can the NHS cope with these types of problems? I went back to Dave Holman at the West Kent Community Commissioning Group. What about the difficulty for parents of children with learning disabilities in getting NHS expert advice? He said that the problem of demand exceeding the supply in the area was known. It was also a national problem and the government had recently reacted by providing some extra funds. He was in the process of releasing some money for extra help. (Although perhaps I should have pursued him about the amount and how much it would cut waiting lists, I did not do so. Against all the other pressures on his funds, it somehow did not seem fair on someone I felt was very committed.) I also went back to the KCC's Clive Tracey and asked the same question. He explained that for the most serious cases (those that are classified as severe or moderately severe), the department did just manage to keep within the government targets of seeing children referred to them within eighteen weeks. ("From Referral to Treatment" is the technical term). They had achieved this timetable in 91% of cases in a recent month.

However, he did agree that for cases where the triage experts felt the need was less severe, there were long waiting lists – nine months on average in Kent overall. I said that the problem seemed to be that no parent who knows their child has difficulties – whether ASD or Aspergers or slightly milder types of autism – will feel happy that the assessment for their child is seemingly put on hold for year or even more. Additionally, other children who have even worse symptoms may be being seen relatively quickly but even the eighteen weeks must seem a long time to parents of children with what appeared to them, the parents, to be a really difficult situation every single day. I did mutter that the delays seemed excessive but again felt it unfair to criticise an individual who I understood was just part of a national system and who had to live within the budget constraints. These NHS waiting lists are by far the biggest concern that I was told about in the treatment of people with a learning disability. The government has said that it knows about the difficulty and that it cares. It has talked about Children's Integrated Therapy Teams. Yet I have never heard of one in the West Kent area. It seems unhelpful to have such delays when all experts agree that early diagnosis improves outcomes and, therefore, presumably saves money in the long run.

Over the past twenty years, the role of the NHS and the role of the schools has gradually changed. Put simplistically, originally the NHS provided the experts and if the parent or the school or the GP thought that perhaps something was wrong, the NHS were expected to organise what was needed to put the matter right – or as right as possible. Gradually, however, the system has evolved, with schools being expected to do much more and the NHS becoming the source of expertise mainly for the most difficult cases. Originally, I suspected that the reason for the change was that the NHS was so short of money and staff that schools were being used to provide perhaps a stop-gap service. I have come to a different conclusion. Nowadays, the schools, with their Special Educational Needs Officers (SENCOs are now in every school), together with teachers and teaching assistants, are increasingly taught about help for children with learning disabilities. So, it means that schools can give support on a *daily* basis for children individually which can be better than going to an NHS expert on an occasional basis.

I talked with the senior NHS paediatric consultant in the area, Dr Sameena Shakoor. She has long experience in the role and over the years has introduced a number of positive advances. Her department comes under KCHCT. Ages of the children referred to her can range from early years/pre-school until eleven, although, in special circumstances, it can be up to eighteen or even nineteen. The children have a range of problems on the autistic spectrum, ranging from severe, moderate and mild autism but including ADHD, Aspergers, etc, plus Down's syndrome children when they have serious difficulties. She also deals with a limited number of children with physical problems. (Children after eleven are seen by a separate group, CYPS – Children and Young People's Service) Her department does not – cannot – deal with children with what could be called straightforward learning difficulties. So, in essence, a child has to have very considerable problems before they are even referred to her department, let alone are accepted by the department. Consequently, there has to be a triaging or screening process. Initially, this is done by the child's GP and/or the school. There are forms so that Dr Shakoor and her team can assess how urgent the case may be. Not all the forms are filled in properly – with the suspicion that sometimes pushy parents have influenced those filling in the forms; and that sometimes schools may hope to get NHS help – which is free – rather than have to obtain extra classroom assistance – for which the school will have to pay. "Severe or moderately severe autism is less common than some people think", says Dr Shakoor. "It is probably only 1% of children, although the often quoted 5% may be right if all the different aspects on the spectrum are included". So, by the time it is agreed the child will be seen by Dr Shakoor's department, a good deal of background information has been gathered, including special assessment tests called 'ATOS'. Once the child is accepted on to Dr Shakoor's list, the boy or less often the girl is seen by the team – usually by themselves, although there are sometimes reasons for the parents to come with the child. A specialist in Dr Shakoor's team will do the first assessment. So, a child with language difficulties will see a speech therapist, and so on. When there are very severe behavioural problems, the child will be seen by Dr Shakoor. After this first assessment has taken place, a report is sent to the parents with an extra copy which the parents are meant to pass on to the school. (The report is not sent directly to the school, not least because the schools do not like to be given suggestions about what they should do. They may not welcome a suggestion that, for example, the child really needs 1:1 support in the classroom – for which the school would have to pay.) There is an annual review of each child, who has reached the assessment stage.

However, the difficulties for Dr Shakoor's team and for the parents who have got through to the team's assessment process are only just beginning. The assessments will normally recommend particular action. For example, seeing a specialist in the area of occupational therapy, a physiotherapist or a specialist doctor, although it is sometimes difficult to obtain enough qualified staff, particularly at consultant level. Dr Shakoor has been training more staff at senior level and has introduced the idea of rotating them to gain wider experience. The national average wait to progress to the stage after assessment is nine months which must seem incredibly frustrating for parents, who have already had a long wait even for the assessment.

From talking to a wide range of parents and specialists in the field, it seems that West Kent does have very long waiting times. It is this delay – not in any way caused by the intensely committed staff – that causes distress and sometimes fury in parents. The KCHCT is trying to alleviate the problem by having group discussions with parents who have similar types of problems. Additionally, parents are increasingly being expected to undertake specified routines at home or with the school before a referral to the specialist can be processed – no bad thing.

I have only mentioned national statistics occasionally. However, the national figures relating to Educational, Health & Care Plans (EHCPs) do seem to be reflected in West Kent. In the 2018/19 year, there was an increase of 10.8% in national requests for an EHCP over the previous year (from 53,307 to 58,950). And, although more requests were granted – roughly 70% – more were turned down than before.[56]

Private assessment/treatment for children – Starjumpz

The complexity of the state system and the often very long waiting lists mean that parents, particularly the better off ones, tend to go private for the assessment and the treatment of their child. All the debates about care in an NHS hospital versus BUPA or private hospitals apply. West Kent is lucky to have one private business to which parents with a child with a suspected learning disability can go for both assessment and treatment. There are also a number of individual clinicians who can provide assessments privately. The private clinic that I visited is called Starjumpz and it is one of the few centres of its type in the country. It is based just outside Crowborough on the East Sussex/Kent border, in a new and well-equipped building, with a sensational view over the countryside. The clinic has been owned and managed for the last five years by Jo Brett, an experienced occupational therapist (OT) but who, in her time, has also worked in a range of jobs in the NHS. She had an in-house staff of six, but she also has twenty experts who work with her regularly – including eight occupational therapists, four speech therapists and two physiotherapists, two neurofeedback practitioners, a behavioural consultant, a nutritionist, and various other specialists.

Very importantly, there also was a consultant neuro-developmental paediatrician, with another consultant about to join.

Parents most often contact Starjumpz because of recommendations by schools or by word of mouth or, less often, from reading about it on the web. I only talked personally with one Starjumpz parent but was given some quotes which – not unnaturally – were very favourable: "Starjumpz has changed our lives" and so on. However, a further recommendation seemed to come from the Social Services across the South East which were referring adopted children with special needs for assessment and treatment to Starjumpz. The NHS, with its current financial constraints, can only deal with children who have more difficult problems. So, a child may have ADD or ADHD but may not be entitled to the NHS support that the parent would want. All these types of circumstances are reasons for coming to Starjumpz which each year helps around 1,000 children.

When families contact Starjumpz, the management team will spend time finding out the parents' concerns, so that the child can be directed towards the most appropriate service or services. Often the decision on which service is required will involve evaluation of detailed questionnaires completed by the parents and school, together with any earlier medical or therapy reports. Once the details have been analysed, the parents will be asked to come for a meeting. This initial consultation usually takes about one and a half hours, either with just the parents but sometimes, depending on the circumstances, also with the child. Then the next stage is the full assessment of the child by the various specialists. A full paediatric diagnostic assessment takes three hours of face-to-face time, with the child and parents. Then the assessment by other appropriate members of the team – occupational therapy or speech therapy or dietician and so on – will take place as required.

I asked about the kind of questions these various assessments included and was given a three page summary which was too detailed to include in this book. Suffice it to say, each specialist aspect has between ten and fifteen sub-questionnaires. The assessment also includes a full physical examination and observation of the child's various types of motor skills. A post diagnostic follow-up appointment is offered to all families so that they can discuss such things as behaviour support or – much less often – to explain the range of medication options available. Advice is always available between appointments. In particular, families who opt for drug treatment for such problems as ADHD, particularly the much discussed Ritalin, are given email/telephone support in between appointments to ensure that any concerns are addressed promptly. Goals are set following commencement of therapy in collaboration with the child and parents, and are reviewed regularly as the child makes progress.

I asked about costs and was told that an average time for therapy treatment would be for thirty sessions of fifty minutes. Each session costs £80. However, when I asked about the not insubstantial money side, Jo Brett pointed out that, as well as the session itself, there is also the planning and recording of the observations and outcomes of the session. People often did not always appreciate how much time has to go into each 'session fee'. Clearly, the clinic does have considerable expenses and Jo does not expect to retire to the West Indies any time soon!

The basis of the help that the child is given is what Jo Brett calls "a holistic multi-disciplinary team approach." The team works together to gain a deeper understanding of the child and the child's needs from the different perspectives of the various specialists. This means that recommendations and treatment will be more effective and 'joined up', and will be based on a range of criteria including establishing the priorities for the child and the family, all worked out in conjunction with the child's school.

I asked Jo Brett to provide me with some examples of the kind of children who had been to Starjumpz, so that readers could understand the range of problems and treatments. I had already asked NHS experts whether they could provide examples but, for reasons I understood, this was not practical. I am almost sure that NHS care – when it becomes available – is very competent. The Starjumpz examples are not given to show that private treatment is automatically better than NHS. And, indeed, one warning was given by someone who had worked in the private sector and the NHS. Although he knew of excellent private centres, he also knew of some not very good ones. He also mentioned that if parents obtained a private assessment and then asked for NHS treatments, the private assessment would not be taken entirely at face value by the NHS triage team, who had seen too many private assessments which had been driven by parents' determination to have their own values and desires included. So, the three Starjumpz examples below are given to show the complexity of the problems which are often faced by the children and the parents; and the successes which can be achieved.

Sam's Story. Sam, a nine year old boy, was diagnosed with ADHD and sensory processing disorder. He had problems with hyperactivity, attention control, behavioural difficulties and motor skills. He also had limited writing ability, together with sensory processing difficulties which meant that he was spending very little time within the classroom and was academically behind his peers. At the assessments, he was found to be a very bright child whose difficulties were having a very negative impact upon his academic performance and on his behaviour. His self-esteem was very low and he was acutely aware of his difficulties with pencil work which made him resistant to doing any writing at all. His significant sensory processing difficulties were seen as disruptive and aggressive by the outside world. He sought strong physical sensations from movement and from activities such as climbing and pushing, but also hitting. Neither his family nor his teachers realised that Sam was driven to do this sort of heavy muscle work because it had a calming effect on his nervous system. Sitting at a desk in the classroom was extremely difficult for him and he would frequently run off to the playground and climb on the apparatus outside. In his occupational therapy assessment, where he was constantly given positive feedback, his mother was astonished when he drew a picture of his family and even wrote their names. The paediatrician recommended that Sam begin a low dose of ADHD medication to help him settle back into school after the summer break. The speech and language therapist recommended that he attend a social communication group as his poor attention, hyperactivity and behaviour were impacting his social communication skills. Over the summer holidays, Sam received twice weekly OT and sensory integration therapy sessions, working on improving his sensory processing, his motor and pencil skills. He loved doing heavy muscle work and using swings and equipment, where he was having great fun whilst gaining therapeutic benefit from the very intense activity. This in turn helped to regulate his nervous system so that he could then play games and participate in activities to develop his motor skills such as using a craft material, 'theraputty', to make models.

Sam began to learn to recognise how different movement and activity made him feel; and what activities could make him calmer, so that he could begin to self-regulate and manage his behaviour and his impulsivity better. His family were helped to understand his behaviour and how to support him. He learned to curb his impulsive behaviour by reminding himself to 'Stop and Think Before Doing'. He began to enjoy art and creative drawing and, as he gradually grew in confidence, he was able to develop his writing. He returned to school after the summer holidays with additional support from a teaching assistant, which included giving him frequent movement breaks to alleviate any anxiety and his need for physical activity. He was also able to join an early morning sensory circuits group to support his sensory needs three times a week. It was agreed that, once Sam was more confident in his abilities and his ADHD symptoms were improved, he would not continue to require a high level of support in school. His temporary ADHD medication also helped his return to school. He became able to adapt much more comfortably and was able to sit in the classroom and to engage in lessons more easily. The Starjumpz occupational therapist visited the school regularly to advise on how to support his needs within the school setting.

The intervention given to Sam has prevented him from being excluded from school, avoiding the possibility of him having to move to another school. He now has an understanding of his challenges and how to manage and overcome them. Additionally, the challenges are understood and supported by his family and by his teachers. As a result, he is a much happier and more confident child who is finding that learning can be fun and that he can be successful.

Harry's Story. Harry is a four year old boy with an NHS diagnosis of autism. When he first came to Starjumpz for therapy, Harry seemed to be in his own world and would wander around the edges of the room, holding tightly onto whatever he had brought with him that day, a book, or a few little cars. He moved very slowly and was fearful of walking across the mats in the middle of the room as he could not adjust his balance to walk confidently on the unstable surface. This gravitational insecurity had a huge impact on his emotional state, making him nervous about exploring his surroundings and anxious about unfamiliar settings. He would not go near a swing. He had few words, limited eye contact and did not like using his hands to play. Helping Harry to improve his body awareness, balance and strength was going to be the key to building his confidence and to unlocking progress in other areas such as developing his play, his motor skills and his language. This involved providing him with activities to stimulate his sensory systems and to improve his attention and coordination. Gradually, by using activities that he enjoyed, he was encouraged into new experiences. For example, he was gently guided to try things by pretending that a very low, solid platform swing was his favourite train, Thomas the Tank Engine. His mother supported him, singing train songs and talking through a story around Thomas; or by holding his hands and gently bouncing with him on a trampette, singing a favourite song, following his lead. These types of songs encouraged Harry to make the actual actions; and moving to music, either stamping or running, helped him to develop his ability to learn by copying. He began to cooperate with the music – banging in rhythm with sticks. With art, he started making marks, especially if it was to put wheels on a huge Thomas the Tank Engine drawn on a blackboard; or drawing either a smiley face or a sad face, finding it funny when his OT spoke in either happy or sad voices. Initially, sessions would be very slow moving and gentle, with the therapist using a quiet, calm voice to soothe Harry's anxiety. However, as he gained in confidence, the therapist injected more energy into her voice and into the speed of movement and activities, encouraging him to be more energetic, confident and louder.

After just two sessions, his mother noticed that he was much more confident when walking outside and was not falling over or tripping up as much. She also noticed that he had started to vocalise more and with more strength. After three months, there was a tremendous shift in Harry's awareness of his surroundings and his interaction with other people and things. He was able to initiate play and talk spontaneously. In fact, he often did not stop talking! He could put together sentences such as 'the crow is squawking on the tree' as he watched a bird outside the therapy room. He was exploring outdoor playgrounds independently. He would arrive at Starjumpz excited before he even got out of the car and would run to look for his OT, grabbing her hand and asking to play.

An important part of the work was advising his school on how to support Harry's new learning. It was discovered that the school had been using some sensory equipment which helps to calm overactive children, rather than what was needed for Harry, which was to encourage his sensory systems with more activity. "The change from a child who lacked energy and was fearful, to one who walked into the therapy room and wanted to pull the therapist out to the swings to play a game was a joy," I was told.

Sara's Story. Sara was fourteen years old and had a Developmental Coordination Disorder/Dyspraxia and Sensory Processing Disorder. She was from the north of England. Her mother had found Starjumpz on-line and Sarah attended the Starjumpz daily intensive treatment programme for two weeks. Sarah's main problems related to poor coordination and slow handwriting, but she had additional difficulties with low self-esteem, poor concentration, poor sleeping patterns and severe anxiety. At the start of her stay, she was lethargic and struggled to maintain concentration. She was given some specialist treatment which helped to improve her sleep; and the OT worked on her motor skills and self-organisation. This included developing a self-regulation programme for her to use with activities which in turn helped activate her sensory systems to become more alert and, at the same time, calmed her to counteract her anxiety. She was helped with how to use web technology and given strategies to improve her organisation and work output. She was also helped to make changes to her thinking patterns to overcome limiting self-beliefs, and to teach her how she could change her physical and emotional state. All this improved her self-esteem and encouraged her to become more motivated.

She returned home with a therapeutic device – the Alpha Stim electro-cranial therapy aid – to help her maintain her good sleep patterns and help reduce her anxiety. After trialling this machine during her stay, she reported that she had fallen to sleep easily and had woken early feeling very energetic and refreshed. She has continued to use this on school nights at home. Her father was amazed at the difference in her. She was more animated and interested in her family and less preoccupied with social media and the confines of her bedroom where she used to spend excessive amounts of time. She was more motivated about her school work and more organised; and she was interested in doing regular physical activity, as well as in making some changes to her diet as she now understood how much this could help her both physically and mentally.

Jo Brett's main concern is how best to help the whole families who come to her. "I try to explain that to allow their child to have fun will raise their self-esteem – which is absolutely vital. Research shows that the amount of time that a child has unstructured play is linked to later academic achievement and emotional well-being." She continues: "autistic children – like any child – do not have to be pushed all the time. They need time to just BE. I try to encourage parents to spend time with their boy or girl, without pointing the child in any direction at all – even if it is only for twenty minutes. Give them your full attention but just follow their lead and don't direct them in any way either to correct their speech, or give to them ideas or to change an activity – within limits of safety of course. Allow them to be creative and interact on their terms in their own time. Actually, it is quite hard. But it will really help."

There are additional ideas about ways in which children with learning difficulties and their parents can be helped. Some of the schemes are provided within the NHS and some by voluntary groups. As the resources within the NHS get more and more stretched with waiting lists getting longer,[57] any extra ideas are worth pursuing. Parents' support groups – where parents can exchange experiences – can be very valuable and can – with some expert help – largely be arranged by the parents themselves. Workshops for professionals to discuss new developments also seem constructive. Meetings for children with similar problems again can be helpful. Extra help for parents of home-schooled children may prevent the child becoming too isolated. And counselling for parents with autistic children – who are almost always under massive pressure – can provide a calmer background for the child – and can even help preserve marriages.

However, there is one type of treatment where some professionals have been perhaps rather too keen to provide help – the use of drugs, particularly Ritalin. Talking with GPs and other experts, it is clear that, at present, drugs are not normally useful for people with learning disabilities (although some new research is being done in this area). Learning disabilities are an inborn characteristic which are not normally going to be greatly changed by drugs.[58] In the past, doctors had sometimes prescribed sedatory drugs for problems which arose from anxiety or depression which in turn stemmed from learning disabilities; and Ritalin has been used for a good number of years to calm down children with problems such as ADHD.

However, such treatments, as well as sometimes benefiting a child when carefully administered, have also provoked a great deal of dubious comment. The number of prescriptions in the UK for Ritalin increased by 50% between 2007 and 2012[59]. I talked with GPs experienced in the field but first a story from one father.

> "Our son was a bit non-stop. He didn't do bad things but he was a bit of a handful – and the teachers did say so, too. But we just thought it was normal. Later the school said they thought he had ADHD and we ought to see our GP. So we went to the GP and he gave us Ritalin. But my wife had heard it had side effects and so she said our son wasn't going to have it until she'd taken it herself. So she took it for two days. She became a zombie – couldn't do anything. So we didn't give it to our son. He seems OK now anyway."

The GPs with whom I talked were surprised to hear of the scale of the increase in Ritalin prescriptions between 2007 and 2012. One doctor suspected that the heavy US advertising some years ago might have some influence but he felt it was more due to so many more children being diagnosed with ADHD. Parents then expected 'a cure'. However, he agreed that perhaps too many prescriptions had been given out. He added that books could be written – and had been written – about the pros and cons of the drug. The view currently seems that there are certainly instances where Ritalin helps individuals but that, as diagnosis for ADHD become more refined and as the side effects of the various drugs have become clearer, the prescriptions for Ritalin are likely to be declining. However, I checked more recent statistics and for any new thoughts from the clinicians. Ritalin prescriptions had doubled in the last ten years, with the head of Ofsted, Amanda Spielman, issuing a warning,[60] saying that the use of drugs such as Ritalin – 'chemical coshes' as they are sometimes called – was still increasing; and that she hoped that parents, as well as doctors, would be more cautious.

There has been a good deal in the newspapers, too, about young adults with severe learning disabilities being kept in adult specialist hospitals – against government policy and in spite of several Ministerial protestations over a number of years that it will not continue. These patients are almost all older teenagers with multiple problems. The severity of some of these patients' problems is virtually never explained in the simplistic newspaper articles or television exposés. I heard of one young woman who was so uncontrollably violent – and very strong – that she had eventually bitten off part of the face of a nurse. She was locked in a special cell and fed with a tray put through a hatch in the door. In spite of various types of treatment, the experts had not yet found a way of helping her. I never heard the outcome. However, for this type of patient, it is not only difficult to find a treatment but to find somewhere for him or her to stay – which should ideally be near their home. When I asked about the position in Kent, I was assured that there were no long-term instances of this type of case currently but that there would always be occasional instances where an under-eighteen who had developed very severe problems could not instantly be found a suitable place to live in a suitable area.

NHS Help for Adults with Learning Disabilities

So far this chapter has concentrated principally on children with learning disabilities. However, there is a separate part of the NHS which supports the adults with learning difficulties. Again, it is run by the Kent Community Health Care Trust, paid for by the NHS Clinical Commissioning Group. The person who heads the department in Kent is Matt Dodwell. For Kent overall, he has a team of specialists who visit these men and women in their homes or special accommodation to give advice. This can cover mental problems – how to cope with their own stresses – or how to deal with other people: or there can be physical problems – which may need physiotherapy or occupational therapy help. An additional service given by Matt Dodwell's team is the provision of a 'Hospital Passport'. This is a medical document which a person with learning disabilities keeps with them at all times and, if they collapse or have to go to hospital, the full details of their condition are shown. In theory, the computerisation of NHS records to include Social Services records should provide information in these cases. However, currently, it appears that the IT system is not yet working – making the Passport even more important. The team also provides training for GPs which should mean that GPs are able to handle the less severe or less complex cases. Currently, Matt says that, although budgets are tight, he does not allow delays to occur.

Also coming within Matt Dodwell's adult department are the Community Learning Disability Nurses (CLDNs, needless to say) – about whom I only heard good things. There are around twenty of them in West Kent, giving support to adults over eighteen. Their initial role for a service user who has just arrived in the area or has just turned eighteen will be to assess what the person needs. Then the CLDNs will provide the support themselves or pass the request on to other members of the team – the physiotherapists, occupational therapists or the speech and language specialists – or, where necessary, outside experts who will be asked to help. One particular aim is to encourage the service user to maintain (or sometimes to improve) their general health. For younger adults, help may well mean liaison with the parents.

Old age for people with learning disabilities can well be even more trying than it is for the general population. So, the nurses will help if the sons and daughters or the house manager or the GP are having difficulty in coping with a relative or resident who has dementia. In addition to these types of services to individuals, the nurses do group counselling and sessions on specific subjects, either for a number of service users and their parents/children, but also to other professionals and outside bodies – not least to raise awareness. But as one community nurse emphasised, it is a very close-knit team who know their patients and work flexibly amongst themselves and with other professionals such as GPs.

I talked with one very experienced Community Learning Disability Nurse, Rosemary Tidley, who remembered the Princess Christian Hospital for the mentally handicapped at Hildenborough in the early 1990s, as well as the existing Princess Christian Farm[61]. She thought the Hospital had given good care by the standards of its time but, clearly, things had moved on and the system was much better today. She also felt the current Princess Christian Farm, which is described later, was and still is a great resource for the area. If she finds she has a 'bad boy', she suggests that he tries to get a place at the Farm. "It can be wonderful for them and they nearly all not only enjoy themselves but get a lot out of it. It meant and it still means that they are actually <u>DOING</u> something, rather than just sitting around back in their room."

GPs

Every GP and GP practice will have a number of patients with a formal classification of Learning Disability. One survey suggested that an average practice with four thousand patients is likely to have a hundred people with a formal classification of a learning disability.[62] Additionally, they will have consulted and tried to advise a good number of others who have learning problems – quite often children. Peter Bench is a GP who now heads the Hildenborough and Tonbridge Medical Group. He is also the doctor to Holly Lodge, the residential home for people with severe learning disabilities. He thinks that each week an average GP would have to advise one or two people who had some sort of learning disability or difficulty. However, the practice he heads probably has more than this, not least because there are a number of ex-patients, now middle-aged or elderly, who used to live at the old Princess Christian Hospital and who were found houses in the local area. And he personally would see the most because word has got round that he is a good doctor to see if there are learning problems. Another GP said that delays in diagnosis were a perennial problem. GPs were not supposed to give a diagnosis of autism: that was meant to be for the specialist doctors. However, as there were "appalling long waits to see the specialists", the GPs just had to do what they could, "although with a ten minute appointment session, you may know what the problem is but it is not easy to actually provide help. It's a real Cinderella part of the NHS – it's awful."

Dr Bench worries that when his patients live alone or in a house without a residential manager, they are not always likely to look after their own general health very well. (Those who live in a home where there is a manager being more likely to be brought to see him, if there are signs of illness or lack of care.) Then the practice's own Community Nurse can keep an eye on them in case they might be vulnerable or just not very good at looking after themselves. Each practice, therefore, has a range of expertise and, while not pretending to be experts, they know how to access the multitude of services that are provided by the NHS or Social Services. They will also understand where responsibility for such things as housing lies; and have some knowledge of schools or further education resources in the area.

One of the services that GPs do already offer is the annual check-over for all people who are formally classified as having learning disabilities. It is voluntary for the patient and it usually takes about an hour. It covers a physical and mental examination. It checks for such things as epilepsy, asthma and diabetes, as well as a review of medicines being taken. Equally important, however, is the chance for the patients (and, where relevant, the parents) to ask questions or to admit to worries. Having asked two GP practices whether the system is useful, they both said that it should be valuable but that quite a proportion of those who should have these checks, never respond to the appointment they are offered. One said, "the check-up is voluntary and we are so extremely busy that if they don't come – which is a pity – we just haven't got time to keep chasing them up." When I asked service users, their house managers or their parents what they thought in general about their GP, almost all said they were excellent.

For many years, another role for GPs was to assess their disabled patients on behalf of the Government to see what state benefits should be given. This assessment process was later given to an outside body but did not seem to prove successful; and, although I only heard about unsatisfactory assessments on a few occasions, two Citizens Advice Bureaux were scathing about the system's problems.

Whether new ways of working for GP practices will emerge –

particularly after the Covid 19 pandemic and with the long-promised integration of the NHS and the care provisions from Social Services – is not clear. What is clear, however, is that new technologies will become an increasing part of treating patients of all kinds, including those with learning disabilities. There is already an NHS system where Cognitive Behavioural Therapy (CBT) can be accessed in real time over the web. There are also GP experiments where a patient feeds in their symptoms and concerns over the web, which are picked up by a duty GP who talks to the patient over the telephone or arranges a visit. Many more advances, some using chatbots, are just around the corner.[63]

Communication and Assistive Technology (CAT)

The KCC and the NHS jointly provide a specialist service called Communication and Assistive Technology, although – as ever – it is bedevilled by everyone calling it CAT. Its basic aim is to use technology, particularly computer-based systems, to make life easier for those with learning disabilities but, particularly for those with speech and communication problems. However, the technology can also help staff with their charges.

The idea for a national service divided into twelve regional units came from NHS England ten years ago. The Kent service is further divided into two – an adult side and a children's side. The children's side has been headed from the beginning by Sarah Lloyd-Cox, a former SENCO, with around thirty professional staff. They get commissioned by various bodies, mainly KCHCT but, because their brief also covers health and education, they have referrals from schools, including from speech and language therapists and from SENCOs. Sometimes an enquiry will come from a GP or a parent. They often help children who cannot speak but who are otherwise able – often very able (the late Prof. Stephen Hawkings is often given as an example). They may be helping a child who has cerebral palsy, has had a tracheotomy or has certain forms of autism. The children helped most often are aged between eleven and fourteen – when they are starting secondary school – but there are increasing numbers of pupils in primary school and they had one child of three and a half. As ever, the earlier that support starts the better but help can be given up until nineteen and even up to twenty-five if the person is still in full time education. Their current caseload in Kent is around two hundred children. Looking at the South West Kent area, there are around twenty-five children who receive this specialist support. "To look after the twenty-five, there are around six staff," says Becky Guntrip in the children's unit. "There is one specialist teacher, one speech and language therapist, one OT, plus one assistant who will be checking on safety and lots of other things. However, perhaps the most amazing people in the teams are the Heath Care Scientists. They are the ones who invent or adapt computers which will operate the machinery needed to help the individual child."[64]

On the adult side, I heard about the work being done from one of their users, Mel Bentley, the manager of Holly Lodge. Relatively recently, the CAT adult team have installed what sounded like a very complex system to help support the five residents. Each has a special television set and control. While the TV can provide normal programmes and virtually any programmes that the resident might particularly like, it can also act as a reminder for him or her to do things at certain times; it can open doors, make shopping lists and generally give the residents, who are not easily able to communicate with actual people on the outside, more independence. Yet the machinery also ensures the staff have given the right medicines at the right time; and monitors the patients' sleep. One resident only sleeps for four hours out of twenty-four. Another will often wake up in a terror. In this type of case, the on-duty night carer will be alerted to go to reassure him. And the motion sensor will even give an indication if one of the residents is having an epileptic fit. I did not talk to the adult service personally but another user with severe problems of fits, was also very enthusiastic.

Another example came in an article[65] I was sent about a local family whose lives had been changed by a variety of CAT machines and advice. The parents were told at the birth of their son that he had cerebral palsy and considerable brain damage. By the time the son was two, it was becoming clear that he would never move his arms or hands and would not be able to walk or talk. Over the next seven or eight years, the CAT team had provided a hugely constructive range of help and equipment. He cannot move his hands to type but, with his computer's help, he can choose his own TV and music; get Google, send emails; and even call for his dog, Pete.

NHS Driving Assessments and Help for People with Driving Problems

Working with the Department for Transport, there is an NHS Centre at Aylesford near Maidstone called 'SE Drive-Ability' which carries out assessments on driving competence and gives advice on such things as cars which are suitable for individuals with physical and mental problems. The Centre tests people with learning disabilities, MS, Parkinson's or dementia; or just old age. They accept referrals from DVLA, health and social care professionals and, even, self-referrals. They claim 99% satisfaction. However, one person who had previously worked in the centre for some time told me that she gave the job up because she found it so depressing to give bad news to so many people.

The Police and People with Learning Disabilities

I have included a brief section about the police at this point because over the past five or ten years, the police have liaised closely with the NHS about the best ways to cope with people with mental health problems or with learning disabilities. An Independent Police Complaints Commission Report from March 2016 covered how the police should deal with people with mental illness. It raised doubts about the way such people were sometimes treated by some police forces and by some individual police officers. Yet I had also heard about the caring and informed way the local police in Tonbridge had dealt with several people with learning disabilities. I wrote to the Chief Constable of Kent to ask how the people from his force were trained in this respect. I was referred to Chris Collins, who has been in the police for many years, and having reached a senior level with Kent Police, was now the Practical Skills Training Manager at the Kent Police College.

> "There have been big changes in training for this type of problem over the last twenty years," he said. "We are now much better at dealing with one-off, difficult situations where a person is not trying to commit a crime but is

certainly creating problems. It is often difficult to instantly assess what is the underlying difficulty or the reason the person is what we used to call 'disturbing the peace.' So we have developed special courses, both at the initial training stage and for all serving officers on the beat which help policemen and women evaluate what is happening and then how best to deal with the person who is often at a crisis point. Every new recruit has a five month training course. Within it there is a two week community placement which covers dealing with situations where an individual is probably 'out of their mind' for some reason. And every policeman and woman has an annual course which includes discussions on how best to cope with these often difficult, but nearly all different, incidents. In the old days someone behaving badly or strangely used to be taken to a police cell to wait for someone – an outside expert – to come and deal with them. As you can imagine, it often made the situation worse. To lock a disturbed man or woman in a cell – however good the intention – was certainly not ideal. Nowadays, we work closely with the experts. The police are often the first on the scene. We try to assess the individual and we either take them to hospital or call in one of two organisations. The first and principal one is the NHS. One of its Mental Health nurses is on call twenty-four hours a day – quite often in a police car somewhere in Kent. Depending on the circumstances, the nurse will either be driven to the scene or the police will take the disturbed person direct to the nearest appropriate hospital. Secondly, we also have a very good relationship – a formal partnership in fact – with the Kent Autistic Trust, which from my own experience, is excellent. It is also interesting from the point of view of your book that our current Police and Crime Commissioner, Matthew Scott, has said publicly that he wants the police to be seen as even more understanding towards people with learning and mental health issues. So, I hope you will feel that Kent Police really have progressed in this area over the last twenty years."

His hopes seemed to have been realised when the head of a Day Care Centre told me that trainee police cadets regularly came to visit. She not only made them welcome but she felt that they learnt a good deal about people with learning disabilities. This aspect of police training was also borne out by the Manager of a care home: police cadets visit her and she explains what it is like when someone with very considerable autistic problems gets frightened; how to recognise when the person may well be in a crisis and unable to understand or respond; and how it is not going to help to lock them in a police cell. She says the cadets genuinely seem to understand.

However, to end on a more pragmatic note. A GP who read this book before publication said that, while I personally may have had a good report about how helpful the local police could be with people who had learning disabilities, his experience "had been appalling." Perhaps his complaints had resulted in the improvement? Additionally, I was also discussing the treatment of people with learning disability or mental problems with a local policeman. I mentioned the good things – rather than the bad – that I had heard. He laughed. Yes, he too had heard about the psychiatric nurse in the police car and, yes, it was a good idea, bearing in mind the kinds of people they had to deal with. But there was no money to do more than the original experiment. On a more positive note, there is what appears to be a constructive scheme which involves people with a learning disability having a Pegasus Card. The Card has a reference number to which the police – or medical staff – can refer and be told about the person's difficulty. These can then be dealt with in an appropriate way. The system usually helps, although it did not do so in one incident about which I was told.

I did not meet with any service user who had had troubles with the law. However, a 2017 report found that 25% of newly committed adults had previous dealing with professionals concerned with learning disabilities and mental health. In July 2020 new guidelines were issued to judges and magistrates about how sentences should take account of these individuals' condition and history.

CHAPTER 7

Schools

The National Picture

Parents in Kent with children who have learning difficulties are in many respects just like any parents. They want the best for their child. However, they will feel different. Initially, they will seek 'a cure' for the particular problem faced by their child. When the likely future for their child is discussed with them, some will accept that there is a problem; others will fiercely deny it. Some parents will be persuaded that the NHS and the maintained schools system will do everything possible to support their child. However, quite often and quite naturally, the mother and father will wonder whether better treatment or schooling could be available somehow, somewhere. They may well go to books or websites or talk to the numerous specialised groups. (There is a large number of each). The question of funding will often come up. Media reports of parents marching to get more money for their schools, gloomy reports by teachers' unions and stories of crumbling classrooms all will raise doubts in the parents' minds about the state system. However, the national picture for schools' budgets may not be wholly negative. On a personal basis, I have not seen a dramatic lack of money for special needs education in Kent. Of course, every school would like more teaching assistants and more training to support Special Educational Needs children but there is more help than there used to be – vital as more children seem to need help every year. Figures in August 2019 said that there have been increases in each of the previous three years, with 20% of children now said to need some sort of extra help in school.[66]

The government has moved towards wanting the NHS to

concentrate their more specialist help on the more difficult cases and it is trying a number of new schemes, some of which seem to provide relatively positive results[67] – although, inevitably, none is providing *cures* for such things as autism or Down's. It is asking schools to make more careful assessments of *all* children's attainments. They want to ensure that no child is slipping through the net – whether he or she has a formal assessment of a learning disability or just some problem of his or her own. The aim is not just to bring each child in special educational needs up to an average across the curriculum, but also to focus on the special talents that the individual child may well have. Repeatedly, I was told of the difficulties caused by Covid 19. It had not only disrupted the school as a whole but had created extra problems for the children who had special needs.

Playgroups/Nursery Schools and Primary Schools

There is a wide range of schools within West Kent. It is not just that there are a good number of grammar schools for both boys and girls; and a large number of fee-paying prep schools and fee-paying public schools. There are free schools and academies as well as mainstream maintained schools; and within these, there are the maintained schools which, although mainstream schools, have special provision for those who have learning difficulties. Finally, there are a number of special schools which cater for children with moderate learning disabilities and a few which look after those with severe disabilities – both learning disabilities and physical disabilities. So, parents have a wide choice.

A small number of children can clearly be identified as having problems when they are born. A much larger proportion are diagnosed between one and three and, as we have seen, there is also late-onset autism. So, it is often at playgroup or nursery school that learning disabilities are first noticed. Parents, who will not always know what is the norm (particularly with a first child) may not have realised that the child is not behaving in quite the same way as other children or is not progressing as might be expected. It is, therefore, useful that nursery teachers are able to make comparisons and to confer with the parents. Then the experts can be consulted – as we have seen – not always the easiest or the quickest of procedures.

(A report in September 2021 suggests that special work undertaken by parents if a child shows early signs of autism, can be of benefit when the child reaches three years old.[68]) By the time the child reaches primary school, there are Special Educational Needs Co-ordinators, SENCOs, as well as the teachers who will be on hand to provide assessment and support.

Primary schools are nowadays increasingly prepared for children who have a wide variety of learning problems. Some of these children can be (more than usually) disruptive – they may have ADHD; or they seem particularly unsociable or anxious. They may be on the autistic spectrum, struggling with reading or maths or with other signs of difficulty which most teachers and particularly the school's SENCO should and usually do recognise. It becomes important for the schools themselves to be as proactive as possible. I talked with a large number of schools about what they do for their children with special educational needs or, as one teacher had said, "children who learn differently". I was impressed by almost all, although the proportion of children who need extra help can vary considerably. The average appears to be around 5%. However, I talked with one teaching assistant in Cheshire (she had a PhD but did the job because she found it so rewarding). Her school had 58% of its children who were formally classified as needing special support. The situation was recognised by the County Council who provided money for ten teaching assistants. Additionally, it had been agreed that her current class should be sub-divided into two, with twenty children in the 'normal' class and fifteen in the SEN class: teaching the two together was not helping either. Initially, I thought it useful to take as an example my own village primary school. I talked with the school's recently retired SENCO, Kay Coleman, who explained the basic principles.

> "Over the past ten years when I have been working in our school, I have seen many changes in the provision of support and the methods of acquiring that support for children with learning difficulties. We can and do make provision for every kind of frequently occurring special education need – for instance, dyslexia, dyspraxia, speech and language needs, high functioning autism, ADHD, and

moderate learning difficulties. There are other kinds of special educational needs which do not occur as frequently and with which the school is less familiar, such as Down's syndrome, or sight/hearing disabilities, but we can access training and advice from outside, so that these kinds of needs can be met too.

Overall, we probably have a bit more than 5% of over 160 pupils who have some type of learning difficulty. (In the past we sometimes have had slightly more or slightly less but the 5% is about the norm for primary schools). The official definition says 'A child of compulsory school age or a young person has a learning difficulty if he or she has a significantly greater difficulty in learning than the majority of others of the same age; or has a disability which prevents or hinders him or her from making use of facilities of a kind generally provided for others of the same age in mainstream schools or mainstream post-16 institutions'.[69]

We formally monitor the progress of all pupils three times a year to review their overall academic progress and there are two extra assessments for writing. Where progress is not sufficient, even if special educational need has not been identified, we put in place extra support to enable the pupil to catch up. Some pupils may continue to make inadequate progress, despite high-quality extra teaching targeted at them and their own particular areas of weakness. For these pupils, and in consultation with parents, we will use a range of assessment tools to determine the cause of the learning difficulty. For example, there is Y1 phonics screening, Speech Link, Language Link and GL dyslexia screening, and the WRAT spelling age/reading age tests. The purpose of these more detailed assessments is to understand what additional resources and different approaches we are going to need to enable the pupil to make better progress. The results will be shared with parents and put on to what is called a 'Provision Map' which is reviewed regularly and refined where necessary. If the pupil is able to make good progress using this additional resource (but would not be able to maintain this good progress without it), we will continue to identify the pupil as having a special educational need. Parents are kept informed of the progress their child is making in school.

It has become increasingly difficult to receive help from outside agencies. In recent years, a child with speech delay or co-ordination difficulties can be referred to the NHS for speech therapy, physiotherapy or occupational therapy and so on, but only if their needs are considered to be severe enough. An outside therapist will then aim to assess them and will feedback recommendations to the school. However, outside support is decreasing, so the schools have to do more to help themselves. There are special courses and workshops for teachers and teaching assistants (TAs) to attend. Where we think that it will be useful, pupils do what are called 'Sensory Circuits'. This programme was created by the physiotherapists to assist children who are not able to concentrate and are over-active, as well as children who have difficulties with motor co-ordination. At our School, we have two senior teaching assistants who have been on a special course at the Dolphin Centre in Tunbridge Wells and they organise the Sensory Circuits for the five or six pupils – usually boys – three or four times a week first thing in the morning. There are a series of exercises which start by warming them up; then exercises which help with co-ordination; and finally we end up with calming them down before they go into class. It works really well. *[There are similar training centres around the country.]*

'Language for Learning' is a scheme which was developed by speech therapists to help children who the SENCO feels are having difficulties with their talking or with their social skills. The Dolphin Centre also helps train up staff to work with these children, although in this case the theory is that <u>all</u> teachers should be involved in providing for the children who have been identified as having these particular problems. Again, the scheme generally seems to work well. We are now much less likely to have outside therapists visiting children in school to provide 1:1 sessions.

The other way to receive outside support is through the Kent Education Authority. A child's case can be taken to a LIFT (Local Inclusion Forum Team) meeting where there are a range of external advisers. These meetings are held regularly at Valence School – our local special school at Westerham. The SENCO will explain the child's difficulties and educational history to this group of specialist teachers; and advice will be offered and, potentially, support from a specialist teacher may be recommended. The specialist teacher will then assess the child and a plan of support will be drawn up. As well as being concerned about our children's physical needs, the School is also very protective of a child's emotional well-being. The school runs a Nurture Group one afternoon a week for six or seven children. The group is taken by an experienced outside teacher who has specialised knowledge and one of our specialist Teaching Assistants. Together they devise a programme to help with the development of social, emotional and behavioural skills. The Nurture Group has proved invaluable for these children. If a child is still not making the recommended progress, then a parent or the school can request an Education, Health and Care Plan – the EHCP. This is normally for our age of children – primary schools – but it can be requested for young people aged up to twenty-five who need more support than is available through the school's or the college's own resources. EHC Plans will identify educational, health and social needs and set out the additional support to meet those needs. In the past, a child with what was then called a 'Statement of Need' would have received funding for extra 1:1 support from the government. (This was where the phrase 'he/she is statemented' came from) The system for funding has now changed and what is called "high needs funding" has been introduced. This requires the school to provide the first £6,000 for the Teaching Assistant's support and the resources that the child needs. Then a case can be made by the SENCO to ask for extra funding to cover the extra support that is required. However, an EHC Plan can only be offered if a child has complex needs and if the parents and school can provide a wealth of evidence to prove that the child's needs are ongoing and that, despite the support by the school for the child in every way possible, he/she is not making progress. At present, we have two children in school with an EHC plan."

I knew that the School has its SENCO but it also has been able to afford not only an expert to run the regular Nurture Groups but a good number of teaching assistants, who, where necessary, have been trained to help with the individual children with learning problems. Money can be a problem and the number of TAs has been slightly reduced recently. I was impressed by the way the school aimed to explain learning disabilities to the whole school. If a child is on the autistic spectrum – has Down's or is very poor at mixing with others, it is easy for the child to be left out. If a child – usually a boy – cannot concentrate and is permanently disruptive, it is easy for other children to find them annoying. I went to a school assembly to find two boys, Dylan and Kallen, both of whom have ADHD, giving an extremely clear presentation about it.[70] I would have liked to reprint all the presentation but it has twenty-six power-point slides. However, I am picking out some of the things that they mentioned. First, there was a clear description of how ADHD makes them feel and act. Dylan says that "having ADHD is like having fifty-nine televisions blaring in your head all at once". Kallen says "ADHD is like having a racing car driving round and round your brain". They then explained how their diagnosis of ADHD initially worried them but, when they had an explanation, it helped build up their confidence. That, in turn, had then enabled them to explain to the whole school why they were like they were.

They showed lists of famous people who had ADHD and gave a list of the positive words which described someone with this 'problem'. It included "intelligent, energetic, creative and determined".[71] What seemed so constructive was that the help being given by the school is not only supporting these boys, calming them down where necessary and giving them back their self-confidence; but is also explaining learning difficulties to the other pupils. I am sure that our school is not unique. Other primary schools, with whom I came in contact, often had various caring provisions in place, although there were some cases where they seemed to be overwhelmed by the numbers they had to try to help and the strain on their resources.

Ines's Story. One family was happy to talk about the excellent service they have received for their nine year old daughter, Ines, who has Down's syndrome. As with the majority of people with Down's syndrome, the girl is usually cheerful but forever on the move, eighteen hours a day. And she, as virtually always with Down's, is not really aware of the pitfalls life has to offer at every turn. Nor is she able to speak in an easily understandable way. However, with the special help she has been given, she is improving and can now use three word phrases at the appropriate time – even if what she is communicating is clearer for those who know her than to an outsider.

Kent Social Services have been watching over her and liaising with her parents (and the caring eleven year old brother). Ines originally attended the local Primary School – always with her own one-to-one carer – now called a Learning Support Assistant. The School was really caring. Ines and her older brother did a presentation at assembly on World Down Syndrome Day (21 March each year) to tell other children about Down's syndrome. However, even with this amount of help, it became clear that she was more than an ordinary class room could easily absorb. The gap between Ines and her peers was growing. After much consultation with her parents, it was agreed that Ines should start going to a special school. The parents visited three possible schools and were successful in gaining a place at their first choice, The Milestone Academy, fifteen miles away.

Now, every day Ines is taken to the school with another child, with a carer to accompany them as well as the driver; and is enjoying herself enormously. When I read her latest school report – a long document – the care she is receiving seems exemplary. The school looks after their pupils at least until they are eighteen. For some time, Ines's parents had naturally been concerned not just about the immediate future but what would happen to their daughter when she was twelve, sixteen and eighteen, and then into adulthood. They are now beginning to feel reassured that there is a system which will look after Ines not just until she is eighteen but, via the Kent Social Services team, when she is an adult. This case reflects well on Kent currently, although always at the back of parents' minds is what could happen if there are even further government cuts. Ines's father added that it was excellent that there was going to be this book that analysed the changes that have been introduced; and gave the general public examples of what actually happens to individual parents and children.

As seen by Ines's story, there are cases where a child has such complicated needs or is so disruptive for the rest of the school that discussion about whether a normal primary school is best or whether a special school has to be considered. For Ines, the decision was to go to a special school where she is thriving and the same applied eventually to Liz Astor's daughter, Olivia. Yet in another primary school, a girl with Down's has continued to stay through the mainstream primary school. She has been much loved in spite of being a year or two below the average skills age – although she will be going to a specialist secondary school when she is eleven.

One specialist helper at a local primary school originally trained as a speech and language therapist. Nowadays, she describes her work as a specialist literacy teacher, helping children who could be considered, in old style wording, as a bit slow, a bit backwards, maybe a year behind (which is now called to be progressing slowly) with their reading or writing. They may or may not be quite on the autistic spectrum.

> "That does not really matter. What matters is that the individual child (usually a boy) gets the extra attention that is needed. We have another specially trained teacher at the school – which is only small – who looks after the children who have more major difficulties – more severe autism or behavioural problems. She is really a counsellor. In her sessions, the child or often several children are allowed to paint or talk but it is always directed towards a specific end – to make the child think about something they do which is

disruptive but in an indirect way. There is also the computer-based literary/phonic programme called LEXIA where a small group or an individual can have their reading and phonic skills strengthened and to help fill in gaps in their knowledge. These spelling sessions are usually thirty minutes per week, although the computer programme is available daily. Overall, it is used by thirty children in the school. Children with severe dyslexia are offered a more specific dyslexia spelling programme and are individually given one thirty minute session a week where the focus is on multi-sensory learning. If a child does have a severe difficulty – autism or Down's or one of the rarer conditions – this will have quite often been picked up before the child arrives. But sometimes, it is only when a child is four or five that the school begins to suspect that there is something not too serious, but nevertheless a potential problem which means extra help is going to be needed. Where the child is clearly going to need considerable extra help, the school can apply for funding which would usually be for an extra, specially trained teaching assistant. Of course, we have to explain all this to the parents – who, not unnaturally, initially react either to deny it or to be horrified. We have to explain that their child *CAN* be helped and, in most cases, there is a good chance that they will grow up a lovely person. The parents nearly always end up being pleased that their child is getting extra help! I remember, too, the son of a friend who was totally awful – the mother was the first to agree. But, with help, he has grown up into a totally charming and very intelligent seventeen year old. So, overall, I am impressed by the extra specialist help that is now available in primary schools which wasn't there even ten or fifteen years ago."

Choosing a School

Parents will initially find that there is a huge list of possible primary and secondary schools in the area. However, on closer examination none will seem quite right. Twenty or thirty years ago the government and virtually the whole education establishment decided that most of the special schools for children with special needs should be wound down and that almost all children who had difficulties should go into mainstream schools where they would be given extra help. Kent and the KCC disagreed. They kept and improved Kent's special schools. They have been proved right. Parents can now choose – with advice from the schools and the experts – what is likely to be best for their child, a mainstream school – where there will be some extra help – or a special school. There is also the choice to be made – if the parents are rich enough – between a fee-paying school or the maintained system.

However, the reality is that at primary school age, the state system quite often will have fuller facilities to cope with a child with more pronounced difficulties than a fee-paying school. Fee-paying Prep schools often have a special needs department and/or teacher but these would normally be to help children who have mild dyslexia or not very difficult learning problems. It is – as so often – up to the exhausted but indomitable parents to go and ask.

Parents, who are already aware or suspect that their child has some kind of special needs, have said repeatedly how difficult it is to choose the most suitable primary school. I found information about all types of schools – mainstream or special; maintained or fee-paying – difficult to find, even on the internet; and, even when I had become relatively experienced, the websites seemed full of the kind of educational-speak that gave me little flavour of the school or its staff. Several tips about deciding on a school were recommended to me. Certainly, get advice. The Kent Autism Trust was recommended by several parents. However, very importantly, try to find other parents whose child has similar problems – not always easy, as most parents do not go round waving a flag saying "my child has a particular learning difficulty". Talk with GPs or community learning disability nurses. Above all, spend time visiting schools and talk not just with the Head but, just as important – or maybe even more important – talk to the SENCO by themselves. Ask about what has happened with other children at the school. How many teaching assistants are there and how much training have they had. And even, if brave enough, when you are fairly near a decision, ask if you can talk to the parents of one or two of the children who have similar problems to your child. If it is difficult and time consuming for any parent to find the right school, it is doubly so for parents with a child who has special needs.

Henny Scott's Story. In 1966 Jill and Denis Scott, who, as we have seen in the description of the Scotts Centre, lived near Tonbridge, decided to adopt some children. First, there was Katie (Katherine), then Charlie and finally Henrietta – 'Henny'. When Henny joined them, she was six weeks old but, almost at once, Jill and Denis began to worry about her. She had a squint and one foot turned in. However, the hospital assured them all would be well. The hospital was wrong. Henny was later diagnosed as having cerebral palsy. Jill started her own playgroup and all the other children there were kind and helpful to Henny. Henny then went to Hardwick Hall, a special school round the corner from her home (now amalgamated into the major new special school Nexus in Tonbridge) until she was fifteen. However, Henny – a very social and cheerful girl – had already announced that she "wanted to go to a sleeping school". It took a big search for the Scotts to find The Mount in Wadhurst, East Sussex – a secondary school based on Rudolf Steiner principles – and Henny went there. It was wonderful. Henny, always very caring of others, had many friends; she learnt to be a good cook; loved making pottery and became a skilled weaver with her own loom. However, the worries of all parents with a disabled child about the future eventually surfaced. The Mount asked the Scotts to come and see them and said that Henny had "outgrown them". It was a shock. Henny was now twenty-four. The Scotts went all over the South-East visiting possible places that could be a long-term home for Henny; but, in spite of taking advice from every possible source, they could find nothing suitable. They decided to do something themselves for Henny and some others like her. The inspiring story of how they achieved their dream is a book in itself. The Scotts Project has already been described and Henny was able to live there happily for the last seven years of her life. She died aged thirty-four in 2000, much loved by those who knew her, some of whom still live at the Scotts Project and remember her with fondness. It is yet another case of remarkable parents fighting to get the best for their child and the difficulties so often faced in finding a suitable school and a rewarding adult life.

Phoenix Centre at Cage Green School

The difficult decision faced by parents choosing between a mainstream school or a special school has been addressed at Cage Green Primary School in North Tonbridge. In addition to the special schools such as the Milestone Academy and some other schools which are described later, this interesting school aims to have children with a variety of not too severe problems partially integrated within a mainstream primary school.

The Phoenix Centre has a separate building which has thirty primary school children who are on the autistic spectrum and have moderate level special educational needs. The aim is that each of the thirty children integrates as much as they can in the mainstream school. Some will be able to spend 70%–80% of their time in the main school classes with their own age group. Some will only be able to spend 10% to 20%. Normally, the time spent in the main school increases as the pupils grow older, certainly up to nine, although quite often this decreases as the mainstream pupils gather pace around ten and eleven. But the whole idea is that the thirty children at the Centre feel part of the main school. They have the same uniforms; they have the same parents' Consultation Day and the same Sports Day; they go on outings together; have meals together; and they have an overarching headteacher. Phoenix pupils also share the computer, PE, art and music facilities as well as after school clubs with the main school. Children in the main school become accustomed to having a boy from the Centre in their class – and, yes, the Phoenix Centre does have twenty-seven boys and only three girls; and yes, the pupils are often good at maths and with computers.

The Centre is overseen by Judi Beggs with huge experience in Special Educational Needs.

"We cater for children from all over West Kent who cannot quite manage in a mainstream primary school but who can manage the National Curriculum with his or her own age group – with our help. All our children have bespoke what are called Integration Support Plans. Pupils will only go to a class in the main school where they can cope or even do well – quite often with one of my teaching assistants there – I have twelve TAs for my three classes as well as the three main class teachers. If a teacher in the main school is covering a topic which he or she knows will appeal to one of my pupils, they will make sure the child is involved. One of my main problems is that we are very over-subscribed with a long waiting list. Pupils seldom leave us during their time here; and as we have only four or five who leave at the end of the primary school years, we are only able to take four or five as new entrants.

"To get in, there is a very strict assessment by outside experts. I get a lot of parents ringing up when they first get the news – the diagnosis of autism. And normally all I can do is to refer them to Jo Blamires at the excellent Kent Autistic Trust. By the time I talk with parents of a child who is actually coming here, I know they have been on such a difficult journey that it is important to make them feel part of a normal school. So, I aim to convince them that we will really help their child achieve as much as they can."

Judi takes me on a tour of the building. It is modern with a large hall, three classrooms and two special sensory play/treatment rooms. It also has its own large, secure outdoor playing area. The classroom for the youngest nine children seems very bare. Judi explains that, particularly at a young age, there needs to be as few distractions as possible.

"We reduce the visual clutter on purpose to stop over-stimulation. We also clarify the purpose of space to ensure that there is as little ambiguity as possible about what pupils are expected to do, and where and when. The only visuals are to reinforce their important things – their timetable in particular". Each child has his or her own little cubicle where they can go to do their own work. However, when I arrive, the children are in a semi-circle listening to a story. We move from Unicorn Class to Griffin Class which has nine children from six to eight. When we get to the top class – Dragons – there are more pictures on the walls but still pointing towards the specific rather than the let-it-all-hang-out artistic. Judi Beggs mentions rewards: "They love charts which show their progress and they love being given stars. It encourages them – especially if they are having to learn something that they can't see the point of. So, we try to use something that they are personally interested in to guide them into learning something which may seem to them quite unnecessary. If a boy is keen on cars, we'd get him to add or subtract cars, rather than just pressing abstract numbers on him". Judi continues: "As well as going on the outings with the Cage Green pupils, we have regular activities of our own. The youngest children – Unicorns – go horse riding once a week at the Bradbourne Riding School in Sevenoaks. It helps their social communication and co-ordination skills. Griffins have swimming at Tonbridge School – the Tonbridge boys are very good in helping us. And the Dragon Class go to formal swimming lessons at the main Tonbridge pool. We are lucky that the Variety Club sponsored a mini bus which really helps. We have two outside specialists provided via the NHS to help individual children – but the help can only be given to those who have a particular need with some specific problem written into their formal EHCP assessment. Some of our children are not very good at communication – their speech needs help. So we have a Speech and Language teacher who comes in twice a week. And a number of pupils have a variety of physical and sensory integration problems, so a specialist Occupational Therapist comes in twice a week. You've seen her special room and you've met her. But we don't really have children with significant physical difficulties."

As well as overseeing the Phoenix Centre, Judi Beggs also does a good deal of training of other teachers from other schools to help them understand autistic children and how best to support them. Additionally, she helps parents via a scheme called 'Early Bird' which is run via the National Autistic Society – for which Judi is full of praise.

I leave the Centre full of admiration for the Kent County Council which has enabled such a school within a school to be set up and run by such a caring and knowledgeable team. The children all seem cheerful and normal but I am aware that there are thirty individual stories under the surface and thirty sets of parents who will each have their own worries, although almost certainly each is relieved that their child is at the Phoenix Centre.

Going to Secondary School

I visited and talked with a number of state and fee-paying mainstream secondary schools. While few of the heads said so directly, they are forced to at least consider their exam results. The relatively new classification by Ofsted, which takes account of the abilities of the child when they reach the school and measures their progress from that start point, should help. However, the newspapers seldom explain the complexities of the new system and most parents are impressed by overall GCSE and A level results.

One SENCO with whom I talked was having a fight with a secondary school which was proud that "it specialised in taking children with dyslexia". (It was a fee-paying school but that did not really affect the main issue). The SENCO, on behalf of an eleven year old girl with dyslexia, was finding the school unwilling to take her. Her dyslexia was said to be just 'too bad'. The parents did not want the child to go to a special school and be – certainly to some extent – cut off from the world but they wanted extra help – and they were prepared to pay. They were seeking legal advice to see whether the school could be pressurised into taking the girl. When I last heard, the parents and the SENCO were winning. However, in more general terms the incident exemplifies the problem for both sides – the parent (and their child) and the school.

Hugh Christie Technical College

Based in relatively new buildings in north Tonbridge, Huge Christie Technical College is – as its name shows – a mixed, non-selective state secondary school. It has over 1,100 pupils. It specialises in providing a rounded education for children with a wide diversity of talents. I have only heard good reports about the school – from several SENCOs, from parents and from children who are there or who have been there. From the point of view of a child with learning problems, a good deal seems to stem from one man, the Deputy Head and its principal SENCO, Paul Bargery.

The school has numerous special facilities for those with obvious and well-diagnosed learning disabilities – special quiet rooms where pupils who are in danger of having a meltdown can go; extra tuition either on a 1:1 basis or in groups; and four groupings of pupils who have different types of special needs. The first is called 'communication and interaction' which provides help for children who are seen to be on the autistic spectrum. The second is 'cognition and learning' which provides extra teaching for those whose scholastic level is low. The third – 'social and emotional' – copes with children with such problems as ADD or ADHD whose behaviour can get out of hand. And the fourth is for children with physical disabilities where the school has powered wheel chairs, lifts etc. (The good disabled facilities were greatly helped when the new school was built). However, as well as these structural grouping, there are things like a breakfast club, often to calm down ADHD pupils – they are expected to do their own washing up; a skills workshop/centre; a homework club and so on, all of which seemed to me to indicate a school with a flexible and positive attitude towards pupils with inherent learning disabilities but also to the larger number of those on the edge of the autistic spectrum or just those who are a little behind or a little worried by life at their current state of development.

One thirty year old I met with not very severe autism, who had been at Hugh Christie, said she still has friends who helped look out for her then and still goes back to the school. However, as I have said, maybe the excellent impression I obtained of the school was just happenstance. Other schools have some or all of the Hugh

Christie's systems and equipment and could be first rate, too.

One aspect of learning disability I discussed with Paul Bargery was the ratio of boys to girls. He said that he had increasingly begun to doubt any major preponderance of boys. He felt that problems just showed differently for boys and for girls. The boys' symptoms were more obvious, more extrovert and more likely to occur within the school. Girls, he felt, probably had as many frustrations, sadnesses and emotional difficulties, but they bottled them up, only telling a teacher they trusted or, more often waiting until they got home. He worries that there is a danger that girls with problems can be overlooked. The more I talked with children with learning difficulties, the more I found this assessment to be likely. (Prof. Anna Vignoles, the nationally known educationalist at Cambridge, echoed this assessment and some research by the University of Exeter published in September 2021 said that there had been a seven-fold increase in girls diagnosed as autistic).

Hayesbrook Academy

I have known a good number of children who have attended the Hayesbrook Academy and who have flourished there. It is another state secondary school but has become an Academy. When I visited the school, they were in the process of finding a new SENCO, so I was joined by the Deputy Head, Gill Ansell, who was in overall charge of the special education needs at the school. She well understood the dilemmas faced by parents of children with milder learning disabilities. Is it better for a child with problems to go to a 'normal' school like theirs; or is it better for the child to go to one of the specialist schools where all the teachers are experts; the classes are smaller; and the other children have somewhat similar characteristics?

We agreed that there could be no one answer. However, Gill Ansell was clear that the policy in her school was to treat each child as an individual and, where any child needed help, the school would support them right through their time at the school. The School has boys up to sixteen, with a separate sixth form which has boys and girls. Out of a total of 788 pupils, the main school has seven boys who have an Education, Health and Care Plan and a further eighty-eight where the boys need some extra help – they will be classified as having 'special educational needs' but that generalisation covers a wide range.

As well as their SENCO, there is a Special Needs co-ordinating teacher; and staff in general are taught how to help the individual boys who are identified as needing extra help in particular subjects or who have behavioural problems. When parents of children with difficulties – even those who have read up a good deal about possible local schools – arrive for a first visit, they are not unnaturally often uncertain about what will be best for their child. The potential pupils and their parents are shown around the school and have a detailed discussion about the extra help which could be available for the child's own particular problem and character.

The syllabus divides into two at fourteen. Half the boys will go on to do GCSEs; the other half will concentrate more on vocational work – although also continuing with Maths, English and Science. The latter will often attend West Kent College one day a week to do catering or IT or other relevant subjects which appeal to them. As a recent example, the School was really pleased about one boy who certainly had his own difficulties but who has now been doing exceptionally well at catering and clearly has a good future in the trade. Two other boys – both of whom were on the EHCP list but with high intelligence – are in the Sixth Form and aiming to go to university. However, as both the boys are on the autistic spectrum, the problem is not the academic work but rather their lack of social skills. They probably could not even go to the bank by themselves. So they are both having special help, sometimes one to one and sometimes in small groups where they can do activities and talk about how to cope with the world.

The Hadlow Rural Community School

I only heard about the Hadlow Rural Community School because I met one of its teachers. No one else in 'the trade' of learning difficulties or education had mentioned it; and it is, seemingly, unusual. It is one of the Government's new 'free schools' and is based within but separate from Hadlow College – a further education college which specialises in rural work such as farming and horticulture. The School takes its approximately one hundred and thirty pupils from eleven to sixteen and aims to provide teaching, not just the basic English, Maths and Science but to give an introduction to a range of rural subjects which will often lead to courses at Hadlow College itself. It caters principally but not solely for the less academically inclined children and, in a rural community such as SW Kent, it provides an interesting alternative. In connection with 'free schools', the Government has said (July 2020) that it intends to set up more, particularly for SEN pupils.

The Judd School

The Judd School in Tonbridge is one of England's leading academic schools. It is a long-established grammar school with a huge demand for places. Nevertheless, the school does have a small number of children with quite clear special needs and the school has its own Special Educational Needs team. In one recent year, they had eight boys who had EHC Plans. Three were visually impaired, one had a hearing problem, one was in a wheelchair, and three were moderately autistic. Cheeringly, of the eight, one went to Oxford; and one, who was clearly autistic, to Cambridge. However, there are also a number of others boys who, although bright, need and obtain extra help on an individual basis.

The then Headmaster, Robert Masters, explained. "I am very proud of the way in which children here who have varied special needs become included within the mainstream of the school. Firstly, we give them a lot of care to start with but gradually lessen it, so that they grow into being independent. Secondly, we are clear that the boys in the mainstream should begin to understand those who are a bit different. As far as we know, there has never been any deliberate bullying but we know that young boys are not always thoughtful. So we aim to get all the boys more mature. We find that our students can change and do change – they do help the school to be properly integrated. We also do a lot of work with the parents of the boys who get the extra support. They are the ones who really know how to get the best out of their own child. You asked whether we get parents demanding a cure for their autistic child but I think that, by the time the boy is eleven or twelve, parents have understood the position and are just aiming to do everything to help the boy reach his own potential and to fit in with society in a relaxed kind of way. We really <u>are</u> proud of what they achieve."

As I was finishing my conversation with Robert Masters at Judd, I mentioned that I thought I would probably talk with the two major fee-paying public schools in the area, Sevenoaks School and Tonbridge School. What did they do to help pupils with special needs? He laughed wryly and said that he wished he had the huge amount of money that fee-paying schools obtained which enabled them to take on large numbers of specialist staff to cope with children who had a range of not too difficult learning problems. As it was, while generally very sympathetic, he had to concentrate solely on boys who were outstandingly bright academically. He was able to help a few who had physical or other disabilities; and that was excellent; but clearly each of these children had academic potential. The school then did all they could to get round their individual disabilities. "So please do not equate the Judd with Tonbridge or Sevenoaks Schools. They are different and can afford to be different."

I, therefore, approached the two public schools, realising that there would probably be a larger number of children with a range of special educational needs than there were at a top grammar school. However, I did not foresee how large the number would be.

Tonbridge School

Tonbridge School is one of Britain's best-known boys' public schools, with high academic results in the national league tables (although normally not as high as Judd for reasons which will become apparent). Out of its total of around eight hundred boys, it has one hundred and fifty pupils who have a variety of learning problems, all of whom get individual extra help. I asked the Head, Tim Haynes, how the hundred and fifty are chosen. He explained that they will come via a number of routes – prep schools or primary schools; doctors or specialists; or just parents hearing by word of mouth. All will have heard something about the School's special schemes. The School will be happy to talk with a young boy who they suspect is bright, although probably not in a completely normal way.

"We try to get in contact with the boys early – well before they might come here. He will need an 'Ed-Psych' – that's a formal report from an educational psychologist – and we will at that early stage give him various non-academic tests. They can be for dyslexia or dyspraxia or dyscalculia: or they could have hearing problems or impaired sight; but we want to be sure that he is bright in spite of a seeming problem, and that he will fit into the School. We will show the boy and the parents round the School, including explaining about our Learning Strategy Department. This is what we call the unit which helps the boys who have these wide varieties of learning problems. It seems better to call it that rather than something like The Special Educational Needs Unit. We have specially trained teachers and a boy will be encouraged, sometimes on a 1:1 basis, sometimes in a group. I don't want it to sound as if we take boys with severe or moderately severe learning disabilities. But we do look after boys who may be bright but who have something that needs individual attention.

"We also try to get *all* our pupils to be socially aware. We have boys who go to help at the Scotts Project which you know about; and the boys take people with severe learning disabilities to our swimming pool or help with drama groups for the disabled at the Oast Theatre in Hildenborough. We want all our boys to realise that the world is made up of a huge variety of people and that they themselves are extremely lucky. I also feel that to build up this knowledge will prevent the risk of bullying or hint of discrimination against boys within the School who are perhaps a bit different. I've certainly never had any sense of problems of that sort. I often feel that one of the most important things that these boys – who are not always obviously in the mainstream – need is confidence in themselves. Because they know they are a bit different, we have to aim to avoid low self-esteem. One of the things that we do is to get these boys, when they are fifteen or so to mentor a child with perhaps similar difficulties in a primary school. So, we always aim to build up the confidence of our children with special needs. That's really important."

Sevenoaks School

Sevenoaks School is another well-known public school in the area, this time co-ed. Their effort to help boys and girls who have mild learning problems is – like Tonbridge – considerable. At any one time they have around a hundred children (2 to 1 boys to girls) who are considered to have 'special learning difficulties' or who definitely need extra teaching help in some areas. These boys and girls are carefully chosen, with questionnaires and interviews before the main interview at which the School's Head of Learning Support is present with the Admissions Department. Once admitted, there is further screening and then help from both the main teaching staff and the Learning Support Department. The school also has weekly classes to support those with poor motor skills.

The Senior Deputy Head, Theresa Homewood, who is in overall charge of their children with special educational needs added:

"Over the last few years, we have had a good number of students whom we identified as having learning difficulties. We have supported them through their school careers and were obviously very pleased that some have gone on to study Medicine at Cambridge and History at Oxford, and to gain a place on a graduate scheme at Price Waterhouse Coopers. Our approach to supporting students like these is reinforced by our commitment to voluntary service, which has been an integral part of the school since the 1960s. So, a number of our students help adults and children with learning disabilities in the community each week. Students with mild learning difficulties thrive at the school. We recognise and rejoice in the creativity and diversity that they add to the school."

However, as ever, the situation is not straightforward. I was telling two people who work with SEN children about Tonbridge and Sevenoaks Schools. They felt that it was perfectly fair to say that these schools were doing well in helping their pupils who had some lesser degree of problems with learning – and sometimes with behavioural problems. However, they were very clear that the kind of problems that these schools faced with their carefully selected 'problem' children were not the kind of difficulties faced by the wider world of education. The mainstream state schools, and the pupils they have to help, would have more severe difficulties, with which a fee paying school – ever anxious about its GCSE and A level rankings – would not be able or willing to accommodate. This suggestion was borne out by several well-to-do parents whose boys were not accepted.

Secondary Age Special Schools

In South West Kent there are a number of special schools for secondary age children with moderate learning disabilities which people mentioned. (It is once again worth explaining that a 'moderate' learning disability means a child and his or her parents are having a <u>very</u> trying time day in, day out). There are cases where even the kind of education given at the Phoenix Centre at the Cage Green School is just not suitable, let alone a mainstream school, however good.

So, the KCC's educational authorities have provided several schools which help boys and girls with somewhat more complex needs. The first is Oakley School which has three parts, a primary school with fifty-two pupils; a secondary school with seventy-nine pupils; and a 16+ Centre with around forty pupils. It has two sites, one in Tonbridge and one on the outskirts of Tunbridge Wells. The majority of its pupils will move from the Oakley primary school, to the secondary school and then to the 16+ Centre. Of the twenty in the 16+ Centre who left last year, seventeen went on to further education, one obtained an apprenticeship and one moved into supported living accommodation. It has twenty full-time teachers, ten part-time teachers and forty teaching assistants. Form sizes are normally eight to ten; and – as so often – 75% are boys.

I understand that the school's policy is to respect the privacy of its pupils and its parents. Consequently, I guess that the school authorities did not wish an outsider like me to contact the Head or visit the school. So, I accept that my request even to talk over the phone was turned down. However, I heard of parents who felt that their children were being well looked after by the school. Additionally, I had a sideways look at one aspect of the pupils and their difficulties. A well-known gardening expert, who lives locally, volunteered to teach propagation and planting in a practical way to the students there. She said that when she first started explaining the subject in the well-kept school gardening area, none of the children looked at her. They gazed up at the sky and seemed totally disinterested. However, as they started the practical work with the seeds and the cuttings, they became involved and were prepared to listen and react to what was being discussed. At the end of the first session, one of the girls came up to the gardening expert and said that she had really enjoyed the lesson. The gardener was pleased but even more pleased, when the teacher who was overseeing the lesson said that the girl never normally talked at all.

A second, KCC-supported, special school is Broomhill Bank. In fact, there are two linked schools, one in Hextable, near Dartford, mainly with weekly boarding and the other, a day school, just outside Tunbridge Wells. The latter is set in woods and landscaped gardens and caters for boys and girls from eleven to seventeen who have 'mild to moderate' learning disabilities. Additionally, there is a Sixth Form which goes up to age nineteen. To be considered, a child has to have an EHC Plan. The schools also give talks to local primary schools via their 'Outreach' scheme. Having heard from a number of current and former parents that the school had been very helpful for their children, I talked with the school to hear more. They explained that when a new pupil arrived, they aimed to give him or her extra support to help them settle in. Class sizes were small – usually ten to twelve – and they aimed to help their children obtain the best GCSEs that each child was capable of getting. Their Sixth Form not only works on the academic subjects but, building upon earlier teaching, develops social skills and how to live in the wider world, including getting a job. The boarders at Hextable are similarly encouraged to become as independent as they can – helped, no doubt, by the fact that they are living away from the support of their parents and have to learn to live – at least in part – independently.

I also heard how good the Milestone Academy was from a good number of parents but I did not visit the school. Nor did I talk with Bethany School, a fee-paying boarding school in Goudhurst which was recommended by several parents who had children with middling learning difficulties.

Ridge View School – now Nexus School

For children who have 'profound special needs', West Kent has an outstanding school – not just because I was given a very impressive visit but also because Ofsted classifies it as 'outstanding'. Ridge View School, until recently, was in North Tonbridge. It has now moved into expanded new buildings on the edge of the town and been renamed Nexus. The school is the area's PSCN School – PSCN standing for Profound, Severe and Complex Needs.

To explain the three definitions to a layman: 'Profound; is a combination of difficulties – multiple physical problems, often with hearing and/or visual impairment, as well as very little or no ability to learn; 'Severe' is pretty bad; and 'Complex' is usually only a little easier but with some ability to learn – in the jargon – "more able in cognitive skills". Ridge View/Nexus helps children aged between two and nineteen with all these different disadvantages.

As I waited in reception, there was a mass of teenagers – quite often in wheelchairs – going out of the building and others dashing around inside in all directions to different parts of the school. A couple of teachers (maybe teaching assistants?) were trying to shepherd one disparate group going out – a good number with obvious mental and physical disabilities with their walking or their talking but all cheerful. The then Headmistress, Jacqui Tovey, gave me a tour. She has worked with learning disabled children for thirty years and has been at Ridge View since1999. She was in charge of the futures of a hundred and ten children, any one of whom most of us would feel scared to have the responsibility of looking after. Because I understood the children had really difficult problems, I was not sure that I was looking forward to the visit. In fact, I found it uplifting and moving – and at the same time down-to-earth and pragmatic. As we walked round, the school's motto "Enjoyment is at the heart of all we achieve" became clear – but is also plainly complex. For each child to go forward to living a life as independently as possible, the School has to try to help with how the child communicates with the rest of the world – not always easy when making what is for us a straightforward, common sense, instant decision, can be a complex, frightening, puzzling matter for a child with major learning problems.

At the start of the tour we pass the well-equipped computer room. Then, at the far end of a long corridor there is a play area for the smallest pupils who can be as young as two but are generally three or four. This is the partially separate 'Oak Ridge Assessment Nursery' to which experts at local primary schools or specialist paediatricians can refer a child who seems very unlikely to be able to cope in a normal school – even with help. By this stage, most will have been put on the KCC's Social Services register. Over the following year or so the staff at Oak Ridge can work out with the parents and the experts what will be best for the child. Some will go on to the main Ridge View School; others to even more specialist schools; and a few to mainstream primary schools. In the adjoining class room there are five very little boys and one little girl at very little desks and chairs. There is a teacher and two teaching assistants. They are all working on 'making decisions'. "What would you like to do next?" asks the teacher showing the children cards with pictures. "Play toy", says the first: the second can't make up his mind. Two things become clear as generalisations: there are many more boys than girls and all the members of staff seem cheerful and patient.

"Yes, 80% of our pupils are boys", says Jacqui Tovey. "When the parents first get told that their child has a problem – has learning difficulties, has autism – they are naturally in shock. They are grieving, quite understandably – particularly if they don't know much about 'being on the spectrum' and all the complex jargon. They very often want to know what the cure is – to demand a cure. We completely understand their distress and bewilderment and we have to try to explain: we will be able to get their child to reach his (or her) best potential but we cannot cure them: it will be a problem all their lives. There is no cure".

We leave the Nursery. Going down the corridor, we pass a small room with one tiny girl and one teacher. Between them is a large blow-up plastic ball. Jacqui Tovey explains that the little girl is profoundly deaf; she cannot see or speak; and cannot walk. "All we can do is to give her some sensory experience".

We move on to the main school. In one class room there are only two pupils – the rest are off doing other things. One little six or seven year old girl is giggling loudly at the end of singing 'Old MacDonald Had a Farm'. She sits on a wooden board eighteen inches square with castors underneath. She clearly has massive problems with walking but her teacher/helper is persuading her to move around on the board. The other small girl sits cuddled with her helper; seemingly without much action or reaction. What on earth are the stories of these small people and their parents?

We now approach the teenage part of the school which has a slightly separate unit for 16-19 year olds – their Further Education Unit – which helps develop their skills for living away from the school bubble. There are three men/boys chatting and at first I am unclear who are pupils and who is the teacher. But Jacqui resolves the issue by asking one what he is going to cook for lunch tomorrow – he is a pupil and they have just come from planning it. The teenager can't remember and there is perhaps a flash of annoyance that he has been asked. However, his friend – all of six foot four – is cheerful about it. He explains laboriously – it seems an effort – but cheerfully that the meal is going to be a special Greek kind of macaroni cheese with herbs. They will get all the things from the shop. "It's a sort of Norwegian Greek version", he adds to help clarify the recipe. In the classroom itself the boys – they are all boys – are working away with their teacher. Jacqui explains that some go to the Princess Christian Farm once or twice a week. I talk to one of them and, to be honest, while he is lovely, he doesn't really understand what The Farm is or what its animals are. I hope he enjoys himself there but he will certainly not be able to become an agricultural worker.

We visit the playgrounds: "I've brought them out there to let off steam", says one of the two teachers of the probably eleven year olds. "They were getting a bit tensed up but now they are all happy". A girl on her knees shows me her exercise book and smiles with delight when I try to praise it. Finally, we end up at the gardening area where a variety of fourteen year olds (I guess) are digging over and raking the soil in the raised beds. "We've got ants, worms and centipedes", explains a girl, adding, "red ants bite". One of the three teachers/teaching assistants says they will be planting potatoes and onion sets next week. "And tomatoes", says a boy.

Jacqui Tovey is keen to explain the continuous assessment that is done for each child on an individual basis.

"Obviously, one of the most important times is when they first arrive and we have to liaise very closely with the parents as I've said. But then, towards the end of their time here, there is a debate about what will be best for them when they leave us at eighteen or nineteen. However, we plan ahead. At around fourteen, we have a special PCR – Person Centred Review – which will involve the child and the parents, the teachers, and various outside experts to start looking ahead for 'The Destination' – what should be the aim when they leave us. There is a range of possibilities, although few of our type of children are ever likely to get paid employment. A few may just continue to live at home; some may be able to go to the very basic Foundation Courses at West Kent College or to the Princess Christian Farm or even a few to Hadlow College itself. Some may have to live in secure accommodation or at least in sheltered or supported accommodation. Some will be able to fit in a bit of voluntary work and a few may go to Nash College – it's residential up near Chislehurst. But for most, it will be a combination of one or two of these things. Importantly, we keep track of them when they leave: they are not sent out into the world without being looked after.

"Staff training is very important whether it is for teachers – we've got thirteen – or teaching assistants – we have got about forty-five, although we're always looking for more. There are outside courses and a great deal of formal training within the school itself. Recently, we had a session on how to restrain a child. It is very rare that we have trouble but you have to be prepared for anything. We get excellent outside specialist help – speech therapy, OTs and physios; we've got a dietician and we have our own nurse. There are educational psychologists and counsellors; and a specialist sports coach. And they don't even come out of my budget – they are paid for by KCC's Social Services. Our only major problem ironically is transport – getting the boys and girls to and from the School, let alone the near chaos with parking each day – you can imagine with two schools, us and Cage Green Primary, together with the Phoenix Centre all on the same site. But we get it sorted. We've even got one child who does the fifty mile round trip from Cranbrook every day. We worry about money, of course, but our big project is the proposed move to the new site on the Judd School playing fields. This will mean we will be able to expand – badly needed." Since my visit, Ridge View, now Nexus, has actually moved into its new, purpose-built premises at the other end of Tonbridge. It can now teach one hundred and eighty-six pupils; and a new satellite school will later be opened, looking after a further forty-eight children."

This extra provision reflects well on the cash-strapped KCC.

To an outsider like me this seems a remarkable School. As I have said, I was delighted to hear that Ofsted had assessed it as 'outstanding'. Congratulations to the Head and the staff; and one guesses to the parents and children as well. They clearly do not have an easy road to travel.

Young Epilepsy and Valence School

The South East is also lucky that, as well as the 'special needs' schools just described, it has two other schools which provide help to children and young adults with even greater difficulties. The first which has been briefly mentioned before is the Young Epilepsy Centre, formerly known as St Piers, in Lingfield, Surrey; and the second is Valence School just outside Westerham, near Sevenoaks.

The Young Epilepsy Centre is one of only two schools in England which specialises in children and young adults with severe epilepsy. (The other is in Cheshire). It has children from five years old up to nineteen, although increasingly they stay until they are a few years older, depending on their individual circumstances. There are around two hundred students, divided into the main school, which has twenty plus day students and over fifty boarders; and the College, which has twenty day students and nearly a hundred boarders. Nowadays, since the addition of a major new building opened by David Cameron in February 2018, all the boarders have their own well-equipped rooms. The new building also has a swimming pool and various other new facilities. There are also some students who come from the outside on a part-time basis.

As well as talking with the school, I talked with one ex-teacher. She adored her time there and joined with everyone else with whom I have met in praising the teaching staff, the many specialists and the whole ethos of the school. However, she added that the financial pressures, the shortage of places for children who should be at the school, together with the huge range of problems that the children faced "did make life a bit complicated."

A former, long-serving governor, David Hodge, also had nothing but praise for the staff. "They are like saints. Sometimes I was almost overwhelmed by what they had to cope with – and they don't get the biggest salaries in the world either, although they are looked after as well as possible by the school. Most of the staff stay for years – and there is a huge range of expertise there – specialists of virtually every kind. My other major memory is the parents. I felt so sorry for them. For a good number – those with children who were very difficult to live with – the parents' lives must be a nightmare." He is proud of the way the Young Epilepsy Centre has progressed. It is not just that the school has been able to obtain enough money to radically improve and expand the buildings; but it is also the care and professionalism that runs throughout it. His only major concern was about what happens to the young adults when they leave. Often they are being supported into their twenties – increasingly so – but still the difficulty remains. How will they then progress? Will they be able to obtain a job, let alone one which is satisfying and will give them independence? It is a problem faced by many schools and in many households who have children with different degrees of learning disabilities or learning difficulties. Finding a job is discussed in more detail later in the book.

Valence School is yet another centre of excellence, in this case primarily helping children with severe physical handicaps. Although not within the main confines of a book about learning disabilities, it does, yet again, give an indication of the care given to children with special needs. I have a personal connection via one of my daughters, who thirty years ago was doing her Gold Duke of Edinburgh Award with the Sevenoaks VSU (the Voluntary Service Unit). She decided to volunteer at Valence and over a period of a year became very close to a boy of her own age with cystic fibrosis, including taking him on an apparently uproarious holiday at Butlins. Sadly, a few months later, he died. My daughter went to Valence to try to help console the parents. On my own visit there, I related the story and two things were – firmly – explained. Firstly, it was not the done thing to talk about death; they aim to look ahead in a positive way. Secondly, in the last thirty years, huge advances in medical care had been made and life expectancy for people with the various physical handicaps they help has increased. However, I was told that, while there has been this progress with improving survival rates, medical advances at childbirth have meant more children with multiple problems are reaching childhood and adulthood. (The advances in recent years were confirmed when I later met the parents of two teenage children who both had had cystic fibrosis all their lives. Although they were on daily medication and regular check-ups, both otherwise led cheerful, normal lives – including sport – and were doing well with GCSEs and A Levels). Valence School has a hundred children from all over the south of England, with ages from four to nineteen – all with complex physical difficulties. Virtually all are in their own specially adapted wheelchairs and many have multiple handicaps, with about half the pupils being unable to speak. This means one to one care is needed most of the time, although it was great to see a seventeen year old going at high speed in her wheelchair between buildings with a huge smile on her face.

The school still has regular volunteers, including the older children from the Sevenoaks VSU. The whole atmosphere of the school is positive, always concentrating on helping each child reach his or her own best potential. There are two hundred staff, including a great range of specialists, and much made-to-measure equipment. In the cookery class the teacher and her helpers were laughing with their class about how to measure out the ingredients for a cake – not straightforward when your mobility is very limited; but even the ovens can be adjusted to any height. The same adaptability is applied to the swimming pool, the IT room, the gyms (it is very important to keep each child as relatively strong as possible), the science lab and the dining room. And all the children's bedrooms can be individually adjusted in various ways, too.

Children and young adults with severe physical difficulties and often multiple other problems will sometimes need help with mental worries or with learning difficulties. In both cases there are specialists at the School to help.

One other story may illustrate the difference between children with learning disabilities and those with severe behavioural problems. It came from a former social worker at the Barnados Home in Southborough, near Tunbridge Wells. He told the story of a particularly damaged teenage girl. She was always rude and disruptive; never did anything to help anyone; and was often violent both to staff and other pupils. The social worker decided to try a new approach. He drove her to a school for severely physically disabled children in Sussex – somewhat similar to Valence School – and left her for a day. She came back a changed girl. And to visit Valence can also be a life changing experience for an ordinary person.

CHAPTER 8

Further Education – 'It Isn't Easy Being Me'

The Difficulty of Choice after School

If mainstream teenagers find it difficult to find something constructive to do when they finish school, it is dramatically harder for young adults who have some form of learning disability. We have seen that the parents face dilemmas in choosing the 'right' primary school and at least as much difficulty in finding the best type of secondary education. It is just as hard – if not more so – to plan what to do after school. The teenage boy or girl with any level of learning disability or difficulty, who has got used to the daily routine of getting to school, regular classes with pupils and teachers he or she knows and a set time home, is faced with a new and completely different type of world. Schools will normally try their best to bridge the gap, particularly if there is a sixth form which goes up to eighteen or nineteen. However, for nearly all young adults leaving school, there is the availability of university or further education. This chapter covers the wide variety of courses which can be taken in further education locally where training and support for those with learning disabilities is given.

The Hadlow Group: West Kent College and Hadlow College

In South West Kent, there are two Further Education colleges. Both come under the umbrella of the Hadlow Group. The first is Hadlow College itself, rated by Ofsted as 'Outstanding' when I looked it up, with over three thousand students. It specialises in agriculture, horticulture and a range of courses for jobs within the rural economy, covering all academic levels, from the very basic to university entrance.

The second is West Kent College in Tonbridge, with nearly five thousand students and with an even wider range and level of courses, from IT to catering, from various building crafts, to fashion, hairdressing, gardening, media, sport, vehicle maintenance, nursery nursing and other caring skills. Courses at both colleges can be taken by students who have very varied levels of learning difficulty.

In the early 1990s, West Kent College was one of the first FE Colleges to introduce special courses for students with learning problems. These courses are today called Foundation Learning and great efforts are made to provide training for young adults who 'learn differently'. This phrase – used instead of 'learning disability' or even 'learning difficulty' was mentioned by the person in charge of 'additional learning support' for both colleges, Karen Richardson. Karen originally came from a Social Services background, including community housing and looking after disturbed adolescent girls. She has a team of sixty staff at West Kent College and a further forty at Hadlow College, many of whom help support students who, as she says, learn differently. The staff includes both teachers and teaching assistants with experience in the field; some communication support workers who, for example, help hearing-impaired students. Specialist tutors are allocated to those with learning problems; and there are also tutors who can teach when English is a second language.

The students can be hugely different in their abilities, some with very minor problems, others who will require a great deal of support. There is a trend, however. Over the last five years, there has been an increased number of students who have an Education, Health and Care Plan (the EHCP), which ties in with the increasing number of children classified as having Special Needs. Perhaps associated with this trend is that when asked in the application process to assess themselves, a significant number – 38% – said that they thought they would need extra help. These concerns can turn out to be groundless but their fears are a sign of insecurity stemming from their work at school.

Each prospective student has a conversation with the staff, usually with the parent present, which aims to lead them towards a suitable course. The tutors build up a good relationship with the various schools and so will often have helpful, prior information about potential students. The colleges have what they call Curriculum Taster Sessions at which prospective students can learn about the courses they are considering. The aim will always be for a course which will lead towards a suitable job. The staff will need to feel that prospective students are really keen on the particular course – not just being pushed by the parents – and that their skills level is going to make the course feasible for them. A relatively new criterion called "Preparation for Adulthood" always has to be at the back of the staff's mind. The four principles that are considered for each prospective student are:

- will the course help lead towards a job (or further useful study)?
- will it help the person to live independently in due course?
- will it increase the chances of the person becoming part of the wider community and forming friendships?
- will it help lead to good health?

There is an annual review of every student, at which they can invite anyone they wish to be present. One of the main objectives of the review is to check that the four principles have been or are being met. However, the review could include worries about bullying or social exclusion. In this respect, both colleges have a commitment to an inclusive culture – including preventing bullying – and it is heavily promoted. Like any school or any workplace, there will be occasional problems but the staff are available to provide help when and if they arise. As part of every course, students have to find themselves suitable work experience. If they are finding it difficult, tutors, who try to keep in touch with relevant industries and businesses locally, will aim to help. The colleges also provide assistance with filling in forms and with interview techniques. To test whether the individuals really have been helped to find a job, both colleges commission a survey to see what has actually happened. Each student has said what they hope their particular course will lead to and, in the January after they have left the college, an outside agency contacts them all to see where they are working.

The results are passed on to Ofsted and to the various local authorities – both Colleges have students from a wide area including South London and Bromley, East Sussex and East and Central Kent, as well as West Kent. The results are also printed in the Annual Reports[72]. (The statistics sound very encouraging – almost unbelievably so – and some doubts are mentioned in the notes).

Within West Kent College, there is a department called The Hadlow Foundation. It normally caters for students who are between eighteen and twenty-four but it has looked after a few as young as fourteen and as old as sixty-four. The range of ability is wide.

Head of the Department, Mandy Hutchins explains.
"We have what we call the three levels of Foundation Learning courses. At present, we have five pupils at the Entry Level 1 which is for those who have very limited skills. Most cannot read or write. All will have Education, Health and Care Plans and our Department will usually have had useful prior liaison with the young persons' individual schools as well as with the prospective students themselves and their families. These Level 1 courses run five days a week for up to three years. Last Tuesday, I was teaching a class about their home addresses; they just didn't know them. We give them a wide range of experiences – but all with the aim of helping them live more easily within the main world. Where possible we try to start on English and Maths but they will also do things in a kitchen, or in a gym. We also do a variety of things with Tonbridge Girls Grammar School. The girls there are amazing. They are working for their baccalaureate exam and, as part of it, they have to plan how and what to do to help our students. For one term it could be things to do with art and the next, science. This year they have done 1:1 sessions with computers but on other occasions they have done woodwork and music workshops. It really is a wonderful relationship – for both sides.

Entry Level 2 is for young adults with slightly less severe learning disabilities. Currently, we have thirteen students divided into two classes. Most can do a bit of reading but usually not much; and they often do not have very good social skills. Again, they are with us five days a week and again we aim to tailor the course work for each individual. We get them to experience gardening and cooking and arts but we are also lucky in having the Princess Christian Farm which is overseen by Hadlow College. At the Farm, there is a wide variety of expertise in agriculture, conservation, animals and so on with its many rural based courses. We have more complex English courses, with various different levels, and Maths courses, also with different levels. But there are no exams – they just couldn't cope.

Entry Level 3 is for people with a few more skills. At the moment we have seventeen students in two different classes. We aim to get them to a standard where they can start on a mainstream college course in the following year. Last year, for example, twenty-five out of fifty went on to a full course at Hadlow or West Kent College. And, occasionally, it can lead eventually to a degree course. I can remember around six people in the five years I've been there.

"But the Department does more than the three Foundation course. We run sessions for secondary schools – both for special schools such as Nexus and Broomhill, but also for mainstream, local schools – usually it's a once a week session for groups of up to ten children who may need help. We take them over to the Princess Christian Farm or round West Kent College or to Hadlow College. And once a month we get together with children who are being educated at home – although I have noticed that home schooling seems to be less common round here now than it was five or ten years ago.[73] And there is the valuable work we do all the time with the regulars who come to work at the Princess Christian Farm. Two of them used to live in the Princess Christian Hospital itself twenty years ago. But all the time we are aiming to help the individual teenagers or young adults reach a better level of understanding of the world – of course, always in conjunction with the families and, where relevant, the schools. We really do aim to tailor-make a plan for every one of the people we are helping so that they can cope with life more easily."

The much-reported Government cuts to Further Education budgets over the past years have not made it easy for further education colleges anywhere, including those in Kent.[74] The government still pays towards pupils up to eighteen and pupils up to twenty-five if they have an EHC Plan but colleges have to find extra money to pay for teaching those with less severe learning difficulties. In spite of the financial pressures, the colleges at Hadlow and Tonbridge are adamant that where the teaching of pupils who learn differently is concerned, they will continue to do everything they can to help each individual student.

Regrettably, since I finished the draft of this book, the Hadlow Group has gone into administration. It is only just becoming clear what will happen in the future. However, the Colleges within the Hadlow Group have gone through similar crises before and it is to be hoped that the services they provide to those with learning disabilities will not be lessened.

The Orpheus Centre

The Orpheus Centre is a very specialist college. It was started by Sir Richard Stilgoe[75] and is for young adults between eighteen and twenty-five who, although they have learning disabilities, will benefit from having help to develop their musical and performance skills. The Centre is in Godstone in Surrey. It now has thirty-six students with learning disabilities of all types, twenty of them living in their own flats and with the rest coming in each day. 83% of the students leave Orpheus with something specific to do – some kind of occupation – a very high figure.

I visited the Centre and I also heard one of their concerts. The concert was amazing. Two things will remain with me. The first was a young man, whom I met later with his mother. He played a long and particularly complex Bach piece on a xylophone but with no change of expression, before, during or after. The second was a song composed by Richard with some of the students – "It isn't easy being me." But the classical singing was of the highest standard, too. The Centre receives some State money – basically for each pupil, but it is nothing like enough to support the enterprise without private donations. As so often, a good view of the project and particularly the stories of some of the students can be seen on the Centre's website.

Words and music by Richard Stilgoe, from ideas by Thomas Puttock and Angus Morton

Richard says:
"This is the lyric of a song written with the help of some students with autism. I have been amazed by the ability of young people like them, who have real problems to express human emotions in prose, but who can sing with passion and insight about those same emotions when they are part of a song – because when they sing, they are accessing a part of their brain their autism somehow doesn't reach. They all knew the song by heart after singing it just once."

IT ISN'T EASY BEING ME

Everywhere and every day
People stare then look away.
I understand – I'd do it too.
If I were you – that's what I'd do.

It Isn't easy being me
The day is full of ups and downs
The road has twists and turns
And I don't know the way
It isn't easy being me
But this is who I have to be
I am me – the same old me – every day.

It isn't easy being me
I'm in a place I can't call home
It has no memories
No seeds have yet been sown
It isn't easy being me
But this is who I have to be
And I have to face the challenge on my own

One step at a time
One beat of my heart
Every step (every step, every step)
A brand new start.

It isn't easy being me
When every face is fresh and strange
I cannot read your mind
And everything is new
It isn't easy being me
But this is who I have to be
Being me – just being me – is what I do.

It isn't easy being me
But this is who I have to be
And I suppose – who knows?
It isn't easy
Being you.

One Orpheus parent with whom I talked explained that her child had mild Down's. When the time came to leave her special school at seventeen, they looked at all the possible courses at Hadlow and West Kent College. The staff suggested gardening. The daughter actively disliked the idea of gardening, so they contacted the KCC Learning Disability experts. As the daughter had always been keen on acting, the Orpheus Centre was mentioned. However, because it was outside Kent, the KCC said that it was unable to pay the fees: nor could they provide transport every morning and evening. A compromise over the fees was eventually reached and the girl had a rewarding three years at the Centre – even if the mother had to drive more than two hours a day as an unpaid taxi driver. It is worth mentioning that the mother was in the caring profession; and without her specialised knowledge – as well as her persistence – the successful outcome would have been very much more difficult.

"Everyday English and Maths"

There is a further education scheme laid on by the KCC called 'Everyday English and Maths' – shortened inevitably to the uninviting EEM. In particular, it aims to provide classes in the two subjects for people with not too severe learning disabilities of any age – not just young adults – who want to progress a little further with basic education. They could be living by themselves, or in sheltered housing, or just be a person with learning difficulties who wants to be more self-sufficient. Talking with the manager of the scheme, he says that people get referred to the classes in a variety of ways.

> "A care manager or the parents or a Housing Association could suggest us; or it could be a Job Centre or the Kent Supported Employment Unit – anyone who feels that a bit more basic education would help the person be more independent or get a job more easily. We call it Everyday English and Maths as a friendly title – we don't want it to sound too complicated or frightening. It is basically two and a half hours on English in the morning; then two and a half hours on Maths in the afternoon. We have an excellent, very experienced lady teacher and the course is free –

Skill Funding Agency money – but you have to pay for the lunch! We need to have ten people to enable us to run the course, so that means we do not have a regular schedule for the courses. But we think we really can help."

Roger's Story: from 2½ to 21 – Aspergers. Roger – not his real name – was two and a half when his parents (well-to-do and intelligent), together with his playgroup teachers started worrying about him. His language development seemed behind the other children; he was inclined to be isolated; and he seemed more interested in things than people. A very helpful lady from KCC's Learning Disability Unit came and gave advice; and, particularly useful was the eventual diagnosis that Roger had Aspergers and/or was on the autistic spectrum. (His mother explained that it used to be said the child had autistic spectrum disorder but the word disorder was thought to be pejorative). The diagnosis may not have been ideal news but at least the parents felt that they knew the position; and, importantly, it gave them the ammunition which would go towards getting the authorities to 'statement' Roger (the old term for what is now the EHCP). This would in turn help get some financial support and access to help in school. It also gave his parents the impetus to join specific support groups where they could talk with others in a similar situation. Roger's mother particularly mentions how helpful the Kent Autistic Trust has been.

The next step for Roger's parents was to find a suitable local primary school and to ensure that the school and Roger received extra, one-to-one help at lessons. After visiting a number of other schools, they chose Weald Primary. The Kent Education Authority (KEA) – rather than the Learning Disability Unit at Social Services – had to give permission for 1:1 assistance to be given. However, the KEA has a large number of requests and initially they said that they were unable to help.

It took the threat of legal action to get their agreement before, at last, aged four, Roger started at Weald with the one-to-one care assistant. For the next two years Roger was relatively happy at school – although it was clear that he was not totally absorbed into the mainstream of school life. Eventually, the mother became concerned that Roger was becoming too dependent on just the main care assistant. The family decided that perhaps a special school where there were other children more like Roger would be better than a normal school where he stood out as different. After viewing various possible schools, the parents particularly liked Browns School, a special school in Chelsfield, and the school said that they were prepared to take him. Roger was not going to have a one-to-one teacher but *all* the teachers were specialists. The money that went with the KEA Statement was given to Browns. Roger was there for five years and seemed happy.

When Roger was eleven, the problem facing the parents was where he should go next. They went to the various secondary schools in the area, one or two of which had units for children with learning difficulties. None seemed quite suitable. One teacher, who was in charge of special needs, even advised against Roger going to the school. After a long search the parents found Laleham Gap School seventy miles away in Margate which catered for a range of children with special needs. Roger became a weekly boarder for the next five years. The parents still feel that he was happy there – although they think that, if one asked Roger, he would not agree. He did, however, get five GCSEs, mostly at reasonable grades – quite an achievement.

At sixteen, Roger's parents were yet again faced with what was best to do to help him and, after advice, tried West Kent College. They were very impressed with the facilities and the people who look after the students who came to them with a variety of learning problems; and Roger did well. There was a one year GCSE type introduction and a further year when Roger successfully did a BTech in Sport and Leisure. At twenty-one he now teaches and helps in a leisure centre. He has ambitions to move on to be a personal trainer – although his parents feel that this would not play to his strengths: and they are wondering how to try to explain this to him. The family, including Roger's brother, a year and a half younger, have had a tough twenty years; and, as so often, it is not over yet.

CHAPTER 9

The Difficulties in Finding a Job

The Problem

However much schools and, in particular, their Sixth Forms do to help prepare their pupils with learning problems for a job; and however much further education does to train their students for work, it is still very difficult to find a job when you have learning disabilities. One GP called it a chasm. To find a fulfilling job is even more difficult. The figures are grim. There are two surveys which quote 6% and 7% as a proportion of people formally classified as having a learning disability who are in paid employment. Two other reports say that only 16% and 17% of those with autism are in full-time employment.[76] The problem can be made even more difficult when parents – or at least some of the parents – have unrealistic expectations for their child. Successful parents, quite understandably, want their child to "do well" but can end up pressurising both the child and the authorities to find a "better" job.

The advice from one very senior KCC expert, who had spent the whole of her life helping those with learning disabilities, stuck in my mind.

> "It's finding the right job which will suit the individual that's important. I had a relatively severely autistic man: he could not communicate with those around him very well but once he got the basic idea of something, he would do it with great accuracy for hours and hours – enjoying it. So we found him a job in a big store in Tonbridge, working a machine which crushed cardboard boxes. He did it brilliantly, once he was properly trained. He loved it and the employers were really pleased, too."

I also remember the opposite kind of story where several parents were very dissatisfied with the advice given by West Kent College and insisted on courses which were not achievable or suitable for the young adult. Liz Astor in her book 'Loving Olivia' also describes the worries and frustrations she felt in trying to find the right level of work for her daughter. Nor is it only young adults. In another case, I was told by the parents about their son with Down's who was by now over thirty. In spite of their earlier efforts over many years and all the suggestions from the authorities, they had never been able to find proper work for their son, although he was good at woodwork and his speech was not too bad. Eventually, they got agreement for the son to work in a charity shop. However, it proved difficult for him to deal with the customers and the customers in their turn were not sympathetic. So, the shop moved him into the backroom sorting things. This was not a success and he went to work at a different charity shop. The work there involved him using a steam iron for hours on end and resulted in his hands getting burnt.

One of the country's leading experts on Learning Disabilities, Professor Sir Simon Baron-Cohen at Cambridge[77], has spoken movingly about finding jobs for the people he cares about. "With autism, the magic bullet is a job… [otherwise they can] languish, not in institutions [as they used to] but isolated in bedsits." The Professor made some documentaries for the BBC[78] which showed the importance of establishing what level and types of skills the autistic person has and then finding an employer who needs those skills. One of the programmes followed a man with severe Aspergers and another with Tourette syndrome. The first had taught himself computer programming but was almost completely unable to talk with anyone. While his intense shyness meant that he had been unable to contemplate any type of job, the Professor was able to persuade the Managing Director of a high-tech computer company to take on the man for a trial period (helped undoubtedly by the presence of BBC cameras). The documentary followed what happened. At first the workforce was dubious about their new colleague who could not join in any conversation. However, when they were talking about a specific computer problem with which they had been struggling for some months, the man solved the problem within a few hours. He still was not able to join in normally with his new colleagues and ate his lunch separately; but eventually the others accepted him as he was. At the end of the trial, the Managing Director said that he would employ the man and the documentary ended with the man himself making his first ever speech to the assembled workforce, thanking them all for accepting him, followed by rousing cheers from his colleagues. It would be tempting to see this first programme as an example which could be followed for all people with autism or learning disabilities.

However, the second programme showed that finding a job, in this case for the man with Tourette's, is not easy. The man, when we first met him on air, seemed cheerful and normal but could suddenly lapse into the most violent spasms and swearing, which can sometimes – but certainly not always – be a signature problem of Tourette's. Professor Sir Baron-Cohen went to great lengths to analyse what might be a suitable job and eventually he obtained agreement for the man to work on a fishing boat. However, in spite of explaining Tourette's to his future colleagues, the experiment did not work out.

I was told about one young woman, whom I later met. She had had a difficult early life and was also clearly autistic to some degree. It meant that she had not obtained good exam results but, more importantly, she found it almost impossible to talk with people. It was more than being shy. It was the inbuilt characteristic which prevented her from communicating about almost anything. Yet once she set her mind to something, she could concentrate and do what was expected of her well. She needed a wage to supplement her not very generous government benefits, so that she could pay her rent and buy her own clothes and food. Going by the Professor Sir Baron-Cohen's aim of finding work which fitted her talents, a job suddenly arrived. She became a chambermaid in a big hotel. She did the work conscientiously and felt satisfaction from it. She never *had* to talk with anyone and the wages, although not large, enabled her to have her own independence in her own flat.

Help in Finding a Job

This problem of finding jobs is not new. In 1900 the group of people trying to help the 'feeble-minded' to have real work set up the Princess Christian Farm Colony. The men – the 'boys' – did farming and gardening – with supervision – but also had carpentry and bricklaying classes. The 'girls' had their sewing and cooking – and, sometimes, farm work – particularly the milking. For nearly a hundred years, this system continued, although it was nearly always within the closed community. It worked well. The men and women were given jobs that they were individually capable of doing and enjoyed the work and the way of living. The coming of 'Care in the Community' meant this small specialized hospital was wound down.

Today, the Government realises that being out of work is not something that the vast majority of people with any type of disability want: and paying for them to be out of work is very costly for the taxpayer. The solution to both problems, as the Government has seen it, is to encourage reasonably paid jobs for disabled people.

In the autumn of 2016, a consultative document was issued. As well as asking for comments, it proposed, amongst many other things, to once again make GPs do more for the one million physically and mentally disabled people and to be responsible for 'fit notes', as they were now to be called. Experts were sceptical about many suggestions but they had a chance to contribute to the eventual November 2017 proposals. The criticism of the second document was more muted. The proposals included a wide number of well-meaning ideas, although none seemed very specific about the Government's own action (or the provisions of extra money), apart from a major drive to increase the role of the Job Centres – nowadays called Job Centre Plus (or JCPs). What the Government was proposing about expanding the role of the Job Centres seemed in theory to be sensible – as long as there was to be sensible funding. Job Centre staff – now called 'Work Coaches' – were to have more training and new schemes were to be started including 'Personal Support Packages' and 'Supported Internships', where "every person with an Education, Health and Care Plan will have a chance to take part in a supported internship to help build up their skills and get work experience". In other parts of the document, the importance of building up the disabled person's confidence was emphasised – an excellent ambition. One further constructive aspect of the document was about localness. "We want to make local support better… [with] local groups and organisations to help us support people into work."

Job Centres Plus

For a person looking for a job, one of the obvious places to try is indeed a Government Job Centre. There are Centres in Tonbridge and Tunbridge Wells. (The Sevenoaks one has been closed which seemed strange when the Government was saying that it wanted Job Centres' role expanded and wished to see more localness). Initially, I was not clear whether Job Centres had any expertise in what is inevitably a specialist task of finding work for someone with autism or Down's syndrome or the many varieties of learning difficulties. The Job Centre I visited sees seven hundred people each week. (During the recession in 2008/9 it was one thousand five hundred). There is a cheerful security guard on duty, although he does not have a formal uniform. He says that he seldom has problems. However, he thinks that his presence helps keep people calm: "It's not like Liverpool Centres where they're always having to ring for the police – it averages about twenty calls a week!" The Centre has two senior staff whose work includes the specialist role of helping disabled people of all types – people with mental health problems or physical disabilities as well as those with learning disabilities. Both seem committed to this work and I was told about a number of Government schemes and given examples of people whom they had helped. The Centre will often need to explain the complexities of possible extra Government payments – originally called the Disability Living Allowance but which were being replaced by the Personal Independence Payment. (It is easy to guess the commonly used abbreviations). If you prove yourself eligible via an outside assessment firm (formerly ATOS but then Maximum), then money will come from the Department of Work and Pensions, which can vary from £21 a week to £140 a week.

'Access to Work' is another Government scheme which aims to let the Job Centres step in to provide help if there is anything which a disabled person would like to do but something is preventing it. One example I was given was of a cerebral palsy girl who they had thought should apply to a local firm who needed a call centre operator. Without interviewing her, the girl was turned down. The Job Centre expert rang the firm, got the girl an interview which in turn led to a job. It is usually quickly clear to the staff if someone with learning problems is likely to produce a negative reaction at an interview. Then the Centre thinks of ways to overcome what is likely to create the difficulty.

"We had one lad who clearly couldn't relate to people. Later, we had him assessed and, as we had guessed, he had Aspergers. Anyway, we knew that what he really needed was a confidence boost. So, we got him working in our office with the team and after a time, when he was coping with life and other people better, he got a job. We also have people in to show them computers and we can recommend computer courses which would be useful to them. We got one man with mild learning problems a job as a van driver with a big chemist chain and another one as a filing clerk. The Royal British Legion Industries in Tonbridge also help us place people. Increasingly, too, we get to know the big firms who are active in seeing what they can do to help. Waitrose and Marks & Spencer, together with The Range in Tunbridge Wells, are all firms we contact when we feel we have someone who might be suitable for one of their schemes.

"There is also a body funded by the Government, called the National Careers Service – NCS for short. They have an office in West Kent and they come round to us two or three times a week to give advice to individuals. Sometimes it's how to fill in a CV or to do mock job interviews. We had a man who now does stock control in a local warehouse and another man who got a job in a shop selling CDs. Because both these two jobs involved remembering where things were with their associated numbers, both were very good – we had guessed that they had a degree of Aspergers. Some of the people we are trying to help are not people who are formally recognised as having learning disabilities; others, though, are definitely 'on the spectrum'. But we try our best to find them all a job."

I asked a good number of people in the learning disability field about the Government's plan to increase the role of the Job Centres. They were not always in favour of the service which was already being provided, not because of the people in the Job Centres but because of the system. One summarised, "People with learning disabilities often have constraints about the number of hours they can work before losing their benefits – usually sixteen hours a week maximum. So the Job Centres do not formally deal with these as their customers. In essence, such people are not seen to be fit to do 'a real job'. The other problem is that Job Centres use a number of sub-contractors as 'advisers'. The advisers are paid by results and this means that they concentrate on the easier cases, with those who have actual learning disabilities or the more complex problems being what is called 'Parked' – or certainly not getting a useful service."

Kent Supported Employment

When 'Care in the Community' arrived in the late 1980s and early 1990s, the authorities – in this case the KCC – were aware that, if possible, jobs for their new 'service users' would need to be found. Therefore, twenty-five years ago, they established a department called Kent Supported Employment (inevitably called KSE). When I first asked people who the best person to talk with about KSE was, they all laughed and said, "You should talk to Mitch – Mitch Mitchell. He knows it all. So, ring him. He'd love to tell you all about it". So I did. And he did. Mitch usefully snowed me under with information (much of what he clearly felt I should have known already) which explained the double job that he and his twenty colleagues around Kent had – first, to find 'clients' who needed jobs; and then, secondly, to put them together with suitable employers. The clients are referred to Kent Supported Employment from various sources – by the KCC team dealing with individuals with learning disabilities; by schools; particularly special schools with whom Mitch and his colleagues have good relations; by NHS specialists; and often by word of mouth. Many are young adults who have just left schools or colleges. The aim is to find a job for them before they become a NEET ('not in employment, education or training').

However, although every client will have different needs, the one thing that all are likely to share is a lack of confidence. It is, therefore, one of the aims of Mitch and his colleagues to make each of their clients feel better about themselves and about their ability to do a job – as long as the right job can be found. The client will not only be helped to write his or her CV so that it will tie in with the job for which he or she is going to apply; but they will also be coached for the particular role and how to explain why their qualities will be useful to the employer – together with possible difficulties. For example, a good number of people on the autistic spectrum are very sensitive and easily distracted by noise. So, the client and the employer need to consider how this could affect a job.

Nor will a person with learning disabilities be able to understand the normal type of questions that would be asked at an interview: "Where do you see yourself in five years' time" and so on. They are usually not able to conceive of an abstract idea or to look ahead into their own future. All this has to be taken into account when coaching the client but also when talking with a prospective employer. One of Mitch's clients had a prospective job but had never had to go from his home to the new place of employment. So, it was necessary to give him 'travel training', with Mitch and his colleagues teaching him how to catch the bus and build up his confidence enough for the man to actually make the journey by himself. However, the team is clear that they cannot go on supporting a client indefinitely. They give themselves and the client up to a year.

Mitch gave a recent example of a fifty year old man who was on the autistic spectrum and whom they had been able to help. However, sometime later the man was having trouble with his employer. Mitch talked with the employer but the employer was unsympathetic: he said that he had a business to run and could not carry someone who needed extra help. Mitch had got to know the fifty year old client well and learnt about his strengths and weaknesses. Having heard about a possible new employer, Mitch went to talk with the boss, emphasising the client's reliability and the great accuracy and numerical skills that he could bring to the job. Mitch was referred to the Service Manager for whom the man might be working. Mitch again described the client and about learning disability in general. The Service Manager agreed to take on the man, saying he now realised that he too was somewhere on the spectrum – something his wife had been saying for years. Not only is the man doing well in the new job but he had ended up earning £7,000 a year more pay than he had been earning with his previous employer. However, Mitch agreed that this kind of result did not always happen. It was more likely that the client had to be found a part-time job to start with – sometimes with a charity, sometimes with a shop. The problem with this type of work was that it was too like the system which had been operating ten, twenty or thirty years ago when the government gave a three pounds a day allowance or helped by providing sheltered workshops. Eventually, it was thought this type of support was providing firms with cheap labour and was perpetuating an almost institutional-type attitude. Instead, the Government thought that what was needed was 'real' work at a real wage. Mitch recalled one lady who had been employed for £3 a day at Tesco's for years. To stop such a system may conform to modern ideas but the new aspirations do have drawbacks. It is clear that people with learning difficulties love working if the job is suitable; and that money is not their major concern. This suspicion was confirmed when Mitch mentioned a man who had recently been given a job with 'Help for Heroes' for three days a week but was insisting on working five days a week for the same money.

I asked how Mitch and his colleagues found firms who might be willing to take on someone who was on the autistic spectrum. Mitch explained that the Kent Employment Service was divided into four areas, North, West, East and South – each with a staff of five or six people. Each area builds up relationships with a variety of local employers. To encourage the employers, there is a scheme called 'Job Carving'. The idea behind it is to make a business realise that to employ someone on a bottom rung will release more time for higher paid staff to concentrate on the more productive parts of their job. (The scheme is not always helped by the legislation). However, overall, it is important that the outside world understands the background to finding jobs for people who have learning problems. Mitch, for example, gives lectures to various employer groups as well as liaising with organisations which have contacts within the world of learning difficulties. He had talked at West Kent College with Karen Richardson's team. They also watch out for jobs advertised on-line; and will even do some cold-calling if they think it could build up a relationship. Mitch thought that it was vital to publicise what they do, not only to make possible employers more understanding but to encourage prospective clients who were seeking work to come to him and his colleagues. The team will each have twenty or thirty people on their own caseloads at any one time and the KSE's aim as a whole is to place around two hundred and seventy Kent clients a year into a job.

Compaid

Compaid is a local charity which has two distinct roles. As we have seen, one is to transport people with age-related or learning problems. However, its other role is to help people with a range of physical and learning difficulties to learn about how computers can not only be fun but also useful to them. They run IT sessions for about five hundred disabled people a year – including quite a few people with learning disabilities.

One man, a jeweller who had been badly affected by a stroke, was not at all keen on computers. He was shown how to find out more about his great love – diamonds – and about his own former work place – Hatton Garden. He realised that he could technically work a computer and what was more, it was stimulating and useful. "It is their entry point into the unknown – whether they have physical difficulties like this man or learning difficulties," says Stephen Elsden, Compaid's Director. The parents of one Down's man in his forties, whom I got to know, says how much their son enjoys his weekly computer session at the Compaid HQ class in Staplehurst. Compaid pick him up in the morning and deliver him back at the end of the day. In the morning, he works on a computer. Then he has lunch. Then, in the afternoons, he socialises and plays computer games with friends he has made – and making friends is never easy for him. The parents are full of praise for all parts of the Compaid service.

The Princess Christian Farm

From Victorian times on, one of the long established forms of teaching an 'unfortunate', whether they were criminals, mad or just unemployed, was to teach people about farming. It meant that they were occupied and, in most cases, that they were productive. It could also lead to 'improvement', a state dear to Victorian hearts.

The Princess Christian Farm, as the name indicates, was and still is an actual farm. It was started around 1900 as a 'Farm Colony for the Feeble-Minded' by a remarkable man, Dr John Langdon-Down (of Down's syndrome) together with his eldest son, Reginald, with the patronage of Queen Victoria's third daughter, Helena, Princess Christian. For over forty years it existed as a residential charity, looking after a hundred men and fifty women in buildings built or adapted for the purpose until, in 1949, the NHS took it over and renamed it The Princess Christian Hospital. When the hospital was wound down and its men and women scattered into 'Care in the Community', the Farm, with its 115 acres, was given by the KCC to the Hadlow Group on a ninety-nine year lease for training those with learning disabilities.

After visiting it on and off for thirty years, I feel it still has the atmosphere of a farm, including the need for wellingtons in the winter. Today, it is a valued asset to the local area, normally catering each day for around twenty-four 'learners', as they are called. The majority comes from the local area. Some come once a week; some for three or four days a week, but never five because that would prevent them doing other things. The degree of disability varies. Out of the sixty men and women on their books (three quarters are men), one is in a wheelchair; one has two support workers and ten have one-to-one help. The rest have so-called 'mild learning disabilities', although, as ever, they all need very considerable help, care and patience. Choosing a learner usually comes after being recommended by a KCC care manager. The prospective learner will be required to visit the Farm to meet the staff and the other learners and to complete an application form. Then they would attend a few taster days and, in general, show a keenness to work sensibly and regularly at the Farm.

There are seven staff including Chloe Brooker, the Unit Manager, and six specialists – all of whom have teaching qualifications (or are getting them) as well as farming expertise. Each member of the team has their own subject. So, one looks after cooking and food; one looks after the poultry; one horticulture; the one in the Farm Shop teaching retailing and so on. Two of the six are also what are called 'TI's or technical instructors. Three act as Tutors to fifteen or twenty learners each, meeting on a one-to-one basis every five or six weeks to discuss how the individual is doing and to work out a plan for their goals over the coming months. Overseeing the whole operation is Liz Read with a BSc in Animal Husbandry and numerous other qualifications. She introduces me to everyone and then explains the various aspects of the farm.

They have five hundred free-range hens; a pig unit which seemed to have about fifty very lively piglets, as well as the sows; sheep and cattle which are grazed on the fields behind the Farm buildings and overseen by Peter, the Hadlow College farmer. ("He's really good with the learners who have an interest in agriculture. They respond well to men as role models," says Liz.) There are four much loved Shetland ponies; three goats and two alpacas. There is a section for small animals – some rabbits, some ferrets, some gerbils, hamsters, degus and rats. There are two snakes, a bearded dragon, some stick insects and geckos, and an African land snail (whose pet name I have forgotten) and even an axolotl of which I had never heard but which is about ten inches long with a toad's front end and a lizard's back half. It seemed friendly. On top of all this, they are breeding tropical fish, although everyone seemed surprised at the proliferation. "We are not intentionally breeding the fish; the fish choose to breed themselves! They have no use but staff take them away as pets!", says Liz. What this zoo is used for becomes clearer when the tour proper begins.

The Farm Shop is well stocked but its primary role is not to make money. Rather it is to teach the learners about shopping. As well as the produce from the farm, they have to decide what is going to appeal to their regular customers. The learners are driven down to Bookers and other shops to buy what they have decided they need, then they have to look after the money side, including a proper profit and loss system. Then they make sure the shop is clean and tidy; and learn how to be good at dealing with people who visit the shop. They thought up the idea of taking photos of their animals and putting them into key rings.

We move on to the kitchen which is large and industrial. It was originally designed to cook meals for the whole community. However, nowadays, the aim is to help the learners to cook for themselves; simple meals that they can make at home if or when they have their own kitchen, including knowing how to work such things as a microwave. Liz Read hopes that soon the room can be altered so that it has five or six units in which individuals can practise. Then I meet some of the learners. David is proud of the prizes the Farm has won at local agricultural shows – a reminder of all the prizes the Farm won in the 20th century. One lady has been coming to Princess Christian since 1984. So, I ask her about the old days. However, in reality, she does not remember, although she says it is good now. Another much younger lady is keen on knowing my name, age and birthday, and cheerfully follows us around on the tour.

However, perhaps the most memorable part of the day was when Liz Read asks Ben, a cheerful man of fifty to show us around the farm of which he is clearly very proud. We leave the big meeting room and visit the main pigsties. Ben explains that he helps clean them out. "Quite a lot of the others don't like the pigs." We then visit the five or six groups of piglets of different ages and I have the advantage of deep litter explained to me by Ben – with only a little prompting from Liz. We move on past various concrete farm buildings and Ben mentions that he helped put them up. One building is the chicken unit, which we reach just as the team responsible for eggs collection arrives. The unit is formally registered and has regular visits from outside inspectors. The automatic egg retrieving machine is started and Liz outlines why they moved from a large battery hen unit to the present free-range system.

> "The battery unit may have produced more eggs but it could get quite dusty, the learners didn't like cleaning it out, and really they didn't learn as much as they can from the new free range unit system. Now we can get the learners to work the egg collections machine, with the safety features (which Ben is pointing out); followed by the washing. Then there is the weighing and sorting the eggs into sizes with a special machine, the reporting sheets and the packing and dating. Each stage has to be understood and practised by the learners."

Ben tells me that you have to stand the eggs with the large end upwards – I didn't know that. We look at the currently empty greenhouses and polytunnels (it is winter) and end up with the small animals, fish and reptiles which are grouped around the main classrooms. Each classroom is designed to take around ten learners. Ben tells me about some of the animals. He knows the name of the boa constrictor – if not the other snake – but is not sure what the axolotl eats when I ask. Liz suggests that he looks it up and, when he has found the correct manual – there are a lot of them – he has a go at reading it out. It is a bit of a struggle. He and Liz explain that he is learning to read. He is justifiably proud that he is improving. The wide variety of animals and reptiles is used by the staff to encourage the learner to understand about the care of each type – its food and its natural habitat. They also have to write records of the work they do. Ben has been coming to the Farm for around twenty years. He is picked up in the mornings from his house, where he lives with his mother, three miles away in Tonbridge. He loves the Farm but has other interests. He explains that he goes to the gym on Mondays and talks about the voluntary work he does on Thursday and at weekends in a nearby nature reserve which has lots of birds. He also mentions a great day when he was allowed – I suspect under supervision – to drive a tractor. "And there was the big blue digger!" He is well aware of the fact that the pigs are there to become food. "They go off to the slaughterhouse. Once some of our people went there but we don't anymore. I don't think they would like it."

As well as the main farm, there is also the horticultural section, where the learners help grow plants for sale but, more importantly, get used to working with plants. The produce, including cakes and quiches made in the kitchen, are sold not only in the Farm Shop but also at the local farmers' market. The learners have the opportunity to work towards qualifications and last year members of the team earned two certificates. I asked Liz Read whether the learners were paid but was told – as I had already heard from the Job Centre – that to pay them would complicate matters and potentially lose them their benefits. As it is, the KCC pays Hadlow College for the training it does.

Probably the last thoughts about the Princess Christian Farm should be left to Ben. In reality, he will never be able to work for a living by himself but he is full of enthusiasm and is still learning – and is an absolutely lovely man. He feels that, although he has his other interests, the Farm is wonderful – even better than it was twenty years ago when he first came.

As I finish the book, it seemed likely that due to its difficult financial situation, the KCC may not be able to continue to fund the Farm – the kind of problem faced by county councils all over the country. However, another charity has agreed to support the Farm.

Spadework and Other Farm Related Schemes

Spadework is an organisation which has been training men and an increasing number of women in gardening and horticulture for over thirty years. The charity was originally founded by a group of parents who felt that 'the System' was not providing enough training or extending their sons' and daughters' skills enough. This was in the days before both Care in the Community and the wide range of support and education provided nowadays. However, in spite of changing times, the charity has continued to flourish, moving away from its original home within the yard at Princess Christian Farm to a large site at Offham. They have expanded the range of training that they provide. In 2003, thanks to a Lottery grant, they were able to open their own café – The Tastebuds Café. It not only caters for the team but is popular with the locals. The team use their own produce which is also sold in their Farm Shop which opened in 2009. The café also enables the staff to teach basic hygiene, cooking and serving at tables. There is a Garden Centre and gradually other courses have been introduced which cover basic computer skills, woodwork in their craft workshop, machinery maintenance and office/retailing skills. Spadework has achieved all this with a basic KCC grant and excellent fund-raising, together with a bit of money earned from the café and shop. When I talked with their relatively new General Manager, Chris Healy, he was particularly proud that in 2017 they had provided 71,463 hours of teaching to their ninety-seven trainees with their twenty-six staff.

Growing Concern

Growing Concern is another small organisation set up by the big charity, *mcch*, again with support from the KCC. It employs around ten people with learning disabilities to learn about and actually do gardening and horticultural jobs in their small nursery at

Staplehurst. There is a wide age range of the service users (nearly all men) – between their early twenties up until their sixties, although two men in their seventies in sheltered accommodation nearby come in with their carers and do an hour or two most days on jobs that they enjoy. There are two permanent, paid staff, who not only organise the normal work in the nursery but also manage the contracts they have to water hanging baskets and do other outside gardening jobs. Any money made from this work goes towards the service. There are regular indoor training sessions once a fortnight – usually fitted around bad weather – with each service user setting his own goals and with a key worker allocated to each to encourage them. The results from the nursery are first rate. I bought a wide range when I met the team.

There are various similar farming-based operations around England, including the Camphill Villages and Little Gate Farm in East Sussex, where people with learning disabilities can enjoy and learn about working with animals and farm work.

Tuck by Truck

'Tuck by Truck' is run as both a business and as a charity. It was set up and it is owned by *mcch*. There are units in various parts of Kent, with the basic idea to get 'volunteers' – the people with learning disabilities – to pack lunch boxes. One local unit regularly has sixteen to twenty-two volunteers, most with their own carers accompanying them. The scheme helps them in other ways, with a key worker encouraging each volunteer to have their own personal goals and working out how they could find other, perhaps more challenging, jobs. For some, it will be possible, probably after further training, for them to work in a shop. For example, one person with Aspergers, who had started at Tuck by Truck, went on to work in an electrical shop and later moved on to a more challenging job after further training at West Kent College. Some people have gone on to work as gardeners, again, some receiving training at West Kent College. Others do useful work on the Princess Christian Farm and then in some cases go on to help with various agricultural or horticultural businesses. However, it is only honest to say that the numbers progressing to full-time paid work is not large and only happens when their further education training has gone well.

The Town and Country Foundation and Gray's Cafe

The Town & Country Foundation is a local charity set up by a large building developer. It aims to help those with learning difficulties, mainly around Tunbridge Wells. It does not have large amounts of money to give away and, therefore, concentrates on acting as a catalyst. They have helped a scheme which raised awareness of the bullying suffered by people with disabilities. Several times a year, they hire the Trinity Arts picture gallery in Tunbridge Wells and enable different groups to exhibit, including 'Mindwell', a small charity which encourages a wide variety of people with difficulties to paint. They have helped groups run courses at the NHS HQ at Sherwood Park in Tunbridge Wells on "How to Take Care of Yourself", as well as providing support for Pepenbury. The Foundation also supports 'Gray's Cafe'. For around thirty-five years, Sue Gray has run a cafe in the village of Brenchley. But it is a cafe with a difference. As well as providing a focal point for the village, the cafe trains about ten people at any one time with learning disabilities. The Foundation is a good example of how business money can support small charities which have excellent volunteers who, in turn, help the people who need it.

Hugh's Story. Hugh had meningitis when he was a baby over forty years ago, and, although charming, intelligent and lucid for ninety percent of the time, it is an almost constant worry for him and his parents every single moment of every day that things will suddenly go wrong. He has very severe epileptic fits – which become more frequent when he feels stressed. He tries to explain his life. His principal feeling is one of frustration. "My typical day? I get up. I don't have breakfast because I go to Café Nero in Tonbridge High Street and drink coffee and have a cake. There are a group of us there. Then I have some more coffee and we talk some more. And then I go home and probably cook myself a bit of lunch. Then I'll go back to Café Nero and maybe end the day watching a DVD before I go to bed. I can't tell you how frustrating it is. I want to work – to get paid for it because I'm doing something worthwhile. I've been on three training courses to learn to help teach art to people with disabilities but because I tell them I get epilepsy, I get discriminated against and they won't have me. It is all a bit sad because I'd written special essays which a top English teacher said were A*. I realise that I can get very upset when I feel discriminated against. Things do upset me but I went on an anger management course which did help. A bit ironic really, because when I was on one of the teaching courses, I sent myself outside the room to calm myself down because of some idiot there. And then they held it against me! I go once a week to help at a centre where there are really severely mentally and physically disabled people. It's called the Thursday Club and it's run by a husband and wife team. And over the last year I have been helping teach art to people with mental health problems with a group called The Mindwell Art Group. We've just had an exhibition at the Trinity Arts in Tunbridge Wells. And I did voluntary work with the YMCA – who do a really good job helping the disabled.

A few years ago, I was co-chairman of a group representing the disabled in Kent. We were meant to tell bodies like the police and local councils what more they could do to help the disabled but it was very frustrating. They sort of listened and sounded interested but nothing seemed to happen and they never got back to us – although I have to say the police in Tonbridge are very good. They have a specially trained Police Community Support Officer and she does understand what disabled people go through. And they provided Victim Support when I got attacked not long ago. It all started in church. (Both St Stephen's and Christchurch in Tonbridge have been great). Anyway, I was in church and I had a fit. And this drunk – whom I had seen before – came over and beat me up. Then the next day I saw him on Sevenoaks Station and he came up to me, punched me down on to the floor, kicked me really badly and broke my arm. There was a retired judge as a witness and it is all on the station's CCTV. The paramedic arrived very quickly – although the ambulance took ages – but, of course, they were worried that, if they gave me pain relief, it could be dangerous for my epilepsy".

His parents take up the story. "By the time Hugh got to the Tunbridge Wells Hospital he was, as you can guess, very upset. And when he gets upset he does often shout at people. Without actually asking him anything, the Accident and Emergency people decided he was a drunk and left him – with a really seriously broken arm for over four hours. When we complained later to the Hospital, it just resulted in an unapologetic reply but the whole incident shows how even an A&E Department can be totally unaware and consequently uncaring towards those with learning disabilities. The police did arrest the man who had attacked Hugh but although by this time he had assaulted another disabled person, they could not do more than warn him off pending his trial. In the meantime, he follows Hugh around and Hugh – he's six foot three – is genuinely frightened".

Hugh continues: "As well as the epilepsy, I'm what is called hemiplegic. I'm not sure how it's spelt but it means that I'm slightly paralysed on my left side. And I know I walk a bit differently to most people. What worries me – annoys me – makes me very frustrated – is that certain people with a low mentality make a point of picking on people who are disabled in any way. It's awful. And I don't think that ordinary people understand – which is why I want to explain the terrible frustration that disabled people have. Ordinary people should be more aware of disabled people – not pick on them and discriminate against them. Ordinary people should understand".

His parents want to explain another example of problems Hugh – and others – have had to face. Hugh received a letter out of the blue from Social Services. It said that his Employment Support Allowance had been stopped as from the previous week. Hugh was distraught and, without going into details, had numerous fits, some of which were nearly fatal. He also tried to commit suicide. His parents meantime got his GP to write a long and very detailed letter explaining why Hugh could not obtain paid employment (something he would passionately like.)

In spite of the GP's letter, the allowance continued to be stopped. His parents complained very strongly. The Tonbridge Citizens Advice Bureau was hugely helpful in providing advice. The GP wrote again – an even stronger letter but using wording provided by the C.A.B. – and eventually the allowance was restored several months later, with a genuine but off-the-record apology from a senior civil servant.

This incident about Hugh's social service money lasted four months. During this period Hugh had seventy three epileptic fits.

These fits – together with his other problems – have occurred constantly over his forty-five years. However, there has been one major 'advance', although on first hearing, it does not sound like progress. Hugh has had all his teeth out. His parents and his GP advised against it but Hugh persisted. The reason is simple. During his epileptic fits, particularly ones that occur in the night, Hugh bites his tongue – not just a bit on the edge which we all know is painful enough, but pieces the size of a five penny piece. The pain, which lasts for many days, is terrible; and often it leads to severe inflammation and ulcers. Hugh decided that he had had enough, had all his teeth out and now has a plate which he can take out at night. He is hugely pleased with the result.

Hugh's life continues. He has his own flat in Tonbridge, bought by his parents, with the aim to help him towards as normal a life as possible. He continues his voluntary work helping disabled people. He continues to see his parents regularly who have supported him in every possible way throughout his life; but, as Hugh said to his mother last month, "what will happen to me when you and dad are dead?" A last word from Hugh, "No one seems to believe what a disabled person says. I cannot tell you how frustrating it is. I feel so frustrated all the time. I cannot get a proper job. I so much want one. But all the disabled are discriminated against all the time. Society should understand more. That is what your book should be saying. I just want the world to respect people who are disabled and to understand them more".

The Employers

However good the sixth form teachers at schools are and however much help is given at the further education colleges and the other courses which are laid on for people who 'learn differently', jobs will not be found unless there are willing employers. I have talked with a number of managers about the problem and perhaps there are signs that there is some improvement, albeit slight. I have not gained a feeling that any employer is actively against considering the idea: just that they have not thought about it and no one has put an actual proposal to them.

I talked with Jackie Matthias, the Director of West Kent Chamber of Commerce and Industry (yes, WKCCI) who was surprised – but quite interested – by the query. As far as she could remember, in the last fifteen years, no one at WKCCI had ever brought up the subject of employing someone with a learning disability. So, although some of their members may be doing so, there were so many other things that a business had to think about nowadays, it was not something likely to be at the top of their agenda. No one from Kent Supported Employment had ever contacted them. However, at one stage the Pepenbury residential home had been a member. Their former Director had persuaded groups from the Chamber of Commerce to look around and he seemed to have made some good contacts. Jackie added that it was perhaps sad in view of my query that Pepenbury was no longer a member, A number of local schools were currently members and they seemed to find the networking possibilities useful: probably it helped the schools to get work experience placements. But, although the Chamber would probably be generally sympathetic to the idea of helping people with learning difficulties, Jackie thought the best way forward was for interested bodies to join the Chamber and meet potential employers that way.

I did hear of one large employer, Waitrose, who has a formal policy about taking on people with a learning disability. I talked to them at both national and local level and, in particular, I heard more about one of their long-serving employees who is highly appreciated by the customers. He is in his early sixties, has a bit of a limp and very considerable difficulty with his speech. Officially, he collects the trolleys from the car park but, in fact, he does more. He helps old ladies with their heavy shopping bags, he assists the disabled and the mothers with push chairs and, above all, he keeps people cheerful. In consequence, a good many customers have been to the manager to say how much they think of him; and some of the older lady customers knit him socks with his name on. He helps out at weekends if needed and stands in if a colleague is sick. He is a full partner of The John Lewis Partnership and has won the Employee of the Month – together with a plaque to acknowledge it – something of which he is proud. He is not autistic – he was brain damaged when he caught a bug in hospital just after his birth. He reads the Guardian and discusses politics avidly with his family. He loves his job and wants to continue to help his friends/his customers – in essence, the perfect match between ability and a worthwhile job. The same store has a profoundly deaf and dumb man who stocks shelves. He was initially shy/embarrassed when – not realising that he was deaf – I ask him where something was but I then realised that he could not talk and I made a (brave) effort to communicate. We end up by making a joke with signs.

At another Waitrose store, there is at least one young girl who probably has learning problems and who was being taught to serve at the till. She did not yet really know where things were but, other staff, knowing the situation, helped her out. I felt that Waitrose is being pro-active and I wondered if they have a local or a national plan. So, I talked with local managers and national officials. When I start asking for quotes, the national policy is full of politically correct language and is structured top down. Yet the system is plainly working. All vacancies go on-line on a national basis, with details of the job, the location of the store and what qualifications are needed for a prospective applicant. The national HR department assesses the applications and sends a suggestion to the store manager. 'Equal Opportunities' comes high on the John Lewis/ Waitrose agenda but, as some people are more equal than others, it seemed to me that there is a bit of a hidden agenda – to help the less obvious candidates. I may be wrong, but in one particular store, I felt they were even more pro-active. It has an arrangement with various local schools and they ask if there is anything that they might do to help an individual who has a learning disability. Where appropriate, the boy or girl will go for a chat – sometimes with a parent or carer, sometimes not. The Personnel Manager not only asks the boy or girl questions but explains about the possible types of jobs and the world of work. Her team will even help by doing mock interviews. If a possible vacancy is found, the person is given a lecture about the particular job. This could lead to a trial period and then, if that is successful, to a full-time job. One young man had not long ago started doing a few hours a week, had then graduated to thirty hours a week and was now a full staff member. The Personnel Manager (who had a dyslexic son) kept an eye open just to see things were going well, not only for the person concerned but for the other staff. I explained to the helpful Press/PR man at

Head Office that I would like to name Waitrose as an example for other supermarkets to follow. He was pleased. I later found that at least one other supermarket – M&S – seemed to have a similar scheme; and then I was later helped by a young lady on the checkout at a Sainsburys. She had a slightly funny voice initially but, after my mild surprise, she could not have been more helpful and friendly. So maybe Sainsburys has similar policies.

AXA/PPP

At the suggestion of Jackie Mathias at the West Kent Chamber of Commerce, I talked with AXA/PPP Healthcare – a large multinational whose headquarters are in Tunbridge Wells. It became apparent that AXA/PPP also have a very detailed diversity policy. It calls itself a 'Disability Confident Employer'. They aim to look after anyone who might feel themselves a bit different at the recruitment stage; and, to follow up, if and when they are having a trial period; or when they are actually employed. They have an internal scheme called AXA-ABLE where anyone having problems with things like dyslexia or autism or Aspergers or a mental health problem can go and seek help. The scheme is also open for parents to come and talk. The firm supports the local Leonard Cheshire home and Remploy and they liaise with special schools locally. Not long ago, they had taken on a young man from a local special school for a one day a week trial; another boy with Aspergers was currently being interviewed for a possible job. And one man with a learning disability was employed in their customer support unit. I did not ask for full details but it was clear that the firm is prepared to adjust a potential job to tie in with the capacity and skills of a potential applicant. Obviously, this will not mean that everyone with a learning disability will be taken on but this flexibility – from a relatively brief discussion at least – sounded commendable.

I have ended up feeling that there are various bodies genuinely trying to help people with learning difficulties to obtain jobs. However, I suspect that the co-ordination between them is haphazard. The Government seems to be proposing that there should be co-operation between the whole range of local organisations, although I did not hear of any government money or effort to start schemes going. This proposed co-operation would presumably mean regular liaison between the county council and the local district councils; the Job Centres; the Chambers of Commerce and employers; and the educational services and the voluntary bodies. To persuade local groupings to work together is not always easy but perhaps more could be tried?

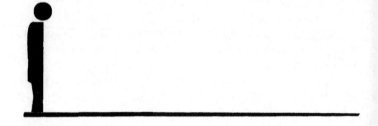

CHAPTER 10

If No Job,
What Do You Do?

If around 5%-15% of people with learning disabilities have a paid job, with some others having jobs with little or no wages; and with maybe a further 20%-35% unlikely to ever be able or want to undertake formal work, that still leaves a huge number who are unlikely to obtain work. What can they do? What do they do? How and who helps them fill the many unfilled hours? There are two types of support available: the first provided by Social Services, particularly with their Day Care Centres; and the second provided by the voluntary sector, some in straightforward ways and some in more unusual ways.

KCC's Learning Disability Department

The KCC's Rosemary Henn-Macrae's job as 'Lifespan Pathway Development Head' involves her in planning new ways to bridge the gulf between education and the outside world. The aim, therefore, is to "take away the cliff edge, particularly for those who are unlikely to find a job", as Rosemary puts it.

> "I have a team and we help via what we call the Lifespan Pathway Scheme. The maximum length of time for the team's help is three months but often it only needs three or four weeks. Sometimes it is just teaching someone how to go shopping by themselves or how to catch a bus or a train. Sometimes it is how the person can do their budgeting and cope with their money. It can be learning about cooking or housework so they can look after themselves more easily; or

it can be how to keep themselves healthy and safe. We sometimes help with how to get on a useful course at a college; and sometimes we help with introducing them to a group or a club where they can make friends. So, there's quite a range of things – all done to suit the one particular individual concerned."

One man who had learnt to go to the shops said how much he now liked to go to the Co-Op to buy the milk for his mum and then go to the café round the corner. Another said how much she enjoyed the walking group she had been recommended to join – not least because she had met her boyfriend there.

Day Care Centres

There are six Day Care Centres in the area, all run by staff directly employed by KCC. I visited two and talked in detail with a third. Some years ago, there were larger units but, after research, the KCC took the decision to make them more local. At the Edenbridge Day Centre – called Evolve – most of the regulars came from the town, with some able to walk or be helped to walk there. It is housed in a newly built Town Centre which, as well as Evolve, has a library, computing facilities for the public, a cafe, the Baptist Church, the local Citizens Advice Bureau and various halls/meeting rooms which can be hired. Evolve is open five days a week from 9am-5pm and has a staff of seven. They have nineteen registered "clients", as Nicki Martin, the Manager, calls them, knowing very well that the official term is "service users". For no apparent reason, the Edenbridge service users ("our people" say the staff) are more physically disabled than those at Sevenoaks or Tonbridge. When I visited, well over a half of the twelve people there were in wheelchairs. Only one or two were able to talk with me with any degree of fluency, although nearly all seem cheerful in a general sort of way. The newsletters from the first six months of the year gave a good idea of the range of activities that the staff provide. On some occasions only one, two or three people want to attend the arranged outing. On other occasions such as the party for the Queen's Birthday or a visit to a film or a local theatre, nearly everyone will go. There are regular dance and movement classes (popular). Twice a week there are cooking sessions with a calm and friendly cookery teacher. "I can only have two people at a time for safety reasons. We have a table which we can lower for people in wheelchairs. They seem to enjoy themselves, even if they can never really concentrate enough to finish off the job".

I watched a craft session – again the concentration could not be called 100% – but the men and women make wonderful pictures out of buttons, after Lynne, the art teacher, has drawn in the basic picture. The work from the craft sessions are sold on a Tombola Day, with the money earned being used to help to buy new children's toys for the Children's A&E Department at the Tunbridge Wells Hospital. The link with the Hospital is a two-way collaboration. Once a month, service users go to the Hospital to have various medical matters explained to them in a friendly, non-worrying way. Last month they learned about plaster casts. At the same time, Hospital staff learn to understand more about people with learning disabilities and how they would like to be treated – something which on occasions seems to be lacking in some hospitals if stories that I have been told are true. A good number of people attended a District Partnership Meeting (DPM in the jargon) for a Keeping Safe Event, which covered such things as bullying; and there was a special trip to the Cycle Park in Gravesend. (Evolve is unusual in having its own people carrier). However, with the financial cut-backs, the KCC cannot arrange transport to and from the Centre. This has to be arranged individually, with people either getting a lift, a bus or a taxi if they cannot walk to the centre.

The clients/service users with whom I talked were only occasionally able to express themselves in much detail. One very tall lady told me about her new flat and how Evolve people helped her go shopping. She mentioned her priest and agreed she was a Roman Catholic before striding off to do other things. A middle-aged man in his wheelchair lives in Paddock Wood with his mother, who, I learn from the helpers, does an amazing job in arranging a huge range of activities for her son. He only comes to Edenbridge once a week, accompanied by his carer. He cannot really speak but while I was with him he leafed through a magazine, looking rather vaguely at the photographs. One lady in a wheelchair, who again could not speak, made her overwhelming wishes quite clear. She wanted food – all the time. Then there were two sisters, both in wheelchairs, who sometimes kept together, sometimes spent half a minute with the craft teacher before 'driving off' to think about something else. One sister, however, was passionately keen on her <u>own</u> wheelchair, which she told me repeatedly was hers. One of the most mobile of the clients there, a slim, dark-haired young woman, walked purposely around the room as if on a mission to deliver a message Although she came up to me three or four times, neither I nor anyone else were ever told anything; nor did she seem to pause to listen to anyone. Another lady was officially making cakes – but <u>would</u> wander off. When I asked her if I could have one of her cakes, she understood, and led me to the tray of newly baked ones before saying she wanted to go out. I was not sure where she wanted to go. Another lady told me that Edenbridge was much nicer than Gillingham where people were not kind. However, by far the most lucid 'service user' there, as well as being the oldest, told me the story of her life, as she did a jigsaw puzzle with great speed. I learned about her upbringing with her parents and grandparents; about a local house, which I recognised from her description, where she had lived with other people and where they were allowed pets – she had a dog, a cat, a rabbit and a guinea pig – "and Sandra had a goldfish". She was very sad that she had been moved away from her friends and her pets into what the powers-that-be almost certainly felt was much more modern and civilised housing in the centre of Edenbridge. She was quietly analytical of all the others in the room – service users and staff – and the care that the service users received or – in her opinion – sometimes did not receive. And she gave me a lecture on hedgehogs which I thought she said were "bicine". Funny old lady, I thought. But I later looked it up. Although I could not find the word in Google's version of the large Oxford Dictionary, in a 1946 Dictionary, there it was "byssine" – fish or animals with prickles. She was quietly, really lovely – and I wish she still had her pet cat. The staff, most of whom I talked with only too briefly, were all caring, all patient and nearly all long serving. As often seems to be the case, a good number had started in the caring profession because of a family connection with someone who had learning problems.

The Sevenoaks day centre was again overseen by Nicki Martin, with around fifteen clients/service users and three/four staff. Their newsletters showed many of the same mix of activities. It is normally held in the Sevenoaks Leisure Centre but sometimes at outside venues. Because the service users/clients were relatively more able-bodied, they had gone to a good number of plays and films – "Suffragettes", "Dad's Army" and "Eddie the Eagle"; had seen "Annie" and "Carousel" at the local theatre; had classes on many things, recently including Emergency First Aid and Floristry. There was also a cheese tasting session (plus cakes) at a Farmers' Market which was very popular. But many other courses and activities were mentioned as available if individuals requested them. Indeed, talking with Ian Haylock, the KCC Manager of Day Services for the area, the list of activities and services that can be provided is enormous. It reads like a telephone directory. Arts and craft, baking, boccia (a kind of boules played seated), bowls, a cinema club, cooking, computer, dance, gardening, golf, gym sessions, horse riding and so on down to 'w' for walks (for different abilities). There is also a wide variety of indoor sports, including swimming. Some of the activities aim to enable people to become more independent, so that, for example, they can become better at using public transport or going shopping.

If a person who is on the learning disability list has other interests, they can tell their care manager who will make sure it is suitable for the individual and will then try to arrange some taster sessions, as well as the associated things like transport. If the service seems beneficial, a key worker will then be allocated who will support the individual to settle in and be the main point of contact. After three months, progress is formally reviewed to ensure that the service is useful and that the individual is happy. The centres also support people with more complex, serious needs such as sensory and visual impairment. Each person using the services will be supported to create their own 'Person Centred Plan' which provides a way of helping them look at all aspects of their life, ensuring that their preferences remain central to their own future.

I also made visits to the Riverside Day Centre in Tonbridge where I met Nikki Drewett, who managed the Day Services there. On the first visit, there were seven 'service users' and three staff. One of the staff had a complex sounding degree and was also associated with pastoral care at a local church but all the staff were knowledgeable as well as sympathetic. Some of the service users live with their parents, others at centres such as Pepenbury but the majority live in sheltered accommodation with two to seven others and with regular help as necessary.

The first service user with whom I talked – or, I have to admit, failed to talk with – had fairly severe Down's. She is probably in her twenties. (It always seems difficult to tell ages for people with Down's). She sat cross legged in an armchair. She was chattering away to herself with her head down. She chose not to join in the general conversation, so her only relationship to the rest of the room while I was there was to stand up. One of the carers, realising what she wanted, took her to the toilet. However, I gather that, on good days, she goes to the Scotts Project Day Centre and takes part in a variety of activities there. She has no family and lives in a house with three other ladies with support from carers. She comes to the day centre three days a week and, on good days, she enjoys going to the coffee morning at the local church, to ten pin bowling, and walking down for a social coffee in Tonbridge. She is making gradual progress towards being more independent and able to do more for herself. But she is still determined not to even try to get on a bus! Her great love is singing – but only when she wants to. (I was not honoured).

The next person I talked with is David. He is wonderful. He is in his fifties and has a 'mild' learning disability. He is partially sighted with a very long white cane. He reacts to what is being said with witty, enthusiastic comments. Until recently, he lived locally with his parents but now lives with three other men in supported living accommodation with staff help available. One of his great passions is Chinese food but he has lots of enthusiasms – his most recent being golf. He now has a free bus pass (which allows for a carer to go free too). He can read and write; likes to cook – and does the washing up. He goes to the gym; and is looking forward to going on holiday with the friends at his house – the first holiday he has ever taken without his parents. He and the others had enjoyed a trip to Leeds Castle, but when they went to Hastings, David thought the seagulls were getting more aggressive nowadays. He wants to try everything – although when his friends there tease him, he <u>nearly</u> draws a line at parachute jumping.

By contrast, another man is quiet until directly asked a question. He has Down's Syndrome, I guess is in his late forties, although, again, it is difficult to tell, and is a bit portly. After David's enthusiasms about golf, he says that he would like to try it, too, but suddenly mentions he likes snooker. He also goes to the local swimming pool, although he likes it to be hot. Tomorrow is his birthday and his family are giving him a party <u>with dancing</u>. (Big applause from the others).

Next I talk to a lady who sits knitting – a fairly basic stitch, I guessed. And a pile of finished squares of different colours is on the table. "We're going to help her put them together into a quilt", says the (graduate) carer with a laugh. The lady has moderate autism. She likes her own space. She did not look up during the general chat until I asked what she likes doing best. Even then, although everyone has cheerily prompted her into saying "knitting", it is the others who say she also does cooking, goes to the library, and they add she really likes the music sessions. Later it emerges that she is a wiz at the internet and prepares her own radio listings. She smiles gently when later I say good-bye.

Then I talk with a lady who is probably in her forties and also has autism. After a cheerful prompt, she announces with huge enthusiasm that she likes "cooking! On Wednesdays!" She agrees that she is really looking forward to going to the musical 'Annie' at the local theatre. Although quiet, she can write and read; and she enjoys looking through the Radio Times and other TV and radio listings. She also loves to spend time on the internet so she can look up things. A particularly popular session seems to be the Tuesday afternoon music which is taken by an ex-school teacher, Alison.

Another activity session which got a particular thumbs up were the visits to the cinema. Here, there emerged a change to the way the 'service users' are supported. Whereas a few years ago a group of eight or twelve would all be organised to go on a particular outing or to a particular film, now the aim is to get groups of three or four friends to choose what they would like to do and then to use public transport by themselves, where practical. "We have moved away from the large minibuses we used to have," says manager, Nikki. I felt that it did show a useful way forward to help get these people into mainstream life, where decisions are learnt about oneself, what one wants to do, who to do it with and how to do it. When one lady said that she had been on a normal bus for the first time, everyone cheered.

On another visit, this time to the specially refurbished premises, there were about fifteen service users, mostly with their carers. I was told that the number of service users had increased to up to twenty a day. The staff had also expanded from four to six. David was there again – still keen on his Monday golf to which he walks by the river with his carer and his extremely long white stick. He also goes all the way to Maidstone for bowling as well as to the local cinema, to a monthly disco at the '6 in 1 Club'. Several attendees are particularly keen on the Friday swimming, where "we get an ice cream after – that's nice". There were two interesting women I met for the first time. Joanna Nelson and Ann French. Joanna explained that she was born with Williams Syndrome[79] and that her parents, who live locally, had started The Williams Syndrome charity. "We're quite famous," she says. She now lives with three other women and likes going into town with its shops and just to be able to walk around. "I do all my own washing and lots of cooking. I did paella here the other day but I can choose what I want to cook." She goes on the Friday swimming trips and is proud that recently she did thirteen sponsored lengths in aid of the Williams Syndrome Foundation. She also explains how she copes when she gets stressed – her friends are wonderful then. Ann is autistic but extremely chatty. She has been married for twelve years and her passion is painting – an artistic trait that she has inherited from her mother who embroiders exceptionally beautiful woodland scenes in silk thread. Ann, however, paints still-lifes in acrylics.

The Centre has had parties at Halloween, Christmas and St Valentine's Day and they have coffee mornings where they raise money for Macmillan Cancer Support. They had a talk and discussion about the importance of hand washing; and a community police officer came for a chat. They participated with the local community in making a large patchwork which toured the area. What cheered me in particular was the mention of how they were known as individuals by people they met regularly. There is a mobile coffee shop where they all are chatted to and, at the Friday swimming, the staff there know the Riverside people by name. This kind of welcome from the 'outside world' is by no means universal. However, the most moving moments of my visit came when I overheard one of the carers discussing the sadness of one of the service users. She had just split up with her boyfriend. I do not want to give more details but it was a very caring conversation between two really nice people.

Helen's Story – Down's. Helen was born in 1991, the oldest of four children. To say that she is a Down's sufferer or suffers from Down's syndrome is completely wrong. She may have Down's but she is very happy with her life, lived mainly at home. Equally, her family totally love her. When I asked if anything was bad about having Down's, she said 'not really' – although it did emerge later that she does not like gardening or even getting her hands dirty. She is certainly not keen on the great outdoors. She seems to have an almost photographic memory. She remembers the birthdays of everyone in the family and most of the family friends. She can also remember every word of the many Disney movies which she particularly likes. One of her favourite books is Yellow Pages which she can leaf through happily as she watches television. "I found you a plumber, didn't I Dad?" She used to do gardening both at the Scotts Project and at Bore Place near Sevenoaks but her dislike of getting dirty meant that she has managed to get out of it – albeit with her usual smiley charm.

Her great passion is drama about which she has been keen since she was eight or nine. "She loves being in the spotlight", says her mother. "She's a colossal show-off," says her father. Helen laughs and agrees with both descriptions. Currently, she goes to the Oast Theatre in Tonbridge every Saturday afternoon as part of the River Drama scheme. There are three age groups there and Helen is in the Academy Group, busy rehearsing for 'Guys and Dolls'. "Last year we did 'West Side Story'".

As well as the much praised main organisers at the theatre and a rota of four tutors, there are lots of volunteers, including girls from Tonbridge Girls' Grammar School and boys from Tonbridge School and Judd School. Most of them are helping as part of the Duke of Edinburgh Awards Scheme but quite a number get addicted and stay on. Helen also does drama at the Scotts Project where she goes two days a week. They are preparing for 'Matilda'. On Wednesday mornings, she helps in the Scotts Project's café – sometimes in the kitchens and sometimes serving coffee and cake.

On Wednesday afternoons at the Scotts Project, Helen is doing some journalism which she likes. She is currently writing an article for the Scotts's Newsletter. "I'm typing it out on my computer". At the River Drama group Helen met her boyfriend, Ian. "He's not my boyfriend. He's my fiancé," corrects Helen. Ian lives at a house for people with Down's twenty miles away, started by a lady who has decided to convert her home in order to help. The residents – six at the moment, but in the process of being expanded – get speech and language help.

Helen has her own social worker, Janice, who has been suggesting that Helen needs to learn more 'life skills' – about shopping, money, cooking and more practical things. Her parents agree. Helen is only partially convinced so far but she has been round Lidl as a start under a new Kent County Council scheme which will aim to give her more practical skills and get her out more into the community. One of the first advances has been Helen being brave and learning to travel by herself to Tonbridge on the train. Initially, she was shown what to do – how to buy a ticket and where to go and so on. Recently, for the first time, she went alone – although there was someone secretly following her. "I didn't know", says Helen. But it is another step along the road. "Are you ever sad?" Helen is asked by her mother. "No", says Helen. "What's the best thing about having Downs?" "Having funny feet", says Helen – showing them. But no one is quite sure why and she just laughs when we ask.

Helen's mother teaches in a primary school nearby. Since having Helen, she has made a point of talking to other parents who have a child with Down's – telling them the pleasures of having a deeply loving boy or girl with their own character, their own likes and dislikes as well as the very hard work which it will mean for them – the parents – over the next twenty or thirty years. Helen's father works from home in order to cope. Helen's mother adds: "Helen is very lucky to live in a village – rather than a town. She confidently walks to the village shop for things and will chat with the ladies there. She also regularly uses the hairdressers in the village, going there by herself. She is known and everyone is so good at looking out for her. As parents, we feel reassured and confident that, should she get into any difficulties, a resident of the village will help her and see her home. Thank you everyone". After I originally talked with Helen, there was a major event in her life. She became a TV actress – something she had worked so hard to achieve. She appeared in the BBC's 'Call The Midwife.' Quite naturally, she became a star within the learning disability grouping locally.

Other Things to do Arranged by Charities and Voluntary Bodies

In addition to seven council-run day centres, there are other similar centres within some of the residential hubs – for example, at Pepenbury and the Scotts Project. However, there is also a wide range of constructive things for people with learning disabilities to do which are run by various charities and outside groups. They are often started and run by volunteers – usually given only expenses or very minimal wages. Very often, the passion and commitment that they give is because of personal experience – their son or daughter or a close friend had a learning disability. The examples of organisations which follow are only those with whom I have talked. I know that there are many others which, I am sure, are good; but these examples give a flavour of the kind of things that can be available.

Edenbridge Friendz is run by a totally dedicated volunteer, Pauline Collins. Although originally part of MENCAP, the national paperwork became so onerous for the Edenbridge group – and other local groups – that they now have a new name and a new structure. (They never received funding from the national charity anyway.) Her main activity is based around the large and active 'Wednesday Club'. Its forty to fifty members meet each week at the nearby residential care home for the disabled, *hft* – 'Home Farm Trust'. There are themed evenings – bingo, quiz nights, musical evenings and so on – and Pauline and her other main helper take it in turns to bake one or two birthday cakes each week – it is nearly always someone's birthday. They have their own minibus – the money had to be fought for – and they have a fair number of other volunteers, who drive the Club members to events. There is a monthly outing

– whether it is just to a nearby pub or further afield to Brighton, Howletts Zoo or the Romney, Hythe and Dymchurch Railway.

Christmas celebrations are a big event. "At one stage we thought having a Father Christmas might be a bit childish", says Pauline. "But there were strong protests: so he still arrives every year. It also means that every year I have to go and buy seventy presents – all under £3 each and all of which have to be chosen for each individual whom we have got to know and cherish". The indefatigable Pauline – who has a disabled son of her own – also arranges to take a group of her Club members – usually around a dozen – to swim at the Edenbridge Leisure Centre on Friday evenings – which, to the Centre's regret, has to charge them £50 a night – yet another thing for which the Edenbridge Friendz has to find the money. Like with so many charities, it is the money and the need for more volunteers that worry Pauline most.

Another charity with which I talked – Kent Friendz – had a very different feel. It was partly because of the work that it is commissioned to do and partly the way it was – purposely – set up to run as a business. Its Chief Executive, Chris Burton, is a former businessman. When we met, he made it clear that his aim was to provide specific, detailed services of the highest standard for which the charity would be paid a realistic sum – which in turn would ensure the quality. He is primarily commissioned by KCC to provide specially tailored help (although he is forceful enough to also obtain money from the local District Council, the National Lottery and Children in Need). At any one time, they cater for around three hundred 'service users' with learning difficulties, half of whom are children and half of whom are adults. They have three year-round clubs for children – 'Kidz' for eight to thirteen year olds; 'Teenz' for fourteen to seventeen year olds; and 'Starz' for disabled children with behavioural problems. There are also weekend and school holiday clubs and outings to a wide variety of places of entertainment, driven in Kent Friendz' own transport. Adults have two clubs of their own, one for younger and one for older 'service users'. Special help can be provided individually either at an outside location or at home. They have nine full-time staff and a further fifty staff specially trained for specific tasks. Kent Friendz also has a 24 hour helpline for emergencies. If they are asked – usually by KCC

– to provide help to an individual where perhaps they have no specialist experience, they will send people on a training course – and charge for it. I talked with a number of families where Kent Friendz had provided support. All were full of praise for the way the staff cared in a professional but individual way.

Although Sevenoaks MENCAP is nominally linked with the national charity, once again all its work and its money-raising is local. Athene Fenn, who runs the group, says her own main role is to listen sympathetically to people's problems and try to advise, based in part on her family's experiences. However, the local charity does more than give valued advice. They run a club each Friday in their own hall. There is a drama group which is normally attended by a dozen people; and they have a "Big Sing" event each December. Mrs Fenn makes the much heard plea – "we badly need more volunteer helpers".

The Woodhouse Centre in Oxted, Surrey, is another example of how one person, supported by excellent volunteers and the community can make a difference. When I go to their workshop, it is like entering an active Women's Institute – except there are men too. The Centre is situated in the middle of the town and presided over by Mrs Sue Graham. The Centre helps a variety of people with ages from twenty-four to ninety-four. There are fifty or sixty regulars, with over seventy on their books. Some just need company. "I've got elderly regulars who probably would not get out of their houses if they didn't come here," says Sue. "Probably a dozen have what you'd call learning difficulties. But everyone mixes in together. We find a range of practical things that some or all can do. We do rug weaving and chair caning and we have a group that makes poppies all the year round for the Poppy Appeal. At present, we are in the middle of getting ready for a big pre-Christmas meal for sixty or seventy." The Centre certainly fills a need in the area: but, as so often, its funding never seems secure.

The YMCA in Tonbridge is another body that helps a variety of local individuals who have learning disabilities, some in a straightforward way and others in more unexpected ways. Rob Marsh, the Chief Executive, talks about the 'surgeries' he holds. Recently, he had been helping a couple with learning difficulties who have a seven year old son. Because they would have difficulty in coping with him, the son lives with his grandmother. However, the mother wants to learn to read so she can participate more in his upbringing. Rob is arranging it. Currently, he also finds himself arranging anger management courses for some autistic people who admit that they have a problem; and sometimes just giving advice to learning disabled people on how to deal with the numerous authorities who have to be cajoled into giving appropriate help.

I have also heard of useful and friendly support given by various local churches to those with learning and mental health problems.

Sporting Activities. A good number of sports are available for those with learning disabilities, although most have to have a carer to accompany them. Some sports are based in mainstream sports facilities; and some are run by charities – the best-known being probably Riding for the Disabled, with over five hundred groups nationally. There are at least two specialist stables in the area – one used by people at Pepenbury and one at Bradbourne in Sevenoaks – which help 'service users' to try riding. I talked with the people at Bradbourne. Their Chairman, Peter Felgate, has been helping people with disabilities to learn to ride since even before the start of Riding for the Disabled. There are a dedicated team of instructors and a large number of volunteers. Other sports include swimming which is provided in a number of places. The Sevenoaks Pool has been trialling several schemes which may be able to provide one-to-one care. And one lady with learning disability had been enrolled in a public aqua-fit class. It seemed to work well initially but when she wanted to go to the toilet, the others in the class had to help – which they did willingly but staff felt was not safe. When I last heard, the staff were working towards a more organised solution. Ten pin bowling was also mentioned as something that can be enjoyable and I also heard about a group at Maidstone Football Club who quite clearly were providing hugely enjoyable sessions for those with learning disabilities. As so often, managers of facilities seemed willing to be pro-active when approached. They understand the problems and aim to find ways of helping. What became increasingly apparent is the number of parents or groups of parents who have initially gone into battle to help their own child or children but have gone on to help other parents and children with similar problems.

I came across some tennis training. It was all slightly eccentric and English but it also seemed to be very pleasurable and constructive. It was a small charity called RASCALS (Racket Sports for Children with Special Needs) which had been formed in 1991 by Mrs 'Chuck' Lugg who was the Secretary of her local tennis club. When her granddaughter was born with cerebral palsy, Mrs Lugg decided that she would set up a charity which encouraged children with learning difficulties to try tennis and, later, squash and badminton – in part to give them an enjoyable extra thing to do but more particularly to help them with exercise. The first school she talked with was the Clifton Hill School for children with learning difficulties in Caterham, Surrey. She started with some ten to twelve year olds who seemed to enjoy themselves; and within two to three weeks the teachers said that they had seen an improvement in the children's general co-ordination. The charity has now expanded into three counties and has been helping schools with children of various ages and with different degrees of difficulty. In the meantime, Mrs Lugg's granddaughter went to a 'normal' school in Tunbridge Wells and, now in her twenties, lives a happy life in a sheltered bungalow in Bognor with five other people who have learning difficulties.

The Odeon Cinema. I was cheered by the Odeon cinema chain. For reasons that no one at the Odeon's headquarters could explain or remember, some years ago the group had started special showings of films for people with learning difficulties. It happens one Sunday afternoon a month. It has films which they know will appeal – Disney, Toy Story, Lego, Batman, Sing, etc. They lower the sound level, avoiding loud noises and leave the lights partially on. The management do not worry if someone gets up and shouts a bit or wanders around – and no one else seems concerned. The cinema showings are extremely popular – they regularly have a hundred people – and it is also a chance for people to get together on a social basis. One regular told me, "It's only three pounds AND you get a biscuit with your tea. I go there with two friends – all together. It's very good."

Charities which Collect Funds. KHOCA is different. It is a charity which concentrates solely on raising money for people with learning difficulties and then, after careful scrutiny, distributing grants for specific projects. It was started over thirty years ago by parents who had personal experience of such problems and its splendidly upper-class committees (it seems to be ladies only when I have met them) have raised many hundreds of thousands of pounds by attracting the upper middle class to Christmas Fairs and Balls at castles and stately homes; and arranging Open Gardens, Bridge and Golf Events. Although Kent-wide, it has been active in helping Pepenbury, the Scotts Project, a group called Upz and Downs, and other learning disability groups locally. However, the same old plea – more volunteers needed.

One KCC staff member also mentioned that the Lions Club in Tonbridge was another group which, rather than physically helping people with learning problems, collects money and give it to specific projects which others organise. I suspect that other similar types of groupings, which raise funds, also consider people with Learning Disabilities.

Citizens Advice Bureaux (CABs). The various Citizens Advice Bureaus help in yet another way. There are four within the area – Sevenoaks, Edenbridge, Tonbridge and Tunbridge Wells. Nowadays CABs get no government funding and often decreasing funds from local councils – surely a false economy. As with nearly all CABs, the majority of the staff are volunteers but each have or acquire specialist knowledge of a specific topic. All the CABs with whom I talked had a person who was a specialist – to a certain but useful extent – in learning disabilities. The most frequent request was for help with government forms.

> As the Manager of one CAB said, "Often it is not how disabled the person is but the answers they give to questions which are not clear. So, a question will be 'can you walk fifteen yards?'. They say 'yes'. But, in reality, it should often be 'but only once a day with a helper and a frame.' But that does not get taken into account. The form filling can make them really anxious – even without thinking about the loss of the Allowance. So, many people do need tutoring in how to fill in the forms to reflect how disabled they really are. Then there are further complexities if they get into the

dispute procedures, which end up with a tribunal. And then, there are massive delays. It can be very complex. And very distressing."

I met one man and his parents who were full of praise for the Tonbridge CAB which had gone into battle to help them about the Disability Living Allowance which had been stopped – without any notice or explanation. Eventually, the Allowance was restored and a (grudging) apology was received from the Ministry of Work and Pensions. Another example: for some time, the Edenbridge CAB has been helping a mother who has a daughter with mild but definite learning disabilities. The daughter lives at home and the mother has found it difficult to cope. The mother has not only the complexities of dealing with how best to help her daughter but the stress compounded by money worries and the problems of dealing with the various authorities and filling in all their forms So, the CAB has spent a good deal of time in helping her – as well as helping the daughter. The particular CAB Manager is especially understanding about such cases having had a child whose problems included learning difficulties.

Other Resources. There are many other voluntary groups and charities and churches locally which all provide practical help and advice. I am sorry that I have not been able to list them all. I think that a full directory of all the resources available could be compiled and put on the web. Maybe it is but I have not found it and no one has mentioned one.

CHAPTER 11

The Strain on Parents: and Respite Care

The Pressure on Families: and Divorce

As will have become clear, families who have a child with learning disabilities or difficulties of any sort face enormous strains. It is not just part-time stress. It is often eighteen or even twenty-four hours a day – almost unimaginable until one talks with individual parents. Their lives are dominated by this one particular child – even if there are other children, although it should be said that I have never talked with or heard about a sibling who has felt ignored or who has not been astoundingly kind and supportive of the brother or sister with problems. Many parents are unwilling to talk about the strain. They feel that, in some way, it will seem critical of their child or to show a lack of love by them for their child. Some even feel guilty. I thought that one article from a magazine[80] outlined the reality. So, I am quoting extracts.

"Forty-two years of pain. [After a difficult birth], I realised something was wrong. A specialist told us that our son John's brain had been damaged ... We had to visit the hospital every week for check-ups ... We endured glares and comments from the public as he became noticeably disabled in his behaviour, while still looking normal. We got up one morning to find that he had daubed faeces all over his room – even on his clothes, which he had promptly put away in the drawers, soiling everything else in there, too. Once he threw a lighter on an open fire which caused an almighty boom. But it was always hard to be angry, especially as John would be dancing and giggling. For my husband and me, there was the perpetual despair as our lives disappeared due to the incessant demands on us. By the time John was fourteen, we could no longer cope. [He went to a special school]. Now forty-two, he is in permanent care [although] recently he was found to have been suffering institutional abuse over the last five years . . . I love John dearly, but sometimes I hanker after a life where he might have been 'normal' . . ."

I remembered, too, Liz Astor's book 'Loving Olivia', where Liz Astor had analysed ten years of almost constant day-by-day, hour-by-hour strain. In spite of her seemingly almost superhuman determination, her ability to afford a nanny and an extra teaching assistant at school, together with her connections which enabled her to consult the most famous experts in the world: despite of all this, she eventually collapsed under the pressure with what someone told her was called 'carer's fatigue'.[81] With support from the family and friends and her own determination to look at new ways forward, she recovered. However, the strain on parents with autistic or disabled children with any type of physical or mental disability can hardly be imagined.

The length of time each day that a child and then, later in life, an adult with learning difficulties needs supervision is a common theme from the mothers and fathers. Regardless of the help provided by schools or colleges; or by day centres and the numerous occupations provided by the KCC and voluntary groups, there are a huge number of hours each day when a parent and/or a carer have to look after the person with the disability. With one parent I had worked out the actual number of hours per week, even in a school term when the wife (and less often the husband) were responsible for the child who, at any moment, could do something which harmed him or ruined something in the house. Out of the one hundred and sixty hours each week, school, including the travel, took up around forty hours. If a further fifty to sixty hours is allowed for sleep (although sleep is often short and random for children with learning disabilities), and around ten hours a week, if one is lucky for support workers taking the child on outside visits, it leaves probably around seventy hours a week in school–term time or one hundred and ten hours a week in school holidays when full-time care is needed. The latter can mean around twelve hours a day or more when the parents are 'on duty'. The parents do not complain; but it is a statement of the time and energy which the parents have to give, hour after hour and day after day, over what can become much of a lifetime. The strain not only on the parents but on people with learning disabilities themselves is enormous. Work by Professor Sir Baron-Cohen's Centre for Autism Research in Cambridge found that two thirds of the autistic people with whom they worked had at one stage felt that they wished to commit suicide.

A good number of people have mentioned (and received wisdom seems to say) that the strain leads to marital break-up, usually with the mother being the one left coping. I did not meet many divorced parents but one of those with whom I did discuss the difficulty was, in fact, a father who had been left in charge. It involved help from the grandparents for many hours each week until, eventually, the father and the elderly granny could not cope and an au pair was taken on.

Dan's Story: moderately severe autism. Another father did talk about the complications of his life over a twenty year period.

To get divorced after twelve years of marriage must be bad enough; to get divorced when you, as a father, have an autistic son you love but are only allowed to see once a month must be much worse; and if, after a further ten years, you are sure the son is not being helped in the right way, it must be really grim. To give full details of this particular story is inappropriate. However, in this case, the son, Dan, was diagnosed as having moderately severe autism at one and a half. For the next ten years, the parents ploughed their way through the massive bureaucracy and the time needed to cope with Dan, although they ended up pleased with the special school Dan attended, where he was much cherished and which he greatly enjoyed. However, there was always a danger that Dan could become so frustrated or so frightened by things he was not used to that he was often on the edge of being violent. The father worked out his own way to defuse these situations. "I didn't know much about autism to start with but, eventually, when I could see he was upset, I taught him to make his hands into great big claws and roar and roar. It's a bit noisy but it stops him hitting people." Yet the strain had told on the parents and it had led to the divorce.

The father was granted very occasional visiting rights and now wishes that he had made a case for much greater access more strongly at the time. His job has taken him far from the district, yet he comes back to visit on every occasion he can. He is very concerned about his son, who is now twenty-three. He feels that his ex-wife is making no effort to help Dan learn to live in the wider world. Dan apparently does not ever go to a day centre and apparently hardly leaves the house. I have not talked to the wife or to Dan, let alone the Social Services, but it does sound a sad story.

It was made even sadder when the father gave me more details. Over the last year or so, he had been trying to get his son out to the shops and to the cinema – not least so that Dan can become less frightened of people. There was a big break through when Dan bought a cheeseburger by himself. However, on a couple of occasions recently, father and son have been to the Bluewater Centre. On both occasions, teenage boys have jeered at the son – to the son's distress and to the fury of the father. Another worry is that the son is very frightened of dogs, particularly if they are not on a lead and they might come close to him. When they are out, the father looks ahead all the time, ready to take action. Recently, he saw a woman with a dog running loose and he went on ahead to ask whether, just for a few yards, the dog could be put on a lead – explaining his autistic son's fears. The woman refused, saying that it was a public footpath. The father wishes people were less prejudiced. He has changed jobs and now works in a care home, even if it is still rather far away, because he feels he is helping people with problems similar to his son's. Ideally, he would like his son to come and live with him.

Respite Care

Obviously, the KCC and all the experts, including the care managers allocated to each person with a learning disability, know about the pressures – both on the child or adult with learning difficulties and on the carers, and most often the parents. They, therefore, have a system of what used to be called 'Respite Care', although the name is being changed, apparently being thought less likely to upset the parents, to the 'Short Breaks Overnight Service'. I went to see both the local respite care home for children and the adult respite care home. Needless to say, the requests for respite care far exceed the availability and the criteria for receiving help has to be fairly tough. However, both services seem much appreciated by those who use them.

Sunrise Children's Centre

When the parents of a child with learning disabilities become registered with the County Council, the child's care manager will assess, amongst many other things, the need for respite care. If the recommendation is 'yes', a number of days a year of respite help is allocated. The average is about twenty-four days a year. The parents and their care manager then start liaising with the Short Break Overnight Service. For the local area, the help for the young is provided by the Sunrise Children's Centre on the Green at Southborough, which was purpose-built twelve years ago with six bedrooms. (There are four other children centres in different parts of Kent).

Initially, the parents are invited to a coffee morning to talk with Jolene Hobden – normally called Jo – the acting manager and her staff. Then the paperwork starts. Forty pages are put together with the co-operation of the parents. The resulting document may look vast but virtually every line provides practical knowledge about the child which will make their stay enjoyable, constructive and safe. Jo will then liaise with the child's school. Next the parents, this time accompanied by the child, have an afternoon tea visit. Once the forty page care plan is adopted and signed off by the parents, the child will have a few daytime visits – including weekends – before coming direct from school, having a dinner there and then being collected by the parents at 6.30pm. Only after the child has got to know Sunrise and its staff, and the staff have got to know the child, will there be the first one night stay, followed by a further meeting with the parents. Then, once the system is seen to be working, Jo and the parents start planning dates for the longer term. Some parents – the majority – request two or three night stays; others ask for five, six or seven days. Bearing in mind the Centre is open twenty-four hours every day of the year, except Christmas Day, this scheduling of the rooms and staff is complex in the extreme, not least because if a child has very severe difficulties, either mental or physical, it may mean that he or she will be the only visitor at the Centre. Alternatively, if there are several children who are relatively able, four or five can be accommodated at the same time. As a result of all these complexities, every six months Jo has to closet herself in her office for a whole week, doing nothing other than plan the stays for the next period. Currently, she has fifty-eight children on her books. They are mainly between seven and eighteen – plus a waiting list. Each child will average around eight to ten visits a year. During the weekday visits, the children will request a variety of activities that they would like to do – depending not only on their preferences but also on safety and their physical abilities. They may play in the garden or in the soft-play area inside the Centre. They may go to the local park or have a go in the Centre's own jacuzzi. There is a specially adapted kitchen where the children can help or actually make food for themselves – carefully supervised. There is also a special sensory room where, as needed, a child can go to relax. And, of course, they can just sag in front of the television or a computer in the special computer room. At weekends, there are numerous additional possibilities, including longer daytime trips. There is also a 'Pat Dog' scheme when a lady specialist brings a trained dog to the Centre – which is much appreciated by the children. To look after all this activity, Jo has around fifteen part-time but regular care staff who are on a four week cycle. The aim is always to have 1:1 care. Every parent is asked to fill in an assessment questionnaire each year to see whether the visits were a success and to make suggestions. There is also a formal, annual inspection by Ofsted – which lasts for two days, with a further interim one. Neither is announced beforehand. It was good to hear that the Ofsted rating for Sunrise was 'Outstanding'.

Hedgerows Adult Respite Care

I also visited the Adult Short Break Overnight Unit, 'Hedgerows', which takes a variety of adult 'service users', although, as Jane Bolton, the lady in charge says, "we try never to use the term, always just calling them by their first name (you can't call them Christian names anymore!), although we'd call them Mr Brown or Mrs Jones if they wanted."

As each person leaves, they are encouraged to fill in a questionnaire. (Some are unable to do so). I looked at the last year of monthly summaries and the visitors are almost all extremely enthusiastic and the individual comments that I read are practical. Only one out of the hundred or so comments I read said anything, even mildly negative. "My stay was OK but I would rather be at home". Virtually all the others scored their stay as ten out of ten and one added "I would tell mother if I was sad". The visitors are all keen to arrange their next stay.

What is Hedgerows like? And what about the staff and staffing numbers? The building is two ex-police houses, well converted, and there is a large garden. It is in a largish village, on the main road, near buses, village shops and the station so there are various things to do within walking distance as well as further afield. There is also a mini-bus for outings when and if the residents/service users want. (The day after I visited, one of the carers had taken two men to Brands Hatch motor cycling). Other visits – where the residents are physically capable – include bowling, trips to a funfair, the seaside and to the larger local towns for shopping. A lady in her late forties was taken to Dymchurch where she watched others on the small gauge railway. One of the staff explains. "At first when I asked her whether she would like to go on the little train for a ride, she said 'no'. But a bit later she changed her mind and loved the experience. She said she had never been on such a fun ride before."

There are five bedrooms – one downstairs with an en-suite disabled bathroom. So, in theory, there can be five people to stay at any one time: but the number will depend on the severity of each of the visitors' physical and mental difficulties. Everyone will be very carefully assessed beforehand, including an interview at the Unit with the parent/home carer there as well. If there are four or five people with only a moderate disability who all want to come at the same time, this is possible. On the other hand, if there is a person with severe, multiple problems, then they may be there by themselves, with all six of the unit's staff being needed to look after the one person. However, in fact, once risk assessments and support plans are completed, they give staff a good knowledge of how to reduce any 'concerning behaviours' during the holiday. Stays are usually Monday to Friday or Friday to Monday; and how many days the person comes in a year is dependent on the assessment made by their care manager. In the course of a normal month, the unit has about twenty visitors.

The five staff under the guidance of Jane Bolton are proud of the way they look after their visitors and the way in which the team works together. I met them while they waited for their next visitors to arrive. All are very experienced in the work and three have been at the unit for many years. I hear about how they look after their visitors as individuals.

"We have one lady who comes to the kitchen to what she calls cook the meal. Really all she does is give a saucepan a stir but she feels she has cooked or helped cook the meal which is the important thing. The staff and the visitor or visitors all eat together and it's usually very jolly. We have some who love to watch TV; some who potter in the garden; some who don't like either. There are some who really want to go shopping and some who want to go on a special day trip – so to Hastings, or the zoo, or swimming, and so on. We try to give everyone what they want. We get to know our regulars who perhaps come here three or four times a year and we get to know the parents or relatives, too. Life must be quite a strain for them. They have been living with the person for twenty-four hours a day for years but we hope we give them a break. They all seem very happy with what we offer. We feel that it is a big advantage to be a small unit, so that all our visitors, our clients, our service users or whatever we have to call them nowadays, can be looked after as individuals. We don't have set routines but – assuming Health and Safety allow it! – we try to fit in things that people find are fun for them. We had beef gravy with fish last night!"

Because of funding cuts – which the staff understand – they do not have a maintenance man anymore. So, the staff have been mending and painting a medicine cabinet, doing the gardening and lots of other odd jobs – not because they have to; but just because they want to make Hedgerows as near as possible to a perfect home and a holiday all in one. The evaluation forms seem to prove they succeed. One elderly couple explained that they were happy to have a little time without the everyday strain of watching over their grown up Down's son and even happier that he enjoyed himself so much when he went to Hedgerows. The father summarises: "Over the years, we have arranged that our son is doing things every single day from 9.30 in the morning to mid-afternoon. That's weekdays. So that's probably twenty to twenty-five hours a week. But we really have to look after him around a hundred hours a week. So, it takes up a lot of our life – although obviously we don't mind because we love him. The care managers, who have normally been excellent and come to see us regularly, agreed some time ago that we could have respite care for our son – twenty-eight days a year which is supposed to be the maximum. But recently, they have increased it to thirty-one days because we can't be so active nowadays. It's a great service."

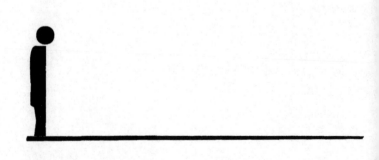

CHAPTER 12

Bullying and Friendship; Sex, Love and Marriage

Bullying and Isolation

Even before I started writing this book, I had heard that people with learning disabilities were often abused or bullied. As I gathered material, I came across very distressing examples and I was reminded of how thin the skin of civilisation is. A favourite poem of my father came to mind.

> *I wish I loved the Human Race;*
> *I wish I loved its silly face;*
> *I wish I liked the way it walks;*
> *I wish I liked the way it talks;*
> *And when I'm introduced to one,*
> *I wish I thought 'What Jolly Fun'.*

The poem by Sir Walter Raleigh (the Victorian one, not Queen Elizabeth I's one) expresses despair not only at mankind's wars and atrocities, but the hurt that can appear in any street. Various reports confirmed the situation. "Disability Hate Crime" which came out in October 2017,[82] said that the situation seems to be getting worse (a rise of 25%); that fear of hostility prevents a third of people with a disability from leaving their homes; and that 30% of people with learning disabilities have had bad experiences. It was not just _fear_ of crime. 18% said that they had been the victims of actual crime but it was the sheer nastiness that they had to endure, which hurt them. This bullying even extended to on-line abuse of disabled people, including children. In March 2021, it was reported that the number of disability-related hate-crime incidents on trains had increased by 24% between 2016 and 2019[83]. The Home Office confirmed the general trends; and Sussex University has suggested tougher laws and better enforcement were needed.

To look first at the situation faced by children. I did not hear much about any physical bullying or picking on boys or girls with special educational needs which was very much worse than the general name-calling or back biting that occurs in many playgrounds. I was told by some people that, in general, the situation has greatly improved in the last thirty to forty years. However, I suspect that it is a reduction in the more obvious physical bullying. In spite of this seeming improvement, 60% of children with autism recently reported being called names because they were seen as different. It was not surprising to learn from the Orpheus Centre that "many of our students have already faced discrimination or bullying as a result of their disability when they join us." It seems to occur even where heads, teachers and playground assistants make great efforts to avoid it. Indeed, all the head teachers with whom I talked were adamant that they will not tolerate any kind of bullying and particularly not the bullying of someone with a learning disability.

However, there is a further aspect in the lives of children with learning disabilities or special educational needs. It is that the child is ignored – isolated and left out of the simple social activities in the school. Furthermore, outside school hours a child can also feel very lonely. I suspect that, nowadays, even if physical bullying does not occur on a day-to-day basis and name calling is perhaps less than in the past, children with learning disabilities find themselves isolated in a way which is different to the teasing of a girl with red hair or a boy who is fat or wearing glasses. The sense of frustration and sometimes outright anger, which some children with learning disabilities sometimes show, is perhaps not surprising.

One story – of many – illustrated the problem of isolation. I met a young woman several times. With me, she was friendly and clear, if a little different in her speech. However, I learnt that she can feel frustrated, particularly if she feels she is being criticised. She had a slightly abrupt way of talking but the fact that she was mildly autistic was not obvious. She had been to a boarding school, where her slightly different looks and the fact that she was a year or so behind on the school work, did not stop her from being 'accepted'.

They were all in it together and she did not feel excluded. It was probably like being in the Army: everyone – however different – gets on with everyone because they are stuck with it – together. However, later in her teens, she went to a further education college. Most of the others on her course had been to the same local schools, talked with the same accent; went to have their nails painted at the same nail bar; watched the same videos; and communicated all the time with each other via Snapchat, Instagram and Facebook. The new girl was different. She was never bullied or called names. She was just ignored. It was not a happy time, although now, two years later, her life is going well.

Earlier in the book, I have described a number of other children both at primary and secondary school who have felt and actually were left out. Perhaps being called names or being left out is not something about which you tell your parents or your teachers. One boy had been very dyslexic and had been rather small until he was fourteen. He had never told his parents or the school that he was being bullied, had been missed out of groups and been called names. He was growing up with a fierce rage which could and did explode. He hated authority: but the one teacher did help. More importantly, he became an outstanding athlete and could run rings round boys three or four years older than himself; and he got himself noticed nationally. In the course of a year, he became a school hero; and his character totally changed. He was still dyslexic but he was now part of the normal world and a cheerful and relaxed teenager. However, not all children who 'learn differently' will have a similar way out and I was particularly pleased when I heard of the active steps being taken to have the problems of various learning disabilities explained to the other school children. At many of the schools where I talked with teachers, there were policies to make the pupils better understand those who were a bit different.

Naoki Higashida, the Japanese boy, the author of 'The Reason I Jump' and 'Fall Down 7 Times, Get up 8', summed up the basic problem in the latter book. "Because children with autism are poor at interacting with others, many of them have next to no friends and some get teased or bullied ... People with no experience of being bullied have no idea how miserable it is to grow up being picked on the whole time."[84]

David Mitchell, the well-known novelist, who worked on Naoki's translation and who has an autistic son, added his own plea for the outside world to be more understanding.

> "When I see a stranger showing a little act of kindness towards my son, it makes me tearful. A woman on a Thames boat trip let him play with her hair: I immediately went into anxious 'dadsplaining' mode and started to apologise, but she chatted quite happily to him." However, David Mitchell realises that this will probably not happen as his son grows up. "A cute boy is an easy sell; a 19 year old with little concept of personal boundaries, less so . . . but whatever my wife and I go through, we have to remember it's not easy being him and it never will be. It would make all the difference if the rest of the world recognised that too."[85]

I asked a good number of teachers about possible solutions, particularly about the difficulties of inclusion. Several said that their school, understanding the problem, had started out of hours clubs "aimed particularly at computer and IT geeks – which included a good number of boys, and occasionally girls, who are autistic or who clearly have Aspergers." A teacher at one of the further education colleges said that she had personally never seen or heard of an instance of actual bullying but she knew the problems of isolation and loneliness. She felt that being part of a large college meant that there were groups which a person who was on the spectrum could join. But she agreed that she had no easy answers except to look at each of their students as individuals and to try to help them. Often they became friends with someone in the college who was similar. But equally often, they did not. Other teachers agreed that there were no easy answers. "We keep a close eye on any child who is being left out of things" was the norm. However, the 'close eye' often did not include what could actively be done when the teacher saw the exclusion. Several experts accepted the difficulty but suggested that mentoring from another child – either of the same age group or possibly from an older pupil – did help. The example set by several secondary schools which had schemes to link some of their mainstream children with children with learning disabilities seemed worthwhile. Perhaps even more constructive was the scheme of mentoring by an older boy with learning difficulties himself.

Turning to the abuse of adults with learning disabilities, the stories I heard reflect the national picture mentioned earlier. On occasions, the rudeness or disregard came from impatience or lack of sensitivity. More often it seemed to come from nastiness. As an example of the first, I was talking with one care assistant who regularly looks after a woman who rides a mobility scooter – the type that can go on roads. The care assistant said how badly car drivers treated a person on a mobility scooter. The woman with the scooter lives at Pepenbury and has to go regularly up the narrow road to the local village. She is constantly tooted and harried by cars. I suggested that it was perhaps because the car drivers were trying to be safe and warning oncoming drivers. She pulled a face and said no: they were just infuriated and aggressive. A slightly more cheering story came from another care manager who had recently taken four men with learning difficulties to Benidorm. People with learning difficulties love dancing and are very unself-conscious. One evening in the Benidorm hotel, the four men were on the dance floor when a young English tourist came in with two girls. He took off his T-shirt and got the girl to video him prancing around with the Down's dancers "to show his friends on the web something funny," the carer said. She was saddened; but she was cheered, afterwards, when other guests came up and said they were sorry about the young man and that it was good to see people with learning disabilities on holiday and enjoying themselves. Two other care managers said that neither of them had had personal experience of seeing bullying at any residential home with which they had been concerned but added that they did know of cases in other parts of the South East. They did not wish to say more and I was not clear whether it was care staff who were the bullies, or other residents, or whether it was the public. Nor did I hear directly of any bullying in a workplace, although I heard indirectly from several organisations who said that they were able to sort out problems that did occasionally occur at work.

As well as the assaults and insults described in earlier chapters, the worst cases that I heard about concerned abuse by the public. They came from the disabled people themselves but the incidents were confirmed by their carers to whom they went afterwards. As the services users are increasingly being encouraged to use public transport, they have their own views on their fellow travellers. A group at a meeting I attended, were swapping stories: how teenage boys threw things at bus drivers, were always swearing and spitting and shouting; they also agreed that they were quite often laughed at and called names and that none of the boys ever offered a seat, even to the most obviously physically disabled. One Down's man said a teenage girl had "pulled up her skirt and showed me her bottom". I was told by several people about an incident on a bus which so saddened me that I followed it up. Several men with learning disabilities were on the bus in St John's Road, a major route through Tunbridge Wells. On the bus there were boys thought (from their uniform) to come from a well-known boys' school nearby. (The care managers later checked on the web for pictures of the uniform). The boys said rude things and baited the men with learning difficulties; and one man with Down's had his face pushed up and rubbed against the bus window. The care manager, having been told what had happened, rang the school to discuss the particular incident and, she thought more importantly, to ask that the general point about not being hurtful to people with learning difficulties be raised at the school. The lady to whom she talked said that it could not possibly have been boys from her school and that to give out anything to the pupils or discuss the matter would certainly not be possible.

When I heard about the incident, I rang the Head but, as he was away, I talked initially with his PA. She was appalled by the story. She said it was against everything that the school stood for and aimed to teach their pupils. She said that any complaint such as this one which came to the school, would be followed up most rigorously. If they had been told at the time the number of the bus route, the time of day and any other details, they would certainly have pursued the incident, almost certainly found the boys in question who would then have been involved – probably with their peer group – in a detailed discussion about why such behaviour was totally unacceptable. While I was impressed with her answer, when I wrote to the Head, he did not reply.

In my experience, adults with learning disabilities are not very ready to describe the slights they endure. However, the most distressing aspect of 'bullying' I read about was in a Guardian article.[86] It reported that, "disabled women are almost three times more likely to be sexually abused than their non-disabled peers . . . children and teenagers are constantly told to respect themselves and others; but if you are disabled, it is likely that many of the adults in your life might never consider you a sexual being, meaning that the usual safety advice and strategies are rarely discussed. You are doubly vulnerable if you can't physically remove yourself easily from an awkward situation."

With these depressing, national experiences on the subject, it was positive to hear that the KCC's day centres had had talks on self-confidence and self-esteem and what to do if they were attacked or had uncalled for approaches from strangers. However, I did not take much comfort from a BBC report[87] which said that attacks on vulnerable people seemed to be increasing and suggested that the only way forward was for the public to be made more aware of the problem. On a local level, I have already briefly mentioned the charity, The Town and Country Foundation, and their scheme to make the bullying of people with learning disabilities more widely known and discussed. "Disabled people almost get used to it," says Jackie Sumner, the Head of the Foundation. "So they are shy of even reporting anything bad that happens to them. We wanted more local groups to be aware of the problem."

Friendship

Parents have repeatedly told me how difficult it is for their child with learning disabilities to make friends. And this applies throughout their lives. One couple was typical. They are now elderly and their Down's syndrome son is middle-aged. He has lived with his parents all his life and, as so often seems to be the case, they were the only people close to him. He had once had a friend of a similar age who had also Down's. They shared a love of computers and computer games. "As well as meeting regularly at the day centre, they would spend hours and hours on the phone together. But, sadly, the friend moved away and fairly soon they lost touch. Now there is no special friend, although he meets people regularly at the various classes that he goes to" the parents said. Nearly all the parents of adults who have learning difficulties say that, apart from themselves, almost the only other friends are their carers or other people with learning difficulties.

I was struck at the day centres I visited by the way all the people there – both other service users and the staff – knew each other well and knew the others' little foibles. They explained about their friends with kindness and good humour. And going to residential accommodation such as the Scott Project. It was noticeable that good friendships combined with helping each other were an integral part of life there. One parent with a twenty-five year old son with mild learning problems had told me what made him sad. "Our son has had a loving home, is kind and intelligent, has a good job and is good-looking; but he's never had a friend." Parents and carers are often the only people who can understand: and the autistic person cannot easily relate to the wider world. Neither side can easily step over the gap.

However, there is a difference between the kind of friendship which the 'boys' and 'girls' used to experience at the Princess Christian Hospital every day of the year and the kind of friendship experienced today. At Princess Christian there were a large number of people who were rather similar to you and they were with you most of the day. The staff were very well known to you. For the last twenty years of its life, at Princess Christian you increasingly had your own villa with your friends. You cooked with them and went out on outings with them. You were part of your own community rather than being directly within the main outside world, although depending on your ability and preference you could go into the main community. And the local people cared about the people at the Hospital. It was a happy place. The aim of Care in the Community was admirable – to take men and women away from the huge mental hospitals and to give them homes of their own in small units, ideally with one or two friends they already knew and, where possible, near any family they had. When they had come from a medium-sized mental hospital such as Leybourne Grange or the even larger mental hospitals, they found more freedom to do as they wanted and generally seemed to prefer their new life.

However, while Care in the Community placed the men and

women in the community, *it did not make them part of the community*. Care in the Community did not mean that the community cared. Time and again, when I asked the leading experts in the field what they wanted to see in the future, it was a plea that the public – the community – would understand and treat autistic people or people with brain injuries or people with Down's or autism as ordinary individuals. It does not seem to happen all that often but it is always pleasant to hear about something which went well.

Del's Story. I was told by two people about a man, Derek Bance. Derek – always called Del – was born in 1938. He was somewhat mentally retarded – as they said in those days – but grew up with his family. In the late 1950s, as an older teenager, he was sent to the Princess Christian Hospital. However, it was clear from the start that he was going to be one of the least learning disabled and he was given a room of his own and was well-known for his collection of records (78rpm) and a life-long passion for cricket. For many years he was the scorer of the Hildenborough Cricket Club. He was allowed to cycle locally and was a well-known figure in the Tonbridge market. After more than twenty years at Princess Christian, Del was told that he was going to be moved into the community. At this point, things could have gone badly wrong, but he was lucky. The Knight family in Tonbridge took him in (as well as three other men) and Del was closely involved with the family for the next twenty years. He worked at various jobs, although he never really learnt to cook. Mrs Elaine Knight and her daughter, Kelly, remember him with great fondness. Kelly says, "I remember him from when I was a child – so I knew him for thirty or forty years. He was absolutely lovely – cheeky, witty, with a heart of gold – just fun to be with." Last year, Del died aged 82 – but the community had made him part of it.

Perhaps it is worth separating the concept of friendship into two. The first and most obvious is the feelings that most of us have when we have known someone for a good number of years: it is easy to be with them and to talk with them. We have attitudes (dare I say it, often class) and nearly always interests in common. This kind of friendship seems to have applied between Derek Bance and the

Knight family. The other type of friendship is much less personal and maybe 'friendship' is hardly the right word. It is the easy acceptance of someone within a community: being part of a group of people who live near each other or see each other regularly – even if it is just in passing. We have seen that, for people with learning disabilities or who are 'on the spectrum', the first kind of friendship is difficult, apart from parents and sometimes people who are similar to them. However, what was once suggested to me[88] was that, although it was always going to be difficult to achieve the first, most obvious type of friendship, it might be possible to do more to encourage the second. He gave an example. A man who is on the spectrum is living in sheltered accommodation in a town. It is highly unlikely that the neighbours next door will become friends in the normal sense of the words. However, he suggested that there were ways in which small everyday gestures – a regular 'good morning' or passing remarks about the weather, the traffic or the blossom on a tree, could bridge the gap between the 'normal' person and the 'outsider' person. It could be enough. Or it could at least be a little bit of a breakthrough.

Another small step forward could come from the parents. It could be helpful for a parent with an autistic child to explain to people that their boy or girl may do something unexpected. It can cause embarrassment or even be counter-productive if the new person is not given some sort of guidance. However, I realise that this cannot be easy. I suspect that every parent will have developed their own explanatory system which they can use in a new situation. I can only suggest that it should be tried more, rather than less often. Outside people will probably be sympathetic and even get a little way towards being understanding if they have a few basic facts given to them – ideally in advance.

Love, Sex and Marriage

The subjects of love, sex and marriage have only occasionally been mentioned to me. People with learning disabilities or difficulties definitely need friendship but, like nearly all the human race, they also want love and sex. It is sometimes said – often with distaste – that people with learning disabilities have a stronger sex drive than normal. However, the world is full of people with either more or less sex drive than the average by definition. A number of parents have told me about the hormones that come into effect when their child reaches puberty. It can be difficult. At Princess Christian, relationships between men and women were formed. "He was very keen on one of the girls" and so on. But the old concerns die hard. It was raised even by the Princess Christian Farm Colony *supporters* in 1910 – "If there is a positive increase in the feeble-minded and lunatics, it is because we are doing our best to breed them." The concern about bringing more children with disabilities into the world continued throughout most of the 20th century. It was not thought sensible to let Down's syndrome men and women marry and distressing stories still circulated even in the 1980s.

A farmer who had worked the land around the Princess Christian Hospital for years told me that all the 'girls' (women at the Hospital were always called 'girls') were on the pill. "Everyone knew that", he said. I mentioned this 'fact' to the senior nursing sister who had been at the Hospital for twenty years. She said that the 'fact' was totally untrue. "I was in charge of all the drug rotas for all the women and none had ever had the pill. Some of the men and women got fond of each other but we were always very careful it didn't go too far." I reported back to the farmer who was crestfallen.

The fact that someone with a learning disability or difficulty has loving feelings for someone else should be regarded as natural. I was told of a Down's man kneeling beside a Down's lady in an expensive, local restaurant. "Will you marry me?" he asked. "Don't be daft. Get up off the floor. And, yes, of course," she said. Everyone in the restaurant applauded.

The long held view that people with Down's will pass on the trait is not true. So, a woman with Down's who marries may well find it difficult to have a baby but, if she does, there is no more likelihood of her child having Down's than anyone else. While autism does seem to run in families in some cases, as far as we can tell, not in all. With so many men and women somewhere 'on the spectrum', it is not practical, let alone ethical, to say that any marriage involving an autistic person should be undesirable.

The more important aspect of marriage is the safeguarding issue. When the Down's lady in the restaurant accepted her suitor, both seemed to the person who told me the story to be admirably clear about what they wanted and neither were in need of 'protection'. Yet not all cases are as straightforward. The authorities may sometimes have to act with care – and delicacy. One of the heads of the KCC Learning Disability team, Rosemary Henn-Macrae, explained that if there is a couple where one or both are considered to have learning disabilities and they want to get married, then certain formal safeguarding procedures come into operation. "The basis is the 2005 Mental Capacity Act," says Rosemary. "There will be a 'Best Interests' meeting where experts from KCC Social Services or the NHS and/or the educational side – whoever knows the people best – can be called and there is a procedure which checks that the mental capacity of the prospective bride and groom is sufficient and that neither side is being exploited." I have been moved by the people I have met with learning disabilities who are married or engaged. I do not need to give any details but it seemed to them to be straightforward and natural; and I came to see it so too.

The question of sex is more private and almost no one I talked with mentioned it. (But perhaps no one I have met over the last two or three years in the mainstream world has mentioned it either?) What became clearer to me came from novels or from radio and television dramas. I have thought how constructive they have been to cover the subject; and how moving and sensitive the writing and acting have been.

Graeme Simsion's "The Rosie Project" novels[89] provide a witty picture of how difficult it is to make friends if you have Aspergers. This very Australian rom-com of a book is not only very funny but, beneath the surface is a serious examination of how an Aspergers scientist tries to find a girlfriend. He uses the most logical forms of dating, usually via the web, advertising himself and the woman that he thinks he wants. He repeatedly gets it wrong. Eventually his sister and brother-in-law go through a long process of explanation and education – leading, inevitably, to him finding the perfect girl, who, after long misunderstandings, finally realises he is lovable in his own special way. Real life may not be quite so easy. (And why do so many of the stories about people with learning disabilities have super-intelligent autistic people as heroes?).

"The Best Laid Plans", a book by Kathy Lette[90] tells the story of a mother with a twenty year old autistic son, Merlin. He is keen – desperate – to have a girlfriend or, at the very least, 'to get laid'. The novel charts the efforts of the mother to help – usually to the horror of everyone from whom she asks advice. Upbeat, witty and apparently at least in part based on a true story.

"The Pursuits of Darleen Fyles" was initially a prize-winning BBC Radio 4 serial in fifteen minutes episodes. It was so successful that it ran for several series before being made into a television programme. Its theme was the day-to-day lives of two young people with learning disabilities. The main roles were played by people who themselves had learning difficulties. In one series, Darleen found herself pregnant. Everyone is so appalled – including the parents and the boyfriend – that she runs away. However, as she learns more about actually giving birth from watching TV dramas, she gets frightened; goes home; and all ends happily with the birth. A low-budget British film, "My Feral Heart", is worth seeking out – not least to illustrate that not all people with learning difficulties are like Dustin Hoffman. There have also been two television series which cover autism and romance well, the BBC series 'The A Word' and 'Atypical' which was shown on Netflix. The latter features a young man's efforts to find a girlfriend and to make love. Although thought good by most of the public, there were two complaints. The actor playing the main role did not himself have learning disabilities; and he was not only particularly good looking but 'high-functioning'. The same complaints could not have been levelled at the excellent BBC series. One hopes that the considerable number of books, films, TV and radio dramas on the subject will have increased public understanding about how very ordinary are the feelings of people with learning disabilities – including their thoughts about love, sex and marriage.

Kelly Holmes and Friendship at the old Princess Christian Hospital

There is no doubt that the old, large mental hospitals were dreadful – in spite of the efforts of the staff; and they were rightly wound down in the 1980s and 1990s. Yet in at least one case, there was a type of friendship that was and still is difficult to replicate in the current 'Care in the Community' structure.

As we have seen, the Princess Christian Hospital had a hundred and fifty people living there. They lived together for many years and clearly had close friendships, as well as knowing the staff on a day-to-day basis. It was a close-knit community – a real community. The villagers nearby mixed with them and, where they were able, they could go to the village or to Tonbridge.

Kelly Holmes worked at Princess Christian before she went into the Army and wrote about the relationships there in her excellent autobiography "Black, White and Gold". It will not be often that today's system – in most ways a huge improvement – will be so full of care and friendship.

"Two of the patients particularly touched my heart. One was a smoker and I spent a lot of time teaching him how to catch the bus to the shops and how to pay for the cigarettes… He came back as proud as punch. It was fantastic to have helped him achieve this new level of independence… The other man, a lovely Down's guy in his late sixties. I used to take him to Rehab and play games and puzzles with him and when he'd finished his treatment he'd walk towards me with a huge beaming smile on his face. Three weeks after I left to join the Army, one of the staff phoned me to say he had died. I was heartbroken. But I've never forgotten him. Helping these men towards little improvements in their lives was one of the most rewarding things I've ever done."

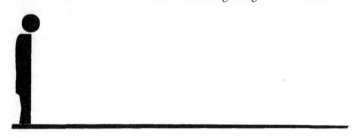

CHAPTER 13

Is Everything Really Going Well? Assessment

It is important to ask whether the many services provided to those with learning disabilities in West Kent are performing satisfactorily. To me, as an outside non-expert, most of the services seemed well run. Normally, too, the service users – a sensible use of this term in this case – agreed, even if they might ideally hope for a little more of something or other. As the book progressed, I asked the people with whom I talked about the oversight of quality, about possible improvements, and about how complaints were dealt with. It seemed important that the large number of services all worked together, particularly as they were provided by different organisations. I was initially dubious about the internal safeguards but I also wanted to hear about the systems of outside assessment.

However, to analyse what happens in a little more detail. Individual children with their parents and even adults with a learning disability cannot know details about all the services which might be useful to them. It will, therefore, need one main, informed expert to tell them. Normally, this would be their care manager who gets to know the individual well on a personal basis, ideally over a longish period. This part of the system normally seems to work and the wide range of help available usually seems to get passed on. GPs can sometimes provide extra suggestions and the Kent Autistic Trust was mentioned several times as being able to explain different ways forward. There is also, of course, the internet, although I found the information on the web to be patchy.

Internal Safeguards

There are several types of internal monitoring or quality control. The first is what could be called the in-house supervision; the second is contained within contracts with sub-contractors. The KCC's Penny Southern was clear that the internal system not only picks up virtually all problems but actively asks for the views of the service users and, where necessary, their parents.

> "You've got to remember the number of people – usually experts – each person with a learning disability comes in contact with. There are the care managers and their teams, the daily carers, the OTs or the physios and so on. Then there are the GPs and the specialist nurses. And all the people at schools or colleges or the day centres, or the sheltered accommodation managers, and even the transport people who ferry them around. All these are on the look-out for problems; and I can say from long experience that any serious issue is picked up pretty early and discussed by the whole team – they keep a detailed file on each person. And, of course, the parents are nearly always more than determined to get the best for their child. The vast majority of concerns, or even comments, really do get picked up in this informal way. Then there are the various outside statutory inspections. The Care Quality Commission (CQC) visits and gives formal grading to various aspects of care; and Ofsted inspects all types of public sector schools. In addition, the KCC has formal contract compliance built into all our legal agreements with our outside contractors; and we have compliance inspections to make sure the contractors are doing what they have agreed."

Another senior KCC Manager, whose staff deal with a large number of service users agreed. "There are the formal, government based outside assessments. The CQC, as well as inspecting many of the NHS services, also inspect some of the KCC's facilities, including our registered care homes – although not our supported living or sheltered accommodation or the day centres. If the CQC finds any faults, it is very public. It is in the Press and with details on the web. So, we hope (and nearly always get) all the facilities in Kent graded as 'Good' or 'Outstanding' CQC qualifications."

Ofsted

The Ofsted reports cover early years schooling, primary and secondary maintained schools and academies and further education provision. (They do not cover fee-paying schools which have their own Independent School Inspectorate). While they assess the whole of a school's achievement in general, they also have a legal duty to look specifically at SEN provision. This reporting applies to both types of inspection – the short inspection and the much longer, full inspection. All schools are required to have a Governor who is responsible for all aspects of Special Educational Needs and Ofsted checks that this aspect of the school is working properly. Children, who are registered as having Special Educational Needs, on average achieve lower exam results than their peers and are absent more often.[91] It is, therefore, important that an outside body which does inspections comments on how effective SEN provision is being; and, as they are inspecting schools nationally, they can make comparisons between the different types of schools.

One of the turning points in the evaluation of this area of schooling was the Lamb Report in 2010 which said the monitoring of SEN pupils progress should be better; that schools should avoid concentrating on the cleverer pupils; that to have low expectation for SEN children was unconstructive; and that parents of SEN children should be more involved. However, I have to add some queries. One Ofsted inspector, with whom I talked, was saddened by changes over the past few years which he felt made the inspections less rigorous and less frequent – he suspected the changes were initiated because of Government financial cutbacks, rather than a desire to improve the system. There also seems unease that Ofsted does not oversee home schooling and that inspections of schools graded as 'outstanding' were then not revisited for many years. (Think how schools can change in two years, let alone five or ten). However, these reservations did not come up in the schools I visited and I was told Ofsted had reacted to some of the above reservations.

Quality Controls for Sub-Contractors

In addition to the detailed contracts with the KCC, the sub-contractors have their own internal quality control systems which include staff performance reviews and training. The KCC checks on what contractors are doing two or three times a year, with an auditor visiting the service to ensure the contract specifications are being met. The auditors speak to people who use the service and their parents/carers to gain their feedback and to ensure the individual's files are up to date and in order. As well as the pre-arranged inspections, there are also unannounced audits. Quite understandably when one is dealing with people who have a variety of disabilities, there are rigorous safety standards and risk assessments which have to be checked. The KCC's aim is "to be performance-led and to have a measurable year on year improvement" says KCC's Ian Haylock.

Service Users' Suggestions to the Authorities; and Liaison between the Providers

There is a system where the service users from a relatively small area – around 200,000 people – come together for a two-way exchange of views and information, with the various service providers. It meets quarterly and it has until recently been called the District Partnership Group. (It is now called – infuriatingly but typically – 'The Valuing People Now Meeting'). I had heard various versions about whether these meetings are valuable. The aim is for those attending to be told about various subjects and events which will be of interest to them; and for the service users to be able to put complaints or suggestions to those in authority. At the meeting that I attended there were about fifty people present, with perhaps thirty service users and twenty staff. I had already met quite a number and was greeted cheerfully.

Many of the service users knew each other and it seemed to be somewhere to meet friends. I was given information about various individuals by other service users – none of it gossipy, just factual. The first formal agenda item was to explain the forthcoming General Election. It did not arouse a great deal of interest, although perhaps this would be a typical reaction from the general public. However, it seemed worth doing and one lady talked about her voting experiences. A Down's syndrome woman was the narrator of a video on the subject that was then shown. There was a list of forthcoming events which moved on to an informal discussion about bullying and bad behaviour towards people with learning disabilities – not a happy subject. However, two useful action points arose. A letter would be written to the local bus companies where there had been problems; and a short film about not behaving badly towards people who acted or looked a bit different would be planned. In particular, the film would be circulated to local schools. (We heard that the Gravesend Group had just been given some money to make four films about bullying).

After lunch there was a discussion about Brexit – another subject which met with little enthusiasm but it led to a discussion on immigration where the general feeling was not in favour. When I asked about whether these meetings were helpful, I was told that earlier in the year, after comments at the meeting, one or two service users went to visit a number of leisure facilities where they made notes about possible improvements which were then passed on to the appropriate manager. For example, the Tunbridge Wells Leisure Centres had been persuaded to make sporting facilities available to more people with learning disabilities. Since then, around two hundred people with learning disabilities have 'had a go' there. Another action point had been a Sevenoaks questionnaire about housing needs which I was told had led to specific improvements. These District Partnership Groups – there are eleven all over Kent – do seem a worthwhile exercise. In spite of some criticism from one man I met that nothing ever changed because of the meetings, the examples I was given and saw on the ground did seem to show that practical improvements can happen. And it was a good social event.

I was also told about various top level committees which regularly brought together the leading figures from the NHS, the Social Services and the education world. (One was called the Kent Learning Disability Partnership Board, but I gathered there were other committees as well). I was told that they were practical and could, where necessary, sort out general problems or even the problems of one individual.

Educational Tribunals

A further safeguard against any wrongful exercise of the power is the Special Education Needs Tribunal system. As we have seen, if a child has what seems to the parents to have moderate to severe learning problems, he or she is assessed by the KCC's experts. Then the KCC will recommend a certain level of care. This will cover how many hours of support, which school or type of school is suggested but particularly whether extra funding will be provided. If the parents disagree with the assessment, there are various levels of further discussions. If, after these discussions, no agreement has been reached, the Tribunal is the last resort. I have only talked with two parents who have gone or nearly gone through this process. It is lengthy, very legalistic and can be extremely expensive. In her previously quoted book, 'Loving Olivia', Liz Astor provides a blow by blow account of her dealing with the KCC and the tribunal system.[92] "Almost every year Kent has more special needs tribunals than any other county." This criticism was, however, made over ten years ago and I was assured that parts of the system have been changed. Nor is it clear whether Kent's educational tribunal system is today particularly difficult. (I did try to contact the appropriate person within Kent Education on numerous occasions but did not hear back).

NHS Complaints Procedures

Complaints about the NHS make news stories with great regularity and the bill for compensation for inadequate treatment has got out of hand. (A knowledgeable accountant friend who had been on a hospital board suggested that the system should be changed so that most of the damages awarded went to a central charity for medical research). However, there are routes for people with a learning disability who need to resolve problems with the NHS, ending up in the most difficult cases in front of an NHS Tribunal Judge who specialises in these matters. Talking with one judge, I got a small insight of the extreme difficulty in balancing the right for an individual's freedom against the right of society, including the staff, to be protected. I do not wish to give the example that I was given off the record but it was grim.

Personal Advocates

I also heard about 'Personal Advocates'. I did not meet anyone who had used a Personal Advocate themselves but I did meet an actual advocate who explained how the scheme worked. Each person who is on the KCC's learning disability list has their own representative who is outside the system – their Personal Advocate – who can raise any question that is worrying the individual or the parents or even the carers. The one with whom I talked was a retired bank manager who had worked for various charities and then had had special training for his new role as an Advocate. He said that his job could involve him in querying matters with various parts of the Social Services or the NHS or in some cases talking with charities or voluntary bodies. His overall conclusion was that the officials with whom he talked on behalf of his 'client' were exceptionally caring and dealt with each query or complaint with great thoroughness. He mentioned his latest case where his client was an extremely ill quadriplegic who could hardly speak but wanted to make a new will. The case involved two sets of solicitors, various branches of the family and a range of medical experts – some of whom were needed to help the patient (the Advocate's client) explain what he wanted. When the matter was eventually successfully settled, the client indicated he wanted to talk to his Advocate. "Thanks", he said. "It's tough this dying" – and passed away soon after.

The whole system of safeguarding and assessment seems a rather British compromise between letting those most concerned liaise amongst themselves; rigorous enforcement of legal contracts; and various Government appointed bureaucracies' oversight of particular aspects. In any case, I personally did not hear of many problems, let alone disasters. Inevitably, there were parents or a service user who wanted to be helped to find something – a job; or a house nearer their parents; or an extra teaching assistant; or to be enabled to do some kind of activity – horse riding or wood carving both got a mention – but, just as inevitably, there are and will be times when the KCC cannot afford what is requested – or sometimes demanded.

However, to end on a less satisfied note. Not everything goes well – always. I heard of two instances where the complexities of life with a learning disability had an unfortunate feel. The first came from a lady who had been a young carer at the Princess Christian Hospital. When the Hospital was being closed, one man she knew well was moved into sheltered accommodation in Tonbridge where there was a manager and where he had friends. She visited him and still visits him. However, she says that, in reality, he is not very conscious of the world around him and is constantly wandering across roads, oblivious to the danger he is in and is causing.

The second instance came from a man whose brother-in-law also used to be at the Princess Christian Hospital. The man takes up the story – told to me when he was furious. "That 'Care in the Community'. It's OK for some. But it's definitely not OK for others. In the old days at Princess Christian, my brother-in-law used to be happy; he felt secure; he knew where he was in life; and, above all, he liked the structure of his life. He did his bit of gardening in houses round about. He liked that. It made him feel useful. He got up. He washed. He had his breakfast. And so on. It was all organised and he had his friends with him – all the time. Nowadays, he lives in his own flat in Maidstone twenty miles away. He's not really with it. Not that long ago, late one evening, he turned up at our house during a thunderstorm. He was in a terrible state – soaking wet and with no proper clothes. He'd got to us by bus and walking somehow. He was desperate. He couldn't understand what was happening to him. He thought he was going to be thrown out of his flat – that he was going to have to live on the streets. Eventually, we found out what was happening to him. He gets government money each week to pay his £20 rent. The trouble was that it all came by GIRO because he hadn't got a bank account. He didn't understand things like that. So, by the time he'd got the GIRO cashed, all the £20 had gone and he'd got into debt. The powers that be – I suppose they didn't understand – were sending threatening letters. No one had been helping him. So, we sorted it all out. We got him a bank account and it all seems to work now. But, as I say, 'Care in the Community' does not work for everyone. And my brother, who is a policeman agrees. He says he's always having to deal with cases like this. And policemen are not trained to help people like this – it's not their job. But they try to help. So, the 'Care in the Community' thing might be working for some people who are a bit, you know, but as I said, it doesn't work for everyone."

I do not know more details of the second story. I guess that the incident was the result of misunderstandings. However, both stories show how difficult it can be for the authorities to get everything perfect all the time.

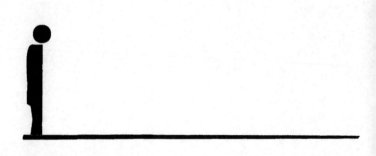

CHAPTER 14

Reflections

I did not want to call this last chapter 'Conclusions'; and certainly not 'Recommendations'. Nearly every one of the people to whom I have talked over the last three or four years knows more about their particular part of the subject than I do. So, this chapter is what I have learnt, with a few queries from an outside observer about the future.

Praise

I am convinced that life for people with learning difficulties is better today than it was in the large mental hospitals of the twentieth century. Even when compared with The Princess Christian Hospital – a very small mental home – which was in many ways a very happy place to live and outstanding for its era – the support given today is normally preferable. I have talked to a wide range of so-called 'service users' and I feel proud to have met them and heard about what they do and how they feel. I remember them all. It is not only memories of the children and adults with learning disabilities themselves which I will cherish. The parents I have met have been remarkable. I have a sense of wonder that their love for their child is so all embracing, has overcome so many obstacles and has often left them exhausted but still fighting and still loving. I have felt sympathy, too, for the well-meaning and knowledgeable experts who try to manage this powerful parental force, which is so determined to get what they see as right for their child. One teacher at a special school said that she knew how to cope with all the different children; but the parents were so often grey with exhaustion that it always worried her.

The heads of every group of experts with whom I talked – from the KCC, the NHS and from within the educational system, to the organisers at day centres or in sheltered accommodation and all their staff, down to the support workers and carers – seemed to be exemplary, although several seemed exhausted. They had dedicated themselves – usually for most of their lives – to the boys and girls, men and women that they were employed to cherish. Some said that there could often be puzzles when each one of their service users was so different but "it was a challenge."

The head of the private firm, Superior Healthcare, Sarah Richards, told me about one young autistic boy that they were commissioned to take out and for whom they had to provide stimulating entertainment. So they started providing two carers who would take him out for the day. However, there always seemed to be a problem. The little boy could not speak but sometimes he would make it clear that he needed to go to the toilet. The problem was that, when he went into beautiful, new public toilets with the support workers, he would have a meltdown. They tried everything to reassure him. They asked the parents. They thought that maybe he had a phobia about toilets which perhaps were not the same type as the one he had at home. Eventually, after all kinds of experiments, they found that what terrified him was the hand-drying blowers. So looking after someone who has learning problems is never dull.

As well as the parents and the professionals, I should also mention the volunteers – both the individuals and the organisations that they run. It seemed to me a false economy by government and local councils to cut back any of the funding for voluntary groups – for example, the CABs – but there are many others. The closeness of voluntary bodies to their community and the kind of localised help that they give is not only inexpensive (or free) but it is personalised.

There could be a caveat to all my praise. I believe that all that I was told was basically true but, perhaps, I was normally introduced to the most enthusiastic people at every level. They felt positive about what they did and I have tried to reflect it. Yet there were occasions when I felt I was being steered away from talking to relatively junior staff; or when I did talk with them, more senior people would have liked to vet what had been said. This was quite understandable as it was not necessarily easy for me to have grasped the full picture, but maybe sometimes I was told only about a perfect world. I met three long-serving middle managers who, I felt, were at the end of their tether with strain and overwork. I did not press them. I also found that the difficulties of finding good staff (sometimes any staff) were mentioned only rarely. I suspected that financial constraints and cutbacks made the care of people with learning difficulties somewhat less good than it could be, even if it occasionally forced new thinking on the services being provided. In one instance, a severely autistic man had lived in his own home – needing twelve to fourteen shift staff and two resident staff to care for him twenty-four hours a day, three hundred and sixty-five days of the year. Eventually, the cost could not be afforded; but it did lead to a new (and better) type of sheltered accommodation. However, no one explained the complexities of this to me. I only heard by chance. I suspect that the whole story was so involved that there was never time to explain one man's life history and the budget allocations that he needed. I have talked briefly with people in six other counties and, on this completely unscientific and biased assessment, would rate Kent as near the top of the Premier League of learning disability care.

The Future – and Funding

However, there seems to be some queries about the future which were worth raising– even if I do not have enough knowledge to call them recommendations. The first concern must be about funding. The Government has delegated more responsibility to the county councils. However, as we have seen, this has put county councils under great strain. Put simply, they have dramatically less money from central government but extra responsibilities are being imposed on them. This has been happening at a time when there seem to be more people with learning disabilities and at a time when, until recently, the county councils have not been allowed to put up council tax to cope with their extra responsibilities. There must be a danger that county councils will be forced to find cuts in the support given for learning disabilities.

Already a number of very useful schemes which are available in Kent have been cut in other counties. There may be the temptation to cut support for the less severely autistic people in order to keep funding for the more severely affected. (Several people mentioned the fact that, as David Cameron had a son with very severe difficulties, it seemed the funding for such children remained at a reasonable level). Another concern expressed to me was that smaller organisations were more likely to be cut, leaving only the large ones to cope with the increasing load. Maybe it can appear that a small organisation takes as much or nearly as much administrative oversight as a larger one. However, I have been impressed by the small groups that I saw, where the personalised and local care, seemed excellent. In reality, the costs of overseeing them must be more than offset by the unpaid work from voluntary helpers. Economies of scale are not always productive and one has seen recently how very big companies undertaking outsourced work for the Government have failed dramatically – at tax-payers' expense.

On the question of wages, I was saddened to hear a number of instances where support workers could not be found because the pay was so poor. This trend has been frequently reported nationally, including in debates in Parliament.[93] The wages are low and need to be increased. The financial difficulties being faced by the Social Services go on to affect indirectly the money available to the NHS to help adults, but, more particularly, children with learning disabilities. The NHS delays in both assessment and treatment of children with learning disabilities are a disgrace. I wondered, too, about carers at home, mainly the parents, who spend so much time and save the government so much money looking after the old, the physically and the mentally handicapped and those with learning difficulties. (One study estimated that these carers saved the country £132 billion a year.)[94] Do we treat them fairly, just because they feel that they must work from a sense of duty and a sense of love? Should society not think of ways of helping those who provide for free what is apparently 90% of the caring in the country? Could at least the poorest of the volunteer carers be allowed more money? Could there be more short breaks for them? I am sure that the home carers that I met were fairly typical. They deserve to be considered more.

Delegation of Support and Volunteers

We all realise government money does not 'grow on trees'. Whichever government is in power, difficult decisions will always have to be made. Britain is not going to become much richer, and, quite possibly, may find itself considerably poorer. Within ten to fifteen years, the dominance of China and probably India is likely to change many of the economic norms which Europe and North America have thought unalterable. More immediately, the authorities have to make tough decisions. Post Covid 19 and post-Brexit they will increasingly have to look for ways forward in the care of people with learning disabilities which produce at least as good an outcome as now but which cost less money.

I put this thought to a number of the KCC's most experienced managers. Several trends emerged. The first was what could be called delegation. For example, Portage teaches parents with young babies to provide treatment themselves. Consultant psychiatrists and other experts are increasingly holding group sessions with parents whose children have similar problems. More teachers and teaching assistants are going on courses to help children rather than expecting NHS experts to give treatment. Pharmacists and specialist nurses may have to take more of the strain from GPs. This kind of delegation and teaching people to do things for themselves will surely have to expand. The role of volunteers should to be encouraged, too. Time and again, I heard pleas for more of them: and they should not be side-lined because they do not have some particular qualification. It is said that there are at least nineteen million volunteers in the UK.[95] They can and should be trained. It would be good if schools used their volunteers who help with children's reading more constructively. If volunteers were trained properly, they could make a much more useful contribution. A splendid, elderly economics professor who has also covered, among other things, the economics of education, Prof. Robert Cassen,[96] sent himself on one of the courses run by a charity called Beanstalk and wrote a witty account in the London Evening Standard about how it had helped him be much more constructive in his local school.

Technological Assistance

In the future, is it likely that technical innovation will be able to reduce problems and provide extra help, not just to the service users, but also to many types of staff? I was impressed by Kent's CAT team and the enthusiasm with which both the residents and the management at one sheltered home liked their new computerised system to control the bedrooms. There is already a four foot robot, Pepper,[97] who asks questions and listens to disturbed people, apparently resulting in significant improvements. Will robots and chatbots actually be able to provide new types of assistance? I suspect so, though I hope this will augment human carers, not supersede them.

I also suspect that websites can be made more useful. For example, it seemed that there could be better information about schools and employment prospects for those with learning disabilities. Many households already have the various machines which provide information when the machine is spoken to; or mowers or carpet sweepers which are self-organised. There is little doubt that machines and AI will soon be able to help look after many of the physical needs of the elderly and disabled. Teaching via the internet, too, will be used much more. There are good specialist websites, although perhaps some of the websites could be better co-ordinated. There is a new simulator for people who have to deal with people who have autism. A doctor from Kent[98] has recently developed an app which has enabled a brain damaged man to speak again. Talking therapy, where the distressed person 'talks' to a psychiatrist in real time over the web sounded helpful; I met one man who found it easier to discuss his problems over the web – in real time – than to visit the doctor in the surgery. This system allows an autistic person time to reflect on what he is trying to convey, without the confusion or confrontation that they can often feel. Artificial intelligence may well bring personalised mental health treatments to the NHS within the foreseeable future.[99] It is hoped that that the NHS is able to provide speedier assessment and treatment for children by using technology better. New technical and medical advances in various, as yet unforeseen, areas will certainly emerge.

Consolidating Services and Localness

Another type of advance which will increasingly need to be considered could be called consolidation or co-operation. Already there is much well-publicised discussion about better co-operation between the NHS and Social Services/social care, particularly, with regard to elderly. This long-promised proposal will probably have been hastened by the Covid 19 experiences. Departmental co-operation and amalgamations are increasingly taking place which look after people with learning disabilities. These changes can lead to top specialists covering a wider area or personal records being more easily uploaded on to the internet – something I was told formally was happening, but other people informally said was chaos. There are plans to involve GPs in a new, integrated scheme – including the possibility of getting them to help people with learning disabilities obtain jobs more easily.[100] (This suggestion for overworked GPs to do more seemed eccentric but . . .). There is also a proposal for the ending of the dividing line between adult services and children's services. The recent expansion of support for the sixteen to twenty-four year olds may well help the service user, although apparently there is no extra staff or funding. Mainstream schools will have to – and are increasingly starting to – have specialist classes or units or groups where teachers, usually with the involvement of parents, can help children with a whole range of learning problems. And might it be helpful to have the boundary between mental health and learning difficulties lessened?

However, with these actual and potential developments about consolidation, there is a potential downside. I found instances where the amalgamation of an NHS department and a Social Services department seemed to have been driven more by the potential saving of money and the reduction of staff numbers than helping service users. Additionally, the amalgamation can mean an increased number of people in the new department who know a bit about everything and a loss of the people who are experts. I also suspect that the localness of the assistance – the nearness to home – is much valued. This will often be lessened if geographical areas are amalgamated. So, increasing co-operation between areas of expertise is a trend which is likely to continue, particularly post Covid, with the likelihood of more NHS and social service integration. While these trends will often be useful, it is hoped that potential drawbacks can be avoided.

Public Attitudes

When I had asked Penny Southern – then the overall head of Kent's services for children and adults with learning disabilities – what the biggest problem she saw for the future, I thought that she might well say 'funding'. Instead she said that she would like to see the public becoming more understanding about the people she and her team help to look after. "Things have improved. It's much better today; but I think that there is a long way to go before my people are treated as the individuals they are."

Rosemary Henn-Macrae, a colleague of Penny Southern, completely agreed but added an extra perspective. "In the future, I hope that there can be a greater recognition that people with various disabilities can very often do more than people expect. Yes – they should certainly be included more into society; but many can also contribute more to society – whatever their level or type of disability".

So, I started wondering about ways in which Penny Southern's 'people' – those who are a bit (or sometimes a lot) different – can be more involved within society. Mick Csaky, an award winning documentary maker, told me about his experience in Iran and Yemen, when making a television series about Islam. He was being advised by an interesting and moderate Imam. One of many things that had surprised Mick was the way in which those with learning disabilities were treated. At meetings, film viewings and conferences, he found that they were given pride of place at the front of an audience. The Imam explained that such people were thought to be nearer to God than you and me, and that they are specially blessed.

In Britain, people with various disabilities are taken care of and supplied with a wide range of help which virtually all comes out of general taxation. This long-distance giving means that the person or organisation providing the funds is far removed from the person to whom the money or services are given. That will mean an inevitable lack of personal connection and, quite possibly, a lack of understanding. If it is right for society to foster everyone – including the poor, the disabled, even the stupid – it is probably more satisfactorily done by being local. Should more taxation go to more local bodies – the County Councils, the District Councils and, even, Parish Councils? Should national income tax be much reduced and more regional and local councils be allowed to expand their taxes – the taxes where they can decide what is most needed locally – and on which they would be judged at elections? This feeling of localness – and often responsibility – was the case in past centuries.

In the 20th century, at the Princess Christian Hospital, the villagers knew many of the people in the hospital and the staff were part of the overall community. Where it was sensible, the two parts – the hospital and the community – met and mixed. Are there ways that this kind of direct relationship can be encouraged in the future?

With our current 'blame culture', one incident can result in a law case. The understandable eagerness for parents to obtain the best for their child, can mean that the parents examine every decision or event to see whether someone was to blame for something they thought was not right. The whole of the medical profession as well as the caring professions need to find ways to explain to parents and relatives that life cannot always be 100% perfect all the time. One local incident which reached the papers stuck in my mind. A young child, who was very autistic and exceptionally over-active, was hurting himself constantly, in spite of wonderful parents and wonderful outside help. To protect the child, the father built a padded frame over the bed. He did not mention it to the support team. The child got caught in the frame and was badly injured. Everyone concerned was blamed by the Press and by everyone else. The social worker was so pilloried, in spite of the official verdict that she had done nothing wrong, that she had a breakdown and resigned. Naturally, too, the parents were blamed. No one seemed to want to say that, very occasionally, there are accidents, there are mistakes. Cannot the blame culture be modified by better explanations and better listening by all sides?

News and Drama: and Public Understanding

The newspapers, and to a lesser extent the other media, do not always help. Almost by definition (or at least by their definition) news nearly always means the bad, the unhappy and – although the public do not seem to realise it – the exception. So, one child in a hundred thousand gets injured in the bed frame; one care worker steals some money from an autistic woman; one pedestrian falls over in an accident; one man or woman is unsuccessfully treated by a doctor – they all become seen by the public as the norm. Politicians, ever keen to be perceived as caring and as 'doing something', rush to build upon the story and think of new legislation based on the unique case. It is not only "hard cases that make bad law". Knee-jerk reaction also makes bad law.

If newspapers and news reports in general have often not helped public understanding of people with learning disabilities, then television and radio, films and plays and sometimes documentaries have often been more constructive. I made a random and unscientific note of material which I felt would have helped give a more realistic and more varied picture of these people to the general public. It was impressive and covered a wide range. Whether it was a situation comedy, a grim or a witty novel, or some of the broadcast dramas I have mentioned, the impact should have made for better understanding. And better understanding should lead towards acceptance – acceptance that these people are as much part of society as anyone else.

Bridging the Gap

As everyone has told me, it should be the aim to bridge the gap between the 'normal' and the 'apparently different'. However, I worry that this generalisation is not very helpful – for either 'side'. Does it have to wait until the children of today, having heard at school about those children who have Down's or autism or ADHD, are more understanding? (One headteacher said that he thought children's attitudes were becoming increasingly positive in this respect).

I tried to do my bit recently. I was playing clock golf with my wife and granddaughter and we were behind two ladies who were helping a six year old boy who clearly was autistic. I said to them how well he was doing and could I perhaps say 'hello'. They were not pleased.

On another occasion, a six or seven year old appeared at a party. He was a disaster. He would not calm down, hit the other children and totally disrupted the occasion. The mother knew quite well that he was likely to lose control but did not like to tell anyone. Had she been perhaps a little braver, the other parents would have understood and tried to help. So, introducing the two 'sides' – bridging the gap – is not straightforward.

Perhaps a clue came from a friend. She is a well-known artist, who has taught at major art schools in this country and in Europe but who has also taught at a school for children with learning difficulties.

> "I much preferred the children. Other people see them as 'having problems' but I found them kind and gentle. I love their straightforward affection. Some time ago, I saw a mother at a tea party with a plainly autistic son. He was about seven. I asked the mother whether I could talk with him but she said, 'No. Let him come to you'. She was right. And, when he did come over to me, we became friends. As he left, he said that he would send me a picture – which he did. And I sent him one back. We exchanged pictures for years. But what the mother said has always stayed in my mind. Don't try to force friendship. Let it happen on their terms – not yours."

The 'Big Society', about which David Cameron talked, should not be forgotten just because the idea drifted away. On the whole, a majority of people *when they actually meet these people for themselves* are moved and will do something to help on the occasion. However, this is not the same as a more long-term commitment to help a person or a family nearby with a difficulty, although is it, perhaps, a peg on which to build a bridge of understanding. It would be sad to think that the Big Society idea could not be developed. Indeed, it may have to be developed as the resources dwindle. I was interested in a Scandinavian experiment called 'co-housing', where a linked group of homes with shared central facilities have been designed for a mix of age, class and ability – including people with learning disabilities.

Probably it is not just that 'the Authorities' should do more. Of course, more money should be spent and new ideas and processes developed. However, maybe the main advance will be a gradual acceptance by 'ordinary people' that those with learning disabilities are as diverse and kind and interesting as 'ordinary people'. And, many 'ordinary people' will probably begin to realise that many of us have some aspect of the traits of people with learning disabilities. Talking with a very influential managing director, we discussed this book and by the end, we agreed jokingly that he clearly had many characteristics of a person with Aspergers, even if, medically, he probably hadn't. So, I end up just hoping that this book can go a very small way to explain the simple fact – as we all know when we think about it – that everyone is different and that differences should not exclude. Differences can be interesting, not embarrassing.

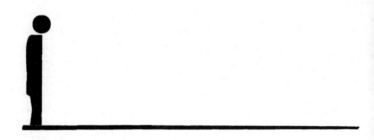

Rebecca's Story

I have known Rebecca since she was eight or nine. Now the mother of a six year old son who is autistic, as well as a daughter who is four, she discusses what her life has been like so far for her husband and herself.

"When you become the parent of a child with additional needs, no one hands you a training manual. No one checks you are clear on the instructions for handling. It's very much a case of learning on the job. Before our son was diagnosed with a rare chromosome disorder – it doesn't have a name – at the age of two, and later aged four, as autistic, I am ashamed to admit I had little knowledge of either – in fact I'd never heard of 'a rare chromosome disorder', and my knowledge of autism stretched little beyond Dustin Hoffman's Rain Man. (Side note: please try not to compare an autistic person to Rain Man. They're not all good at maths – although that said, our son does seem to have a passion for numbers that definitely can't be attributed to me).

"So, when we were first given his diagnosis, I did feel catapulted into a whole new world – one that was unknown and frankly, a bit terrifying, all while processing the news that slightly throws life as you know it completely off kilter. And initially, it did lead to a sort of bereavement on my part; the mourning of a childhood and a life that I had envisaged for my son. If you are lucky enough to become a parent, and then for that child to be healthy, all you want is for them to have everything you've had in life – and then some; the same highs and lows, experiences and memories The stuff that has filled your photo albums and become family folklore, that has shaped the person you've become. When your child is diagnosed as having special needs, there comes the knowledge that they will most likely have a very different life to that which you imagined for them. That they will face challenges that you have never had to. And although, while my son is young, I can try and protect him from that to a certain degree, I won't always be around.

"Fast forward a couple of years to the present day, he is now six – and I'm not going to pretend I find it easy. A lot of the time, I really don't. There is a saying that gets circulated on social media and particularly within support groups for special needs families, that goes 'you only get dealt what you're strong enough to handle'. But I don't agree. I don't think I am any better or worse equipped to care for a child with additional needs than the next person. While I know how lucky I am to be a mum, my years as a parent have in many ways been the most challenging of my life. They have tested me to my very limits, drained me emotionally and physically and revealed sides of myself that I am not so fond of. (I always thought that I would be that calm, patient, almost Zen-like mum. Turns out, not so much.) I have never been more tired and never worked so hard at something, often without feeling I am making any progress.

"But would I like to wish away my son's autism? Absolutely not. And I can say that without hesitation now, whereas even a year ago, I'm not sure I would have. When he was first diagnosed, a friend reminded me the label of 'autism' didn't make him any different to the child he was the day before. And she was right. I don't want my son to be defined by his autism, but similarly I never want him to be ashamed of it. It's not an illness, it's part of him – and many of the things I love most about him and am most proud of are qualities that he probably has just because he is on the spectrum. If he wasn't autistic would he still be able to bombard strangers in the Post Office queue with facts about asteroids, or remember what day of the week his birthday fell on two years ago? Would he still laugh until he is almost sick when his dad stages a bath time puppet show? I don't know where the autism begins and ends, but I'd hate to lose any of the things that make him 'him'.

"After discussing it with my hugely supportive husband, I gave up my full-time job to become self-employed. And while I won't claim to be anywhere near an expert on either autism or rare genetic disorders, I am trying my damnedest to be an expert on my son. And so no, I wouldn't take his autism away. But I would like to see the world become a more accepting, easier place for him to grow up and thrive in. No one person on the autistic spectrum is the same, but they do all process the world differently. And so, for my son, much of what goes on around him can be bewildering and stressful, set up as it is for us neurotypicals. By making society more inclusive we would ALL benefit. I want my children to grow up knowing that not everyone is just like them and to recognise that is a really, really good thing. To know that everyone has something to contribute, everyone has something they can teach you, everyone has something that makes them special regardless of how they look or their abilities. Just think of all that fantastic potential we could unlock if we changed some attitudes and adapted something so they don't just suit the norm!

"But I don't want to end on a negative. Because I think I am past that and, as my son continues to learn and thrive at school – with excellent help from the staff – I acknowledge more and more how much I am learning – everyday. And it is thanks to him, my boy, my precious boy. What has he taught me? Way too long a list. But let's just say what I don't now know about dwarf planets isn't worth knowing."

CHAPTER 15

An Update: 2023

This book was first published in the spring of 2022. However, I had listened to quite a number of the three hundred or so contributors before COVID – sometimes three of four years before publication. I wondered what the changes there might have been over the intervening years.

The first conclusion was that, for people with the wide variety of learning difficulties, not a huge amount had changed for them personally. In essence, they were still the same people. However, they had been affected by the difficulties that so many people had faced with COVID; and with the financial problems forced on all the bodies that provided them with support. So, just as children in mainstream schools were having their education disrupted, so were the special schools. Even though all types of schools which I contacted, had gone out of their way to help children with special needs, the parents had found the lost school days very difficult.

When I had originally talked with the Kent Social Services, they were worryingly short of money. This difficulty had only become worse with central government cuts and extra responsibilities imposed upon them by the government – including dealing with immigrants and particularly immigrant children. (Nationally, it is reckoned that central government funding has decreased by 37% over the last ten years. Kent is likely to have been hit particularly badly). However, it seemed that over the last three or four years the KCC had continued to provide good care for children and adults with learning disabilities in spite of some definite problems which parents in particular explained in the original book.

However, in November 2022, there was a joint Ofsted/CQC

Report about SEN provision in Kent following up on their earlier report in 2019. This second report was increasingly critical. (It is available on the Ofsted website). It is eighteen pages long and while it mentions a few positive points about the services provided by the KCC and the NHS, it concentrates – repetitively – on failings they perceived. Some of the criticisms mentioned by parents, with whom I had talked originally, are confirmed. The parents had great difficulty in obtaining assessments for children who probably have a learning disability; and even longer delays for the prescribed treatments – a national problem. One GP told me, "The situation is terrible. We have been told the delay can now be three years". The Report also focuses on how difficult it is to get hold of the appropriate person with whom to talk. Finally, there was criticism of the way in which the various bodies/departments in the NHS, the Social Services and Education liaise. All these concerns had been mentioned to me for the first edition of the book and clearly they have continued. However, on a personal note, I did find the Report extremely negative and with little reference to the kindness and practical help which I had been told about by the people in the original book. (It is ironic that while Ofsted was, perhaps with some justification, critical of Kent's NHS and Social Service provision, it had failed to detect the most scandalous children's home in the country for many years, classifying the appalling Fullerton House in Doncaster (where there had been over a hundred adverse safeguarding reports over three years) as "good".

I was also puzzled by a separate CQC report on a small housing complex which I had thought outstanding. The CQC criticised it as being a rural ghetto: they said what was needed nowadays were small groups of three of four rooms in a town. This principle – not always accepted as the sole way forward and inclined to make at least some of the people with learning disabilities feel without friends – seemed to ignore the happy, communal life provided by this and other similar group housing projects – where not only the people living there but the parents and staff seemed very satisfied.

In 2022, the KCC had a further problem with its SEN provision. Its transport planning went wrong and left some children stranded. I had not heard about this, with the only feedback on transport that I was given being a new taxi service provided for a Down's lady who needed to get to her Day Centre three times a week.

One further development by the KCC has been proposed. They wish to close thirty-eight Children's and Youth Centres. This has been presented as a cost saving measure to help the financially challenged County Council. However, while the scheme may well save money by selling off actual buildings – which are only partially used – the KCC has made it clear that it will provide at least as much support for the children and young adults but in other buildings and often in more localised locations.

On the subject of evaluation, I recently heard positive things about a national organisation 'Healthwatch'. There is one main branch in each county, which have groups of professionals to assess and advise medical bodies ranging from hospitals to GP practices.

The feedback I received from the individuals to whom I had listened for the first edition of the book, was, on the whole, not surprising. Isabella, who had provided such a moving but factual account about herself for her teachers when she was going to secondary school (page 125), was now a more confident young lady. The young boy who feature in the Postscript (page 273) has not had an entirely straightforward last few years. He has had to make the transition from a local primary school, which he loved but where he was increasingly unable to cope, to a special school. His mother explains. "It took a very lengthy battle with the local authority to secure him a place at a special school that we hope will now enable him to thrive and realise his true potential, and, ultimately, be happy." More surprising was Hugh's experience over the last three years. Now in his forties, he has had a difficult life (page 201), with his inability to find a rewarding job and more particularly his severe epilepsy. He decided that, against medical advice, he would dramatically cut back the increasingly large doses of anti-epilepsy drugs that he was being prescribed. The result has changed his life. He no longer feels permanently not-all-there but is able to enjoy life more. He has even sold some of his pictures – thanks to the publicity from the book. So certainly not ideal, but better.

Hugh's story raised the oft-experienced problem of finding a job – something that Prof. Sir Simon Baron-Cohen had said was the silver bullet for people with learning disabilities. I heard that Matthew, who had some clearly unsuitable jobs but had got himself retrained, was now employed as a computer expert with the NHS – which he found satisfying. Another young man, Roger (page 183) had not yet found a job he wanted but had sent himself to university to gain more qualifications – and, maybe more life skills? I had always hoped that employers would be more flexible and positive about employing young people with learning difficulties. In a general way, I suspect that there has been an improvement and that the public are perhaps a little less surprised or worried about being served by someone with, say, autism. I was also pleased to see that Aspens, the group that had amalgamated with the housing charity, Pepenbury, was having a 'reverse job show', where prospective employers were invited to meet with potential employees from Aspens.

COVID – and lack of funding – had undoubtedly affected schools and colleges. A good number of people mentioned what they saw the Government's lack of support for education. There was now less money for teaching assistants. "They can earn more money stacking supermarket shelves;" and even teachers were leaving. "It is now longer than ever to get children with ASD and ADHD assessed… and we get even less support from outside experts such as OTs and physiotherapy…"

However, COVID seemed to have initiated one development. An NHS head of department responsible for all types of children with disabilities said, "I continue to be short of the staff needed to do a good job. I know the financial problem facing the NHS but…". "Although COVID initially created additional difficulties for both my staff and those they looked after, gradually after being thrown into more texting, emailing, WhatsApp groups and ZOOM meetings, it became an easier and, quite often, a practical way of working. For example, it can save money and travelling time and often make our comments clearer. So now, although I still have a backlog of a hundred families, I think that with this additional way of working – where appropriate – I may be able to reduce my backlog a bit – and a backlog is a terrible thing to have…". Other people with whom I talked, including a GP, echoed this trend to use the various types of web-based communication in new ways – which was foreseen in the first edition of the book (page 266). One go-ahead tuition company (www.right-tuition.co.uk) which helps children aged 5–16 of all abilities including children with SEN, had summoned all its teachers to a meeting on the Sunday before lockdown and taught them how to do all their tuition by Zoom. They continue to do some Zoom teaching and the company is expanding. However, one GP was more despairing about the effects of COVID on an already overstretched NHS. He felt COVID had put and was putting strains on services provided for those with learning disability, just as it had on GP practices, the hospitals and all the specialist support the NHS currently tries to give.

When I talked with various organisations that provide housing for those with a learning disability, they were nearly as dispirited. Their major sourced of funding continued to be money for each of their individuals from various county councils. The Chief Executive of one group said that he had to have detailed discussions with each of the nine councils from whom he receives funding and that he had "usually persuaded them to be realistic… most of them were promising a 9% increase." However, what was more worrying was the even larger increases in his costs. His wage bill had been increased by 10.2% last year. He thought his staff deserved the rise but it had meant extra costs of £700,000 a year. His other costs were increasing in a similar way. The position was made more difficult by the scarcity of staff. "It's a real crisis for all the organisations like mine." Additionally, his organisation was being asked to look after more people with 'profound and multiple learning disabilities', who needed more care and, therefore, extra funding.

Another smaller housing group, which I had thought outstanding, shared all the same concerns but was even more worried about the future. Government promises, which had repeatedly said that more money would be given for social care, had been broken time and time again. Their County Council money had generally only increased by 3%-6%, yet costs were around 10%-15% higher. Wages alone had been increased by 10%, both this year and last year. Heating costs had doubled and so on. Additionally, COVID had meant that absences had increased, putting pressure on staffing which had been already been difficult. Additionally, it is becoming more and more problematic to find new staff locally, who nowadays often needed increasingly complex training – something that is quite rightly becoming more regulated. But this again increased financial commitment. Even though the charity had in the past raised a good deal of its own money, within a year or two their reserves would have run down. This manager – who was outstanding and who had been committed to working with autistic people for over thirty years – said that he had never been so dispirited.

A Day Centre, not directly run by KCC staff, was somewhat more optimistic. They catered for a wide spectrum of abilities and provide a wide selection of courses. They had raised extra money privately which had enabled them to overhaul their buildings; and had meant they were able to increase the number of people they helped. However, although proud of what they achieved over the last three or four years, it was not going to be easy to survive.

I was cheered by one different type of Day Centre, the Princess Christian Farm, near Tonbridge (page 194 on). At one stage, it looked as if the whole organisation would have to close due to the withdrawal of further education funding. However, it had been taken over by Kasbah, a charity which supports people with physical and learning disabilities. The charity had been able to find extra resources, including for building work and, as the need for day services has grown, and with more SEN schools need help for young adults, they had developed a new range of courses. They have even introduced a respite flat for people transitioning away from living at home. They receive many requests to work at the Farm. Being unique helps. However it is not always easy to find people who have the right mix of skills both to look after people with learning disabilities as well as an aptitude for work on a farm. All the people who go to the farm with whom I talked continue to love it there. Most eccentrically, they have become a national centre for rescued reptiles – which are cared for by the students.

For the first edition of the book, I had talked with several Citizens Advice Bureaux in Kent. Going back to them now, they said that the last three years had not been easy. They had lost around half of their volunteer advisers, many very experienced, although numbers were beginning to rise. In this period, their requests for help had increased sharply, including queries about learning disability matters, particularly housing – all this at a time when their funding, mainly from local councils and greatly appreciated, had not been able to be increased.

Conclusions

It is difficult to reach definitive conclusions about the ways in which people with learning disabilities have changed in the years since the book was originally written. The individuals with learning difficulties (and their parents) have been affected by COVID and the cost of living; but they still seem the same kind, gentle people that they were. Nothing in the book about the provision of services seems to have changed, except that there is less money for virtually every aspect of the support offered. Staffing has become increasingly difficult and a fair number of people who provide support feared for the future. The Government has faced considerable problems over the last few years and the outlook is not encouraging. Decisions will have to be made about priorities. President Kennedy – himself with a family who knew about learning disabilities – said:

> *"One of the highest achievements of a civilization is the way in which it cares for its handicapped members".*

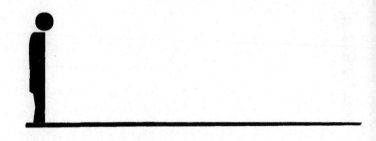

Why, When and How the Book was Written

Chaucer ends his Canterbury Tales saying to his readers that if there are things in the book that they like, give the praise to Jesu Crist. But if there is anything they do not like, it is his, the author's, fault: all that is written is written for our edification and that has been his intention.

I feel rather the same way. What has pleased or helped the reader of this book is due to those with whom I talked. Where I have got it wrong, it is my fault and I apologise.

Between 2015 and 2017 I had gathered together material for a book about a small but unusual mental hospital near Tonbridge. It was originally established around 1900, when it was called "The Princess Christian Farm Colony for the Feeble-Minded" – feeble-minded being the medical and legal term for the not too seriously mad, although locally, its residents were called 'barmy' after the large local lunatic asylum at Barming[101]. The resulting book "Just a Bit Barmy", covered not only the first fifty years when the Farm was a charity but also the NHS period when it became the Princess Christian Hospital. By the 1970s and 1980s the hospital had gradually developed into what was, in many ways, its own type of Care in the Community. It was starved of money and staff – its buildings were not up to the standards of the day and they had dramatically fewer staff than the minimum laid down – but it was setting an example for kind and practical care of its 'boys' and 'girls'. They were always called boys and girls whatever their ages.

As I moved towards the end of "Just a Bit Barmy", I began to wonder how the people like those who had been at Princess Christian had fared when they were moved into 'Care in the

Community'. By 2017, I began taking notes from people I met and by 2018 I had started asking for interviews.

As the research progressed, it became clear that the new book should be for the general public. It was not going to be a medical book and not even a book aimed primarily at the learning disability world. All the people with whom I talked – a huge range – were clear about one thing: the general public were not very understanding about them or the subject in general. They longed not only for the public to see them as individuals, but also for each of them to be thought of as a part of society – the wider world. They should not be seen as embarrassing or 'un-normal'. So, this book is for everyone.

Because this book has taken several years to write, some of the people I talked with have moved into other roles or have retired. I think of one man, Roger Gibson, who has retired as the Director of Pepenbury, where a wide range of people with learning disabilities are supported. Roger may no longer be at Pepenbury, but what he told me – taught me – is still true now. The important point is not whether I was told about the day-to-day life of a man or woman in 2017 or 2021, or even about a particular person in one part of the country. Their story will be much the same today all over the country – although, looking into the future, government financial support may become even leaner post Covid 19 and post Brexit.

Acknowledgements and Thanks

There are a huge range of books about learning disabilities but the two which moved me most were "The Reason I Jump" by Naoki Higashida (translated by David Mitchell and K A Yoshida[102]); and "Loving Olivia"[103] by Lady (Liz) Astor. I commend them both. The constructive "Making A Difference In Education: What The Evidence Says" by Professor Robert Cassen, Professor Anna Vignoles and Professor Sandra McNally, and Steve Silberman's "Neurotribes", a huge, journalistic examination of the subject – mainly in the US – were stimulating. (See the following notes for full details).

However, the interviews were my main source and I am particularly grateful to all who talked with me. Where they wished, I have quoted them by name but many preferred to just pass on their experiences without specifically being named. So, thanks to all in the social services, in the NHS and all the educational people who were so helpful in the middle of over-busy lives. Thanks, too, for the time that people in the charity and voluntary sector spent explaining their involvement, whether it was within the large housing groups such as mcch or Avenues; or the small charities, often mainly organised by one or two driven people. Particularly moving were the interviews with the people with learning disabilities and their astonishingly patient and brave parents. The people at the KCC Day Care Centres, together with the Orpheus Centre were wonderful, too.

I have also really appreciated all those who have made helpful comments about the book before it went to print. So, in alphabetical order, my thanks to Margaret Allison, Sir Michael and Lady Bett, Loris Clements, Matthew Cock, Kay Coleman, Janet Court, Dr John Ford, Martin Gulbis, Peter (and Ben) Hoare, Dame Kelly Holmes,

Sandeep Katwala, Russell Long, Irene Morgan, John Morgan, Helen Scott, Dame Stephanie Shirley, Dr Adam Skinner, Rebecca Thomas, Jo-Jo Tulloh, Lord (Tony) Young and last, but certainly not least, Mark Walker. There were a huge number of others who gave advice and I am sorry that I cannot mention each of them. However, Nick Polkinhorne, the manager of the Sevenoaks Bookshop – the Independent Bookshop of the Year – gave encouragement from the start.

As I went along, I endeavoured to give all contributors a copy of what I have quoted them as saying. If I have failed with anyone, I am truly most sorry.

My thanks, too, for the help on the editorial side, particularly Mike Bowers.

I am also most grateful to Jay Woods and his colleagues at Thieves Kitchen for all their help with the cover design, publicity and marketing.

Amanda Hawkes has continued to be wonderful in the design of the book, as she has done with all my other books.

However, my especial thanks to Joyce Field who has been so patient and efficient (and cheerful) over the past fifteen years interpreting and typing all my appallingly scribbled writing which have become books.

Names and Phrases for 'Mad' People – What to Call People who are Differently Able?

As I wrote the book about the history of the Princess Christian Farm Colony for the Feeble-minded, "Just a Bit Barmy", I started to jot down the names from 'feeble-minded' to 'service user' that have been used for 'mad' people over the last one hundred and fifty years. The problem of giving a name or a classification to types of people who are a bit different is illustrated by the huge number of English language words and phrases that have emerged. The list that follows of nearly four hundred words or phrases can pose three challenges to readers of this book as well as the earlier book:

- Can you think of even more words?
- Grade them from one to a hundred in terms of what you perceive as the severity of the person's problem. So, perhaps 'psychopath' and 'subhuman' in the top five; and 'barmy' as somewhere near eighty and 'inept' about ninety five.
- And what do you call such a person when you see them – or even talk with them.

Some of these terms have origins in Greco/Roman words; some originate from Early English, Germanic, Mediaeval and 15th-19th century words and there are a number from rhyming slang (r.s. in the list). There are one or two from India, for example, 'doolally', and a few from Ireland and the USA. There are typically irreverent ones from Australia and one from Donald Trump. Increasingly, as society gets more sensitive about labelling people, the formal descriptions get vaguer while the medical terms get more detailed. Perhaps my favourites – for a variety of reasons – are 'differently able' (sounds sensible); 'a kangaroo loose in the top paddock' (wonderfully appalling); NFA and PDDNOS (look at the list for the definitions). The new favoured term seems to be neurodiverse. Some medical terms are given in the list, including a Victorian term, 'West's disorder'.[104] The wide variety may give some indication that it has always been difficult or embarrassing to categorise those who are different from the ordinary – different from 'us'. So, if you do at least glance down the list, it will remind you of the men and women who, in each generation, and still today need help and, even more perhaps, need understanding.

I have not included a large number of medical words which denote difficulties which concern learning, mental and physical problems. Just look at some of those beginning with 'A'. There are Agnosia, Alexia, Amnesia, Aphasia, Aphemia, Aphonia, Anosmia, Appraxia, Ataxia and so on.

Abnormal
Abnormality of the Mind
Additional needs
Afflicted
Alexithymia
Alternative Language
    Difficulty
Articulation
Aspergers
Assisted Needs
Attention Deficit Disorder
    (ADD)
Attention Deficit and
    Hyperactivity Disorder
    (ADHD)
Augmentative Communication
Autistic
Autistic Spectrum Condition
Autistic Spectrum Disorder
    (ASD)
Away with the fairies

Backward
Barking/Barking mad
Barmy
Barmpot
Basket case
Batso
Batty/Bats
Bats in the belfry
Baying at the moon
Bazoodi
Below par
Berk
Berserk
Bi-polar
He's a bit – you know ....
Blockhead
Bollock Brain
Bonehead
Bonkers
Boob/booby
Borderline Personality
    Disorder (BPD)
Boron

The 'boys'
Bubblehead
Buffoon
Buggy
Bungalow (i.e. nothing on top)
Buttercup and Daisy (r.s.)

Cabbage Head
Case
Central Auditory Processing
    Disorder (CAPD)
Certified/Certifiable Person
    with Challenging
    Behaviour
With a Chromosome
    Disorder
Chump
In cloud cuckoo land
Clown
Clumsy Child Disorder
Cocktail Party Syndrome
Cognitive Disorder
Communication and
    Interaction (C&I)
Compulsive Depressive
    Disorder
Conduct Disorder (Irish)
Coot
Crackers
Crackpot
Crack-minded
Crank/cracked
Crazed
Crazy
Cretin
Cripple
Cuckoo

Daffy
Daft
Daft as a brush
Deedle
Defective/Defective Personality
Deluded
Dense
Deranged
Developmental
    Communication
    Disorder (DCD)
Development Language
    Disorder
Developmentally Disabled (US)
Differently Able
Dickhead
Dilbert
Dilly
Dim
Diminished Responsibility
Dimmo
Dimwit
Dink
Dippy
Disabled
Disordered
Disturbed
Div/Divvy
Doink
Doolally (Indian)
Dope
Dottard
Dotty
Down's syndrome
Dozy
Dromgo (Aust)
Dumb
Dumb-cluck

Dummy
Dunderhead
Dunce
Dungers
Dwarf
Dyscalculia
Dysmorphia
Dystonia
Dyspraxia

Echolalic
Education, Health and
    Care Plan (EHCP)
Educationally subnormal
Edwards Syndrome
Emotional Disorder
Emotional Stability Personality
    Disorder (ESPD)
Eros and Cupid (r.s.)
ESN

Fantacist
Feeb
Feeble-minded
A few annas short of a rupee
A few sheep short in the top
    paddock (Aust)
A few snags short of a barbie
    (Aust)
A few threads short of a jumper
Flaky (USA)
Fool/Foolish
Fragile X syndrome
Freak
Frenzied
Fruit and nutcase
Fruit cake
Fruity

A fruit-loop
In the funny farm
Funny in the head

Ga-ga
Galoot
Gawnie (Irish)
General Anxiety Disorders
    (GAD)
'My Gentlemen'
The 'girls'
Gone bananas
Goofy
Goon
Gormless

Handicapped
Has problems
Have a screw loose
Haywire
Head basket
He's…. (tapping the forehead)
High Functioning Disability
HSAM (Highly Superior
    Autobiographical Memory)
Hyperlexia
Hysterical

Idiot
Idiot-savant
Imbecile
Impaired
An Inadequate
Inept
Inmates
Insane
Intellectually challenged
Irrational

Jackass
Jughead
"Just call me John?"

A Kangeroo loose in the
    top paddock
Kanner's syndrome
Keith Moon (r.s.)
Kilkenny Cats (r.s.)
Kit Kat (r.s.)
Klictz
Kookie/kooky

Lacks capacity
Lakes of Killarney (r.s.)
Lame
Lamebrain
LD (short for learning
    disabilities)
Learning Differently
Those with learning difficulties
Those with learning disabilities
Those with language
    impairment
Those with speech and
    language disorders
Lennox Gastaut syndrome
Lights on but nobody in
Loco
Loghead
Lombard
Loon/Loony
(In the) loony bin
Loopy
Lost his marbles
Low mental order
Lump of school (r.s.)
Lunatic

Lunk
Lunkhead

Mad
Mad as a box of frogs (Yorks)
Mad as a Hatter
Mad as a march hare
Man on the moon (r.s.)
Maniac
Marches to a different drum
Mazawattee
Those with a mental health
    condition
Those with Mental Health
    Difficulties
Mental
Mentally defective
Mentally deficient
Mentally disabled
Mentally disordered
Mentally impaired
Mentally irregular
Mentally retarded
Mentally subnormal
Microcephalic
Microphily
A Misfit
Missing a few cough drops
    (Suffolk)
Moderate Learning Disability
    (MLD)
Mong
Mongol
Monomaniac
Monotropic
Mood disorder
Moonstruck
Morally defective

Moron/moronic
Motor moron
Multiple Personality Disorder
  (MPD)

Narcistic Personality Disorder
Natural Fool
Neuro-atypical
Neurodivergent
Neurodiverse
Neurotic
NFA (Normal for Andover)
NFC (Normal for Chatham)
Nincompoop
Nitwit
No one at home
Non compos mentis
Non-verbal
Not all there
Not right in the head
Not quite the full quid (Aust)
Not the sharpest tool in the box
Numskull
Nutcase
'A nut job' (D. Trump)
Nut
Nut rock
Nuts
Nutter/nutty
Nutty as a fruit cake

Object prominence
Obsessive Compulsive
  Disorder (OCD)
Odd
Odd ball
Of unsound mind
Off his bonce

Off his chump
Off his head
Off his noodle
Off his plonk
Off his rocker
Off his trolley
Off kilter
On the autistic spectrum
On the spectrum
One flew over the cuckoo's nest
One sandwich short of a picnic
One screw loose
One tack short of a tool box
  (USA)
Out of his mind
Out to lunch

Paranoid
Pathological Demand
  Avoidance (PDA)
'Patients'
Pelmans
A penny short of a bob
Personality Disorder
Persuasive Development
  Disorder (PDD)
Persuasive Development
  Disorder Not Otherwise
  Specified (PDDNOS)
Pillock
Plum crazy
Poop
A potato cake short of a packet
Potato-head (E.Anglia)
Potty
Prader-Willi syndrome
Prannock
Pratt

Profound Learning Difficulty (PLD)

Profound and multiple learning Difficulty (PMLD)

Profound and multiple learning Disability (PMLD)

Profound, severe and complex needs (PSCN)

Psychopath/Psychotic

Rabid

He's radio (r.s)

Raspberry (r.s.)

Raving

Receptive language difficulties

'Residents'

Retardates

Retarded/Retard

Rett syndrome

Round the bend

Round the twist

A sandwich short of a packed lunch

Scapegrace

Schizoid/schizo

Schizophrenic

Screw loose

Screwy

Self-locked-up Disease

Sensory Processing Disorder

Severe Learning Disability (SLD)

'Service User'

Sick in the head

Silly

Simple

Simple minded

Simpleton

Slightly short of East Ham (i.e. one tube stop from Barking)

Slow

Slow at keeping up

Slow-witted

Social Communications Disorder (SCD)

Sociopath

Soft

Soft in the head

Spastic

Spackers/spac

Spaz/Spazzer

Special Educational Needs (SEN)

Special Language Impairment

Special Needs

Speech and Language Disorder

Statemented (of special needs)

Subhuman

Stupid

Sturge Weber syndrome

Subnormal

Suitable case for treatment

Supportee

Taken to/Gone to Macclesfield (asylum there)

'Tenants'

Thick

Thick as two short planks

Touched

Troubled

Twat

Two ounces short of a pound

Tuppence short of a shilling

Turner syndrome

Unbalanced
Unhinged
Unsane
Unsound
Unstable
Up the pole

Verbal dyspraxia
Village Idiot

Wacky/Whaky
Wacko
Wally
Wazzock
West's disorder[105]
On the Wessex Scale (I-IV)
Williams-syndrome

XYY syndrome

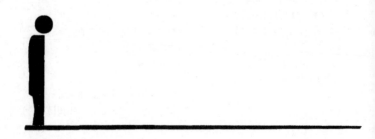

Summary about SEN Schooling

Although this book looks primarily at West Kent, it could be useful to summarise some of the national trends within SEN schooling and some general advice. Many of the points below come from work done by Professor Anna Vignoles in the Faculty for Education at Cambridge.

- Diagnose as early as possible.

- The number of children being classified as having Special Educational Needs and having the more serious Education, Health and Care Plan is increasing relatively quickly. However, extra teaching back-up is also increasing.

- The very disturbing NHS waiting lists for assessment and treatment of more serious cases are known about by government. There are suggestions about how to improve the situation – but very little extra money. Certainly not an ideal situation.

- SEN/EHCP pupils should <u>never</u> be automatically expected to be lower achievers. Do everything possible to boost confidence. In spite of the numerous tests/exams/league tables, all children, whatever their seeming likely level of attainment, should be helped equally; and all children should be monitored regularly and individually.

- Pairing of students; and mentoring by an older student can help.

- It is too easy to say many more boys than girls need help for SEN, behavioural difficulties, etc. They just have different symptoms. Almost certainly, the problems faced by girls are much underestimated.

- Many schools need to provide more information about their SEN processes.

- Teaching Assistants often need more specialist training and need to work with the form teacher.

- There needs to be equal help given all over the country. The richest areas or the richest parents should not get the best/fullest treatment. (Poorer families are more likely to have a SEN child).

- Alleviating social disadvantage would have a major impact on the number of children with special education needs.

- Parents need to get as involved as possible: there are worthwhile schemes for parents to help with the wide variety of individual problems.

- More research needs to be done into what actually works (and does not work) – particularly as little extra funding is likely.

- Most/all organisations – whether state, private or voluntary – have websites. The National Autistic Society can provide excellent overarching information and there are separate societies/associations for separate learning disability problems. There are schemes to help with reading; and specialist help for reading by children who have Down's.[106] One national charity, Beanstalk, helps volunteer readers in schools. Additionally, advice about behavioural problems has at least one helpful course/programme 'The Incredible Years'; and there is help available for ADHD/ADD.

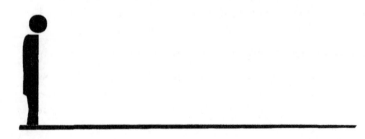

Notes

[1] Sir Richard Stilgoe OBE DL was born 1943 in Surrey but he was brought up in Liverpool. He was in a group which played at The Cavern. 1961 Clare College (and Footlights) at Cambridge. Over the next thirty years, a huge variety of TV, radio and cabaret, the latter often with the late Peter Skellern. He wrote the lyrics to Starlight Express and Phantom of the Opera, and the non T S Eliot parts of Cats. Massive amount of charity work. Founding Orpheus in 1998 in his former family home in Godstone, led to an OBE and he was then knighted 2012 for charitable services, particularly via his Alchemy Foundation – which supports overseas work, including water; together with support for disability and social work; penal reform; medical research and respite care. Married to opera singer, Annabel Hunt, for forty-five years, he has five children and fourteen grandchildren.

[2] A Glossary of Historical Terms for 'Madness': see www.langdondownmuseum.org.uk The UK Mental Deficiency Act of 1913 categorised learning disabled people as follows:
- Idiots – Persons in whose case there exists mental defectiveness of such a degree that they are unable to guard themselves against common dangers such as traffic or fire.
- Imbecile – Persons in whose case there exists mental defectiveness which, though not amounting to idiocy, is yet so pronounced that they are incapable of managing themselves and their affairs or, in the case of children, of being taught to do so.
- Feeble-minded – Persons in whose case there exists mental defectiveness which, though not amounting to imbecility, is yet so pronounced that they require care, supervision and control for their own protection or the protection of others. Or, in the case of children, that they appear to be permanently incapable by reason of such defectiveness of receiving proper benefit from instruction in ordinary school.
- Moral Defective – Persons in whose case there exists mental defectiveness, coupled with strong vicious and criminal propensities and who require care, supervision and control for the protection of others. These people include unmarried mothers.

Other terms in common use in the past
- Cretin was the oldest term, from the French, referring to those with both physical and intellectual incapacity.

- Moron referred to an adult with the intellectual development similar to an 8 to 12 year old child.
- Retarded came from the Latin retardare, meaning to make slow, delay, keep back. Mental retardation was a general term which covered all levels of learning disability.
- Mongolism was a medical term first used by Dr John Langdon-Down in the 1860s to identify someone with what became known after the Second World War as Down's syndrome.

[3] Penny Southern who was Director of Disabled Children, Adult Learning Disabilities and Mental Health when I first talked with her but later assumed even wider responsibilities at the KCC before her retirement.

[4] 'The Reason I Jump' by Naoki Higashida, translated in 2013 by K A Yoshida and David Mitchell. Originally written in 2007. Published by Hodder and Stoughton Ltd ISBN 978 1 444 77677 5. Also 'Fall Down 7 Times Get Up 8', published in English by Sceptre 2017, ISBN 978-1-444-79908-8.

[5] The Oakwood Asylum at Barming was built in 1833 on a grandiose scale with all the mod cons of its age. (See "Just a Bit Barmy" by Chris Rowley ISBN 978-0-9539340-4-1)

[6] Mental Illnesses:
  i. Generalised Anxiety Disorders (GAD) cover such problems as:
    – Clinical depression, acute anxiety, suicidal thoughts
    – Agoraphobia and other phobias
    – Self-harm
    – Eating disorders
    – Drug and alcohol abuse
  ii. Other Types of Mental Illness
    – Bi-polar disorder and schizophrenia
  iii.Sometimes also included are:
    – Obsessive Compulsive Disorder
    – Tourette's syndrome
    Although these are also sometimes considered learning disabilities and autism.
  iv. Also, the grouping known as SpLD – Specific Learning Difficulties:
    – Dyslexia
    – Dysgraphia
    – Dyscalculia
    – Dyspraxia
    – Dysmorphia
All the above have sub-divisions and nearly all have three or four letter acronyms. Schizophrenia is complex: I found that, for a layman to understand it better, it was useful to read a remarkable novel by Jasper Gibson "The Octopus Man": publ. Weidenfeld & Nicholson 2021.

[7] Ibid.

[8] Dr Lorna Wing OBE FRCPsych (1928-2014) was a pioneer in the field of developmental disorders. She advanced the understanding of autism worldwide.

With her long-term collaborator, Dr Judith Gould, she revolutionised the thinking about the prevalence of autism, particularly in children; she coined the phrase 'on the autistic spectrum', realising that it was not the simple 'he/she is autistic/not autistic'; she introduced the term Aspergers syndrome in the late 1970s; was involved with the founding of the National Autistic Society; and was concerned in 1981 with the establishment of the first diagnostic centre for autism – now named in her honour. Sources: various, including Wikipedia.

[9] Figure from Autistica (see note 34)

[10] Monotropism was a theory posited in particular by Dr Dianah Murray (1946-2021), whom the NHS described in her obituary as "an extraordinary autistic woman… ". She felt that autistic people were not good at processing multiple things at once and, where tasks require a broad attention span, including social interaction, a monotropic person will miss things outside their attention tunnel, (Wikipedia and obituary). Also see 'The Passion of the Mind' (2011) by Wenn Lawson.

[11] At one stage, when this chapter was in draft form, I was still not entirely clear about the many definitions I had been given by probably twenty exerts. So, I consulted with Dr Adrian Winbow, MB, BS, FRCPsych.DPM, a leading consultant psychiatrist who had held senior positions in the NHS and private practice. He very kindly corrected the text and explained many things. He also gave me my own copy of ICD10 which in 374 pages summarized the European classification of mental illness. (I was not given, nor did I need the US version). However, all the faults and comments are my own not his. But my thanks.

[12] The web has large good number of papers/articles about the subject. However, it seems the current thinking is that there is some genetic/family link but that it does not seem to be inherited in the usual way. Dr Leo Kanner's paper in 1943 – which used the term 'autism' for the first time – was influential in largely debunking the Freudian theory that such people had problems because of bad parenting/frigid mothers, etc. Prof. Francesca Happé has produced new research on the subject of genetic links. (see websites)

[13] Award-winning US investigative reporter, Steve Silberman, in his remarkable book 'Neurotribes: The Legacy of Autism and How to Think Smarter', publ. Allen & Unwin 2015. ISBN 978-1-76011-3636, has a chapter on this not very edifying development.

[14] Dr. John Ford: retired senior partner of large GP practice and medical historian.

[15] Quoted from The Washington Post website.

[16] Francesca Happé, Professor of Cognitive Neuroscience at King's College, London; and Director of MRC, Social, Genetic and Developmental Psychiatry Centre at the Institute of Psychiatry. She has written three books as well as papers. Listen also to BBC Radio 4 Life Scientific Tuesday 15 September 2020.

[17] Prader-Willi syndrome was first identified by Dr John Langdon-Down, the leading Victorian doctor in the field of 'madness'. The classification of Down's syndrome in the 1960s was named in honour of him and his two doctor sons (see Chris Rowley's book: "Just a Bit Barmy", published 2019, ISBN 978-0-9539340-4-1)

[18] "Loving Olivia" by Liz Astor, published 2006 Rodale International Limited. ISBN 10:1-4050-8815-X and 13:978-1-4050-8815-Z. Out of print but second hand copy worth acquiring.

[19] National Geographic June 2017. "Why We Lie" by Yudhijit Bhattcharjee.

[20] The supposed cures included not only expensive special diets but stroking with feathers and the banging of actual or electronic gongs.

[21] 'The Reason I Jump' by Naoki Higashida, translated in 2013 by K A Yoshida and David Mitchell. Originally written in 2007. Published by Hodder and Stoughton Ltd ISBN 978 1 444 77677 5. Also 'Fall Down 7 Times Get Up 8', published in English by Sceptre 2017, ISBN 978-1-444-79908-8.

[22] The Hadlow Group oversees this and a further education college in the area and is described – with particular reference to its support for people with learning disabilities – in Chapter 8.

[23] BBC Website News Magazine: 29 September 2016 and interviews with specialists.

[24] Figures/symptoms largely from NHS website. The association, OCD UK, say there are three quarters of a million people in the UK with severe symptoms. (There are also expensive sounding experts who promise help). A BBC Radio 4 programme (available on BBC Sounds) from 9.30am Tuesday 13 April "One To One" had constructive suggestions.

[25] NHS and other websites

[26] See Wikipedia and numerous books about him.

[27] From "Making a Difference in Education: What the Evidence Says" by Professors Robert Cassen, Sandra McNally and Anna Vignoles. Published April 2016 by Routledge. Prof Vignoles CBE FBA is Professor of Education at Cambridge, focussing on the economic value of education and equality in education.

[28] From 'Neurotribes', see note 10.

[29] See note 7.

[30] The Times 30 March 2016 in an article about Prof. Sir Simon Baron-Cohen FBA by Helen Rumbelow.

[31] Available along with much more information on the National Autistic Society (NAS) website.

[32] Quoted on BBC Radio 4 26/27 October 2016, amongst other places, and including Guardian 16 November 2016 in a John Harris article.

[33] From Roger Gibson, former Chief Executive of Pepenbury; and other sources.

[34] Autistica is the UK's leading charity working on research into autism. Founded in 2004 by Dame Stephanie Shirley, CH, DBE, FREng, FRCS, it purposely does not undertake the work of the National Autistic Society (NAS) which concentrates more on the service needs of autistic individuals and their families.

[35] An NHS report from September 2010, analysing work done in the Yorkshire and Humber region (www.healthyambitions.co.uk)

[36] Websites and Radio 4, 5 November 2015

[37] See NHS Chapter later in the book.

[38] A wide variety of people and websites.

[39] From House of Commons 23/25 June 2020: there is a national shortage of all types of care workers/care assistants, with "well over 100,000 vacancies" and a very high turnover. Additionally, Unison suggests that while there are currently two million care workers, a further one million will be needed by 2025. See also note 86.

[40] 'Shared Lives' is an NHS scheme which supports adults with learning disabilities and mental health issues. There are groupings widespread in the UK – although none in SW Kent.

[41] At the end of my researches, I was told about a website called 'Kent Local Offer' which has a helpline called IASK. The 2014 Children's and Families' Act mandated county councils to provide amongst other things a website which is meant to include everything about the services provided for people with physical disabilities and learning disabilities. Having been told by a good number of parents (and several educationalists I asked) that there was no comprehensive list of schools which contained various levels of provision for children with learning disabilities, I have recently been told that a list is included in this website www.kent.gov.uk/education-and-children-special-educational-needs-and-disability. There is also the KCC Information and Advice Service on 0300 413000 about which I again only heard at the end of my discussions. Several parents also mentioned how useful the Kent Autistic Trust is at helping with the maze. There are many similar groups around the country with particularly useful local knowledge.

[42] At the time of this interview, Paul Carter – now Sir Paul – was Leader of the Kent County Council (KCC) – and, in effect, also its CEO. He retired in October 2019 after fourteen years in the role, but remains a councillor.

[43] There could easily be several chapters about the money provided by Central Government to the KCC over the last five or ten years. The systems and the amounts have seemed to change virtually every year and, in recent times, changes have taken place more frequently. This makes analyzing like for like comparisons very difficult. Excluding schools, over the past 6 years, the KCC has normally spent very approximately £1.4 billion to £1.5 billion a year. On the face of it, this hasn't changed very much over the six years. However, within this total, there have been numerous changes with the council becoming responsible for additional services which were previously funded by central government, e.g. some new learning disability services, Surestart children's centres, concessionary bus fares for older people, council tax benefit for low income households, etc. In 2010/11 approximately 40% of council spending was funded from council tax; a further 41% from central government and the remaining 19% from other income raised by the council. In 2015/16 the headline equation was very similar, with 48% funded from council tax, 43% government grant and 19% other income. However, due to the changes in function already outlined, this represented a £181m reduction in central funding and £55m increase in council tax. After taking account of increased costs and increased demand, this represented a 32% reduction in the spending. These figures are consistent with

the NAO findings in their report on the state of local authority finance published in October 2016, which concluded over the same period that local authority funding nationally has declined in real terms, i.e. measured against index linked inflation, by 23.4% (of which the decline in central government funding was greater at 36%, compared to real term decline in council income of 4.5%). *[My own suspicion is that the KCC may not want to complain too stridently about the numerous sleight-of-hand changes imposed by a Conservative Part – which most KCC Councillors support – for fear of having even worse and every more devious plans introduced to help balance the Treasury's books. But this, of course, is a personal view. CR].* This change in the relationship between Central Government and Local Government is made particularly difficult for the Shire areas such as Kent as much more money is given to city areas. For example, Inner London receives £361 per person and Metropolitan areas £317 per person compared to county/unitary areas such as Kent which only receives £225 per person (based on 2016/17 Settlement Funding Assessment.)

[44] In addition to spending many hours a week on his wide range of public service jobs, Mr Carter had always been and still is a businessman, running a number of firms in property, construction and retain business in London. As well as having been Leader of the KCC, he has been Chairman of the SE Regional Authority and its replacement SE England Councils.

[45] The detailed KCC plans for adult social care are in a policy statement 'Adult Social Care, Vision and Strategy 2016-2021'. For 2017/18 the budget included an additional £28 million for adult social care, half of which included extra payments and increasing fees paid to contractors/care providers, a quarter to support rising costs (including National Living Wage and inflation) and to tackle market sustainability, with the remainder to meet rising demand and legislative requirements. However, Government changes announced – without consultation in the February/March 2017 budget – are so material that major adjustments to the adult social services budget had to be made. The substantial difficulties arising from the 2020 Covid 19 pandemic will put further strains on resources. The effect of Brexit is unclear.

[46] In 2009/10 KCC paid £91,000,000 for 'Commissioned Elements' (i.e. the outside specialist contractors). This sum had increased to £152,000,000 for 2016/17.

[47] These figures for typical wages were from 2018. They may well have been increased slightly; and the 2020 Covid 19 pandemic and Brexit, as well as the parliamentary or public disquiet, may or may not bring improvement.

[48] "Adult Social Care Workforce in England" publ. 8 February 2018

[49] See various newspapers, Tuesday 4 July 2017

[50] There are a bewildering number of non-school/non-university qualifications, run by various organisations. However, both QCF and ILM are formally recognised by Ofqual. While the outside world would not normally understand the graduations and worth of each qualification, the appropriate employer/manager normally will.

[51] Ibid.

⁵² There have been five CQC reports on the two hospitals in the last nine years. They are detailed and lengthy. In one year, the summary had over one hundred and thirty recommendations. Only one related to learning disabilities. It suggested that communication with people who had learning disabilities should be improved. (Full reports appear on the CQC website).

⁵³ Princess Christian Hospital – originally the Princess Christian Farm Colony for the Feeble-minded – was in Hildenborough, near Tonbridge. See Chris Rowley's earlier book "Just a Bit Barmy", ISBN 978-0-9539340-4-l.

⁵⁴ See note 25.

⁵⁵ CQC Report – Out of Sight – Who Cares? Restraint, Segregation and Seclusion Review: 22 October 2020. "Creating a package of care to meet the individual's needs was often seen as too difficult to get right… Starting at a young age… parents waited, sometimes years, to get a diagnosis of autism… and even when they were diagnosed… they did not get the care and support they needed… .

⁵⁶ The I Newspaper, Saturday 28 December 2019 and the National Autistic Society.

⁵⁷ One NAS report suggested that the average wait for a child who probably has autism to have a diagnostic assessment is now three and a half years: from ITV programme 'This Morning' 9 October 2017 quoting NAS figures. On a personal basis, I heard of one couple from Essex who were told they would have to wait six or seven years. The most pressing cases will be seen sooner: but that is little consolation to the others. See also other comments and examples in other parts of this book about this subject.

⁵⁸ It is now thought by some experts that certain types of learning disabilities are to do with neural pathways 'not firing normally'. Research is, therefore, looking to see whether these pathways can be restored.

⁵⁹ Wikipedia gives a number of references about this apparent increase.

⁶⁰ Amanda Spielman – Chief Inspector of Ofsted – Tuesday 26 June 2018 speech.

⁶¹ See Chris Rowley's book "Just a Bit Barmy" ISBN 978-0-9539340-4-1.

⁶² British Institute of Learning Disabilities (BILD), published by DES.

⁶³ Chatbots, or the use of computer-based speech to ask questions/provide answers were being developed even in the 1960s. In the UK, 'Babylon Health' assesses patients' needs after a 'chat'; and 'Wobot' is a US based CBT system (at $39.99 a session).

⁶⁴ For a further source of information and support, contact 'Communication Matters' (CM), a charity for those who cannot talk.

⁶⁵ Article by Julia Rogers in KCHCT magazine. For more information see www.kentcht.nhs.uk/child SLT

⁶⁶ Professor Anna Vignoles in "Making a Difference in Education: What the Evidence says". Chapter 9, pages 135-154 which includes a list of over 50 books and articles. Published by Routledge 2015. £25 paperback.

⁶⁷ Ibid.

[68] Report by Austistica following research in Australia, published 20/21 September 2021.

[69] Special Educational Needs Code of Practice 2014.

[70] Details given with permission of the school, the parent and, above all, the boys themselves.

[71] For those needing a more detailed view of ADHD, what it is and how to cope with it, see a clear thirty-six page booklet prepared by the KCHFT Community Nurses called "An introduction to ADHD – ADHD understood" Leaflet code 00980 published 2015.

[72] I asked top management for figures but met with great reluctance. This puzzled me – particularly as it was meant to be a public statistic. I was eventually given a figure – over 90% – after I had mentioned the Freedom of Information Act. It seemed amazingly and cheerfully high. Only later did I talk to someone who worked in the administrative department of a further education college. She laughed at my experience. "We all had to adapt: the funding depends on it", she said.

[73] Home Schooling: while West Kent College may have found home schooling is decreasing, nationally the figure is increasing and, because home schooling has little supervision, there is considerable pressure for some regulation to be introduced.

[74] A report in March 2021 says the number of part-time, post-school students fell by over a half between 2009 and 2017. Those most affected were the least educated. 49% in the lowest socio-economic groups have had no training since school; and the vast bulk of government funding for post-19 education (93%) goes to help those with at least A-level qualifications. In the UK, nine million or more have low levels of numeracy and literacy. (Source: The Guardian 29 March 2021)

[75] Sir Richard Stilgoe OBE DL – see note 1.

[76] Yet another version of the statistics comes from E. Emerson and Chatton in a report for the Centre For Disability. It says that over 80% of people with a learning disability are out of work. Mencap, with a slightly different approach, says that 65% would like to work – with the other 35% presumably realising that they would not be able or want to do a job. A BBC Radio talk (15 March 2020) by Ewan Thomas said that only 6% of people with a formal learning disability have a paid job.

[77] Prof. Sir Simon Baron-Cohen, one of, if not the leading academics in the UK in the field of autism. He is a Professor in the Department of Psychology and Psychiatry at Cambridge; and Director of the Autism Research Centre there. He has written many books and articles and made TV programmes and award-winning DVDs on the subject. His clinic has helped over 1,000 patients with their disabilities.

[78] BBC2 "Employable Me" – first series of three documentaries broadcast March/April 2016. Further information on BBC website.

[79] Williams Syndrome is a rare developmental disorder that is present from birth. The condition is characterised by mild to moderate learning disability, distinct personality characteristics and facial features, a range of cardiovascular problems and other difficulties. There is no 'cure' but symptoms can be eased. See Williams Syndrome Foundation website.

[80] From 'Third Age Matters': Winter 2017. Article 'Our Lives Disappeared' by Louise Cooper.

[81] 'Loving Olivia' p.208: see note 16.

[82] Leonard Cheshire Disability Report 17 October 2017. MPs on the Petitions Committee backed the call by Katie Price to have tough and enforceable laws against on-line hate crimes against the disabled (Jan 2019). Matt Hancock, as the then Culture Secretary, said that he understood but that it was difficult to control the tech giants. Separately, a report (March 2021) said that hate crime against disabled rail travellers had increased from sixty-three per year to seventy-eight between 2016 and 2019 – the reported increased of 24%. The numbers may be small but, again, such reportage increases anxiety among the disabled, making them less willing to travel. (Source: the web and newspapers)

[83] From RMT report 28 March 2021.

[84] 'The Reason I Jump' by Naoki Higashida. See note 19.

[85] Daily Telegraph interview by Judith Woods, July 2017, quoted earlier.

[86] Guardian Article: Family Section article by Emily Yates entitled 'Young, disabled and sex' 15 October 2016.

[87] BBC Radio 4 10.30pm 28 July 2016.

[88] Dan Gower-Smith of Avenues.

[89] 'The Rosie Project' was the first of a series of three novels by Australian novelist, Graeme Simsion, the follow-up novels being 'The Rosie Effect' and 'The Rosie Result'. First published in Australia in 2014, they are all now available from Penguin Books/Random House.

[90] 'The Best Laid Plans' by Kathy Lette (published by Penguin Books ISBN 9780 59307 1366) has an autistic son and has given a number of moving interviews including on BBC's Woman's Hour.

[91] Prof. Anna Vignoles in "Making a Difference in Education: What the Evidence says", by Robert Cassen, Sandra McNally and Anna Vignoles. See earlier notes.

[92] Liz Astor in "Loving Olivia" p208-209 and 225-229. See note 16.

[93] In parliamentary speeches on 23-25 June 2020, various figures were quoted – the high turnover of care staff said to be 30%-40%; the shortage of care staff – said to be 100,000; the reliance on immigrant care staff – said to be 1 in 6; the high proportion on zero hours contracts – said to be over 25% plus the normal minimum wage. The Government spokespeople replied – as has so often been said before – that all these matters were being addressed. (Sources: Hansard and speech by Sir Simon Stevens 5 July 2020). The 2021 figures are that 75% of care workers/support workers do not get paid the Real Living Wage (£9.50 per hour/£10.85 in London). 25% are over fifty-five years old. Approximately 65% are women. (Sources: I Newspaper Saturday 13 February 2021). See also note 37 earlier.

[94] From a letter by Don Brand of Staplehurst, Kent in the Telegraph, February 2017. He added that the total NHS budget was £139 billion and that local councils in total spend only £17b gross on social care.

[95] In letter from Jennifer Ball in the i newspaper Saturday 17 April 2021.

[96] Prof. Robert Cassen OBE, Oxford, Harvard and LSE. British economist with a range of specialisations, including working for the UK Government and the World Bank, both in Britain and overseas, particularly India. Professor of Development at Oxford but more recently involved with the economics of education and low achievement.

[97] 'Pepper' has been developed by the University of Bedfordshire and Middlesex University in association with Advinia Health Care. It is the largest ever investigation into the use of autonomous social robots for supporting older people in care.

[98] Dr Benjamin Chitambira, who worked in various Kent hospitals and has spent the last two years on light therapy treatment. From BBC South East news, Tuesday 8 September 2020.

[99] Professor Mirelle Toledano and her team at Imperial College, London are analysing the vast amounts of data collected about individuals in order to use AI to work towards personalised help with mental disorders. (From news report in the Weekend i newspaper by Tom Bawden on 24 April 2021).

[100] Paper announcing a consultation for Disabled People's Employment 31 October 2016 from Damien Green – Work & Pensions Secretary; and the November 2017 proposals which followed up the consultation.

[101] See note 5.

[102] See note 4.

[103] See note 16.

[104] I have added West's Disorder as an early example of a specialised medical term because, firstly, it has lasted a hundred and fifty years and, secondly, it has a Kent connection. Dr West was a respected Tonbridge doctor whose son, E J West, was plainly mentally ill. He was sent to the Earlswood Mental Asylum under the care of Dr John Langdon-Down in 1860 and his condition given his name. He died of TB with Dr Langdon-Down and the matron at his bedside. Information from Dr John Ford, retired head of GP practice and Tonbridge medical historian. For further details see Journal of Medical Biography Vol 11 May 2003 pp.107-113.

[105] See note 100.

[106] See note 91.

Index

In this index, the names of people and organisations are included but not every specific medical condition. Nor have the many mentions of social services, NHS, KCC or most Kent place names been included.

Index

Quotations from the book

"*Maybe surprisingly, for me the biggest problem for the future is not funding. It is getting the public to become more understanding.*"
Director of Kent's Learning Disability Service

"*I don't think of my caring as a job: just going out each day to be with my friends.*" **Support worker at a care home**

"*We kids with autism would like you to watch out for us – meaning, please never give up on us.*" **Higashida Naoki**

"*Middle/upper class parents obtain more help for their children with a learning disability than the less educated.*" **Prof. Anna Vignoles**

"*No one seems to believe what a person with a learning disability says. I feel so frustrated all the time. I cannot get a proper job. I so much want one… Society should understand more.*"
40 year old with autism and epilepsy

"*Initially we support workers have to explain to parents that we can usually improve things but not provide a cure.*" **Head teacher**

A report found that 25% of newly committed adults had had dealings with professionals concerned with learning disabilities or mental health.

We pass a room with one tiny girl with a large blow-up ball. The Head explains that she is profoundly deaf, cannot see or speak or walk. "All we can do is to give her some sensory experience."

"I used to live at Leybourne Hospital, but I'm not naughty now."
Old lady with Down's

"I earn about a hundredth of what I used to earn in the City. But it's great." **A volunteer**

One GP reminded me of the old Yorkshire saying "All the world is odd save me and thee: and thee's a bit queer."

I worked out the number of hours a week where a parent was solely responsible for their child – it was a hundred and ten. **The author**

"If I don't give you eye contact or answer you if you are talking to me, please don't think I'm being rude." **10 year old girl to teacher**

"When I see a stranger showing little acts of kindness towards my son, it makes me tearful." **Father of autistic boy**

"She was hurt if she was laughed at and… continuously on the edge of great anxiety." **A mother**

"Things have improved [for people with a learning disability] but there's a long way to go before they are treated as the individuals they are."
Senior social worker

Individuals with a learning disability should certainly be included more into society. But many can contribute to society. **Social worker**